Experimental Economics

Method and Applications

Over the past two decades, experimental economics has moved from a fringe activity to become a standard tool for empirical research. With experimental economics now regarded as part of the basic tool-kit for applied economics, this book demonstrates how controlled experiments can be useful in providing evidence relevant to economic research. Professors Jacquemet and L'Haridon take the standard model in applied econometrics as a basis for the methodology of controlled experiments. Methodological discussions are illustrated with standard experimental results. This book provides future experimental practitioners with the means to construct experiments that fit their research question, and newcomers with an understanding of the strengths and weaknesses of controlled experiments. Graduate students and academic researchers working in the field of experimental economics will be able to learn how to undertake, understand and criticise empirical research based on lab experiments, and refer to specific experiments, results or designs completed with case study applications.

Nicolas Jacquemet is a full professor at University Paris-1 Panthèon Sorbonne and the Paris School of Economics. His research combines experimental methods and econometrics to study discrimination, the effect of personality traits on economic behaviour, the role of social pre-involvement in strategic behaviour and experimental game theory. His research has been published in *Econometrica, Management Science, Games and Economic Behavior, Journal of Environmental Economics and Management, Journal of Health Economics* and *Journal of Economic Psychology*.

Olivier L'Haridon is a full professor at the University of Rennes 1. His research combines experimental methods and decision theory, applied in the study of individual decision-making as affected by uncertainty. His work has been published in *American Economic Review, Management Science, Journal of Risk and Uncertainty, Theory and Decision, Experimental Economics, Journal of Health Economics* and *Journal of Economic Psychology*.

Experimental Economics

Method and Applications

NICOLAS JACQUEMET

University Paris 1 Panthèon-Sorbonne and Paris School of Economics, France

OLIVIER L'HARIDON

Université de Rennes I, France

CAMBRIDGE
UNIVERSITY PRESS

University Printing House, Cambridge CB2 8BS, United Kingdom

One Liberty Plaza, 20th Floor, New York, NY 10006, USA

477 Williamstown Road, Port Melbourne, VIC 3207, Australia

314-321, 3rd Floor, Plot 3, Splendor Forum, Jasola District Centre, New Delhi - 110025, India

79 Anson Road, #06-04/06, Singapore 079906

Cambridge University Press is part of the University of Cambridge.

It furthers the University's mission by disseminating knowledge in the pursuit of education, learning and research at the highest international levels of excellence.

www.cambridge.org
Information on this title: www.cambridge.org/9781107060272
DOI: 10.1017/9781107446786

© Cambridge University Press 2018

First published 2018

A catalogue record for this publication is available from the British Library

Library of Congress Cataloging in Publication data
Names: Jacquemet, Nicolas, author. | L'Haridon, Olivier, author.
Title: Experimental economics method and applications / Nicolas Jacquemet,
    Paris School of Economics, Olivier L'Haridon, Université de Rennes I, France.
Description: Cambridge, United Kingdom ; New York, NY, USA : Cambridge
    University Press, [2018] | Includes bibliographical references and index.
Identifiers: LCCN 2018007008 | ISBN 9781107060272
Subjects: LCSH: Experimental economics.
Classification: LCC HB131 .J33 2018 | DDC 330.072/4–dc23
LC record available at https://lccn.loc.gov/2018007008

ISBN 978-1-107-06027-2 Hardback
ISBN 978-1-107-62977-6 Paperback

Contents

Figures

Tables

Illustrations

Focuses

Abbreviations and Symbols

Abbreviations

AD	Aggregate Demand
ATE	Average Treatment Effect
ATT	Average Treatment on the Treated
BART	Balloon Risk Analogue Task
BDM	Becker-De Groot-Marschak
BMI	Body Max Index
CADI	Constant Absolute Decreasing Impatience
CDF	Cumulative Distribution Function
CE	Certainty Equivalence
CHM	Cognitive-Hierarchy Model
CRDI	Constant Relative Decreasing Impatience
CRRA	Constant Relative Risk Aversion
DARA	Decreasing Absolute Risk Aversion
DA	Deferred Acceptance algorithm
DGP	Data Generating Process
DM	Dissonance Minimization
ECU	Experimental Currency Unit
FPRP	False Positive Report Probability
FR	Fully-revealing game
FTC	Federal Trade Commission
FW	Fixed wage
HSD	Honestly Significant Difference
IEC	Institutional Ethics Committee
IOS	Inclusion of the Other in the Self
IQR	Interquartile Range
IRB	Institutional Review Board
IV	Induced Value
LHS	Left-Hand Side
LSD	Least Significant Difference
MARS	Meta-Analysis Reporting Standards
MD	Mean absolute Deviation
MLE	Maximum Likelihood Estimator
MOOSE	Meta-analysis of Observational Studies in Epidemiology

MPCR	Marginal per Capita Return
MSE	Mean Squared Error
MT	Amazon's Mechanical Turk
MT	Mechanical Turk
MT	Western Educated, Industrialized, Rich, and Democratic
NR	Non-revealing game
OLS	Ordinary Least Squares
PEEM	Portable Extensions of Existing Models
PE	Probability Equivalence
PGG	Public Good Game
PRISMA	Preferred Reporting Items for Systematic Reviews and Meta-Analyses
PR	Piece-rate
Q-Q	Quantile-Quantile
QRE	Quantal-Response Equilibrium
RDU	Rank-Dependent Utility
RHS	Righ-Hand Side
RIS	Random Incentive System
UBG	Ultimatum Bargaining Game
VCM	Voluntary Contribution Mechanism
WEIRD	Western Educated, Industrialised, Rich, and Democratic
WTA	Willingness to Accept
WTP	Willingness to Pay
WVS	World Value Survey
WVS	World Values Survey

Symbols

$\bar{y}$	sample average
Δ	variation
δ	exponential discount factor, parameter
ℓ	effort
η	decision error
$\hat{\theta}$	estimator
λ, γ	parameters
$\mathbb{E}$	expectation
$\mathbf{B}$	bias
$\mathbf{T}$	test statistic
$\mathbf{X}$	matrix of individual observations, e.g observable characteristics
$\mathbf{y}$	vector of the observations on the outcome variable
$\mathcal{I}$	beliefs in bayesian estimation
$\mathcal{L}$	sampling distribution
$\mathcal{N}$	normal distribution
$\mathcal{S}$	state space
$\mathcal{T}$	treatment

$\mathcal{X}$	inputs
$\mathcal{Y}$	outputs
μ	mean
Ω	variance-covariance matrix
$\omega()$	probability weighting function
B	Binomial distribution
dCor	distance correlation
dCov	distance covariance
F_l, F_u	critical values of the Fisher distribution
Φ	standard normal cumulative distribution
ϕ	standard normal density
π	profit
ε	vector of error terms
ρ	Pearson correlation coefficient
σ, ψ	standard deviations
Θ	parameter space
$\mathbb{V}$	variance
ε_i	individual error terms
a, b, A, B	general purpose parameters (actions, prizes, bids...)
b_L	lower bound of confidence interval
b_U	upper bound of confidence interval
c	threshold in hypothesis testing
$c_e()$	cost of effort
d_0, d_1	decisions in hypothesis testing
DR	decision rule
e	endowment
$F(), f()$	functions
$G()$	cumulative distribution function
$g()$	density
h, i, j, k, s, t	indexes
H_0, H_1, H_a	statistical hypothesis
K	number of samples, treatments, classes...
$L()$	likelihood
$LL()$	log-likelihood
m	number of observable characteristics, median
N	population size
n	number of observations, sample size, number of modeling features
$n_{\mathcal{X}}$	number of inputs
$n_{\mathcal{Y}}$	number of outputs
p, Pr	probability
$p_{(k)}$	rank-ordered p-value
q, Q	price, returns
r	rank
rr	rate of return

S^2	sample variance
SS	sum of squares
T	time, date, period
t_α	critical value of the Student t distribution
$U(), V()$	preference functionals
$u(), v()$	utility functions
w	wage
X, Y	random variables
x, y	realization of random variables
$Y_{(h)}$	ordered value of Y (with order h)
Z	dummy variable
z_α	critical value of the normal distribution
α	Type I error
β	Type II error
θ	parameter(s)
E	event
p_τ	tremble
R	rejection region in hypothesis testing
$W()$	event weighting function
x_{ij}	observation for subject i and variable j
y_i	observation on the outcome variable for subject i

Preface

There is an experimental-economics paradox. Inside the community of researchers carrying out laboratory experiments, these latter are seen as no more and no less than a tool for empirical research. From the outside, however, the method is often perceived as part of a particular sub-field, behavioural economics, which applies insights from both economics and psychology for the better understanding of economic behaviour. Experimental economics is also usually taught this way in most programmes, as part of behavioural-economics classes.

It has, however, long been recognised that experimental and behavioural economics are not the same. Behavioural economics is a research programme with a clear ambition and a well-defined objective: improving economic analysis using realistic psychological assumptions about human behaviour. Experimental economics, on the contrary, is not, per se, a research programme. Rather, it is a research method based on experimental control, applied to the typical topics in economic analysis.

The aim of this textbook is to help close the gap between the perception and reality of experimental methods in economics. We cover experimental economics, i.e. controlled experiments used as a tool to provide empirical evidence that is relevant for economic research. The structure of the textbook thus mimics the way many econometrics textbooks have been written for decades: the coverage focuses on applied statistical methods, the use of which is illustrated with economic results.

There are, however, a number of (good) reasons for this confusion between behavioural and experimental economics, which is at the heart of the experimental–economics paradox. First, behavioural economics emerged partly from the use of experiments – although the contribution of early experiments (such as the Allais paradox and the Chamberlin and Smith market experiments, described in Chapter 1) was to both behavioural economics and mainstream economics (for instance, neoclassical market analysis). Second, the experimental economics method is particularly suited for the study of the phenomena of interest to behavioural economics. In a nutshell, control offers researchers a way of identifying departures from the neoclassical explanation of behaviour. Third, not only behavioural economics but also experimental economics owe a great deal to the accumulated knowledge in experimental psychology: controlled experiments have been used for a long time in this field, and most methodological discussions took place before they even appeared in economics. In addition, the experimental method is taken as part of the psychology research toolkit across the whole community of researchers.

The scope of this book has been greatly influenced by the place that experimental economics occupies between neoclassical economics, behavioural economics, psychology and statistics. First, our methodological discussion mainly focuses on the use of experiments to understand economic behaviour. We complement this fairly standard view in applied economics by regularly devoting space to insights from, and some discrepancies with, psychology. We also cover a number of standard experimental results that are generally seen as part of behavioural economics.

Second, we mainly focus on laboratory experiments rather than field experiments or randomised controlled trials (see Chapter 3, Section 3.5 for the definition of these). This restriction reflects at least three factors. First, one textbook cannot suffice to embrace the large literature on methods for both laboratory experiments and randomised controlled trials. Second, this restriction also comes from our own limitations in expertise. Last, but not least, laboratory experiments are a convenient step in the study of controlled experiments in economics. Laboratory experiments can be seen as an extreme case of controlled experiments; they allow the accurate identification of behavioural phenomena, but at the cost of a highly artificial environment. Due to this artificiality, laboratory experiments provide answers that are sometimes hard to interpret – and are often challenged by non-experimentalists. Other kinds of experiment offer a way of loosening these limitations by implementing the same empirical method in less artificial contexts. We thus believe that laboratory experiments are a good starting point for anyone who wants to learn about controlled experiments in economics. Many of the discussions in this textbook aim to clarify the most appropriate cases for each type of empirical method; for example, whether observational or experimental data are required and, if it is experimental data, how close to the field the experiment should be.

Structure of the book

This textbook is not the first experimental-economics book by a long way, with respect to both methods and applications. Our predecessors can be split into two groups. First, textbooks/handbooks written for students and academics provide extensive surveys of experimental results. This applies to the textbook of Friedman and Sunder (1994) and the two seminal handbooks edited by Plott and Smith (2008) and Kagel and Roth (1995). In the same spirit, a number of books propose reviews of existing results from laboratory experiments with more specialised perspectives: Camerer (2003) contrasts behaviour in the lab with predictions from game theory, Cartwright (2011) and Chaudhuri (2009) mainly focus on social preferences and behavioural economics, and Angner (2012) provides a detailed overview of laboratory experiments regarding decision problems. These are all required reading for anyone wanting to learn more about experimental results. On the other hand, a few advanced books on the methodology of experiments have recently appeared. These are state-of-the-art collections of papers, written mainly for academics working in the field. This is the case for Guala (2005), Bardsley et al. (2009) and Fréchette and Schotter (2015).

This textbook is an attempt to build a bridge between these two kinds of reference: it provides a detailed presentation of the methodological aspects of economic experiments for readers (students, academics and professionals) who want to enter the field. To this end the book inverses the usual way of presenting the material, as the experimental results are used to illustrate methodological issues – rather than spreading out the methodological discussions over the presentation of various experimental designs. The content of the book is set out at the end of Chapter 1. We are aware that 'Methodology, like sex, is better demonstrated than discussed, though often better anticipated than experienced' (Leamer, 1983, p. 40). Mimicking the approach in applied economics and econometrics textbooks, the concrete applications of the method that constitute the core material in existing textbooks are here introduced as illustrations of the main material. To this end, the book contains three types of side material describing particular experiments, results or designs: case studies, illustrations and focuses.

- **Case studies** are sections devoted to the detailed presentation of a particular strand of experiments. They seek to illustrate the methodological discussions provided in the corresponding chapter – identified as such in the table of contents.
- **Illustrations** are boxes providing a presentation of one particular experiment or result, to illustrate the point discussed in the text. Illustrations are often provided in sequences, showing how the literature has evolved according to the different dimensions discussed in the text.
- **Focuses** are boxes providing a more detailed and/or formal presentation of a point discussed in the text.

These together provide examples of most of the applications or results that are generally seen as essential in the field – as described in Section 1.4. To help readers bring together all of the information on one particular topic, they appear as specific index headers (see p. 431).

Audience

There are three natural audiences for this book. Its first purpose is as part of a graduate course, describing methods in experimental economics. The organisation of the book closely follows the typical outline of an 8 × 3-hour course. Chapters 1–4 cover the material that would serve as an introductory lecture to laboratory experiments. These chapters describe the main objectives of laboratory experiments and provide examples. Chapters 5 and 8 provide core methodological insights that would best be split in two lectures each. Longer classes could include a discussion of the statistical analysis of experimental data based on Chapter 7 and a discussion of the insights drawn from behavioural economics in Chapter 9, and/or use case studies to devote some lectures to applications that illustrate the main material. In particular, a thorough methodological course would probably feature some lectures devoted to risk preferences (Section 7.4), time preferences (Section 6.6) and belief-elicitation methods (Section 5.6).

Second, the book more generally seeks to provide future experimental practitioners with a broad picture of the toolkit that they will need. By providing the rationale for the general method and setting out in detail each particular choice of design feature, we hope that readers will be able to construct experiments that fit their research question well. A good understanding of the methodological challenges is also an important requirement for becoming an informed reader: this book may help to interpret the results from laboratory experiments or the writing of referee reports on papers using the experimental method. Third, we hope the community of academics who are new to this literature will find it a useful summary of the current state of the art about what experimental economics can tell us, and under which conditions it provides valuable answers to research questions in economics.

Acknowledgements

The book was written using the course material for PhD/master 2 courses in a number of different places, and in particular at our home institutions. We are more than grateful to the students who attended these classes for their commitment, remarks, scepticism and enthusiasm. We gratefully acknowledge the support from the Institut Universitaire de France.

It is likely that the book would never have reached its final stage without the encouragement, help and remarks from, and discussions with, Jay Shogren. The writing process took such a long time that we will certainly omit many people whose contributions at earlier stages were much appreciated. This also meant that we have worked with many research assistants, whose help very often exceeded what was expected. Our thanks to Lisa Simon and Solene Delecourt for their work on early drafts of some of the chapters; Sophie Cottet for producing the graphs and figures; and Alberto Prati, Guillaume Royer and Shaden Shabayek for their work on some of the boxes. Last, an incredible number of PhD students and colleagues spent a great deal of time reading the first drafts of different parts of the book and provided us with invaluable feedback. We gratefully thank Arthur Attema, Aurélien Baillon, Han Bleichrodt, Aurélie Bonein, Elias Bouacida, Béatrice Boulu-Reshef, Arthur Charpentier, Paolo Crosetto, Laurent Denant-Boémont, Antoine Hémon, Justine Jouxtel, Antoine Malézieux, Elven Priour, Kirsten Rohde, Angelo Secchi, Benoit Tarroux and Adam Zylbersztejn.

While the field of behavioural and experimental economics is sometimes described as over-competitive, it is also one in which researchers from all over the world cooperate on methodological and bibliographic issues, thanks to the ESA discussion group: the discussions there provided us many insights and ideas for which we gratefully thank all contributors. Our gratitude also goes to Sandra Freeland and Andrew Clark for their thorough proofreading of the manuscript, and the editorial team at Cambridge University Press, Phil Good, Neil Ryan and Chris Harrison, for their continuous support and outstanding work.

Part I

What Is It? An Introduction to Experimental Economics

1 The Emergence of Experiments in Economics

> There is a property common to almost all the moral sciences, and by which they are distinguished from many of the physical; that is, that it is seldom in our power to make experiments in them.
>
> Mill (1836), cited in Guala (2005, p. 2).

This statement by John Stuart Mill, or similar remarks, introduces virtually all texts on the methodology of experiments in economics. At the time, and for a long time after that, controlled experiments in the social sciences, and especially in economics, were considered impossible to conduct; it appeared that experiments were reserved to the natural sciences, and that the testing of social and human behaviour in the framework of a controlled experiment would prove completely unworkable. Nowadays, experiments are a widely accepted means of generating knowledge in economics. Among many examples, it is shown by the fact that experimental or behavioural economics is part of the graduate programme of most universities, there are many books, handbooks and textbooks focusing on the field, and even a well-recognised academic journal ('*Experimental Economics*') is specialised on research using this method.

Before moving on to a detailed discussion of why and how laboratory experiments are performed in economics, we will explore this intriguing trend. What happened between the time experimental economics first came into existence and when it finally became an established member of the community? We will start by highlighting the progress of experimental methods in economics, from an area that was thought impracticable, meaningless or uninteresting, to an accepted and widely used process in economic research. In describing the reasons why there was such a sudden change of interest in and attitude towards experiments, we will examine some of the very first examples of experiments in economics. These examples are interesting not only from a historical point of view, but also because they underscore the main reasons for the change and how experimental economics has grown since – both in terms of the research questions that are addressed and in the type of answers it provides. These will be followed by three more recent examples which illustrate what the research programme has become today – a unified and also very diverse area of study.

The most obvious and powerful unifying factor of all works using laboratory experiments is, in fact, the methodology applied: a controlled environment allowing use of the observed behaviour of human beings to produce knowledge about economics. As the last section will show, a thorough study and presentation of this methodology requires a wide-ranging knowledge of economic theory as a whole, and its relation to different application fields, analytical tools and approaches. It will soon become clear that no single textbook can possibly cover all these aspects: this chapter will offer a road map of everything this book is unable to cover, or can only cover in part. Perhaps more importantly, this chapter will try to convince you that in order to fully understand the rationale, contribution and practical lessons of the results generated by experiments in economics, the first step is to be aware of the choices of methodology and the reasoning behind them: this is what this book is all about.

1.1   The End of a Long-Standing Regretful Impossibility

Even if experiments in economics were considered impossible for a long time, they were nonetheless the object of considerable wishful thinking. If experiments could be implemented, they could be designed and put in place in order to provide empirical evidence and serve as a basis to enhance theory. This is implicitly acknowledged in a celebrated remark made by Friedman, 'We can seldom test particular predictions in the social sciences by experiments explicitly designed to eliminate what are judged to be the most important disturbing influences' (Friedman, 1953, p. 10). Experiments in the social science are seen as a very attractive, though impossible, way of testing theories. If feasible, experiments would allow researchers to neutralise all forces driving behaviour that are outside the scope of the theory. In that case, experiments would help elicit the empirical content of theory, and therefore identify the main driving forces of behaviour. This opinion was shared by many eminent economists long after 1953. In their groundbreaking principles textbook, Samuelson and Nordhaus noted that 'economists cannot perform the controlled experiments of chemists or biologists because they cannot easily control other important factors' (Samuelson and Nordhaus, 1985, p. 8). All of the remarks cited above show quite clearly how recent the appearance of experimental economics as a *bona fide* field of study is and also underline how desirable experiments are for research. Fortunately, the long-standing and powerful belief in the impossibility of experiments in the social sciences, however regretful, is now a thing of the past.

As a matter of fact, in a later edition of their textbook (which appeared less than ten years later) Samuelson and Nordhaus had already adopted a new and different mindset: 'Experimental economics is an exciting new development' (Samuelson and Nordhaus, 1992, p. 5). Between these two editions, economists had managed to set up experiments similar to the ones conducted in the natural sciences. But, even more importantly, the results generated by these experiments began to be considered by an increasing number of specialists to be sound empirical evidence.

From then on, the pace and scope of the changes taking place increased so rapidly that today the situation stands in sharp contrast with the earlier views expressed above. This phenomenon is illustrated, for instance, by the rise in the rate of academic publications related to experimental economics over the years. Figure 1.1 shows the results of a survey carried out by Noussair (2011) concerning the percentage of articles including experiments that have appeared in major academic economic journals. The survey

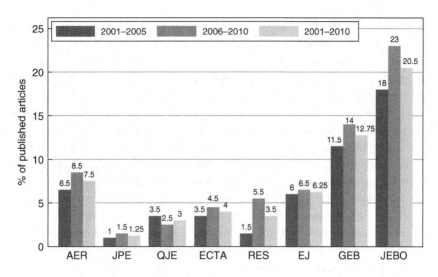

Figure 1.1 Trends in academic publishing in experimental economics
Note. Percentages of experimental articles from those appearing in the journals: *American Economic Review (AER), Journal of Political Economy (JPE), Quarterly Journal of Economics (QJE), Econometrica (Ecta), Review of Economic Studies (RES), Economic Journal (EJ), Games and Economic Behaviour (GEB), Journal of Economics, Behavior and Organization (JEBO).*
Source: Noussair (2011, p. 8).

covers the top five journals (*AER, JPE, QJE, ECTA, RES*) which experts acknowledge as the leading supports in the field; three other journals were added to the list: *EJ, GEB* and *JEBO*. These are more specialised and/or lower-ranked journals, but which are, nonetheless, highly influential and open to experimental works. The chart shows the change in the rates from 2001–2005 to 2006–2010. The first ten years of the new millennium saw a slight increase in the percentage of articles in the sample. More importantly, the share of experimental papers is very significant in most of these leading journals: from 2% to 7% in the top five journals, and from 5% to 20% in the more specialised ones. This a clear indication of the growing acceptance and recognition of this type of work by the academic community.

The four experimental economists who have been awarded the Nobel Prize in Economics in the first decades of the new millennium, who we will come across a number of times in this book, are another example of this recognition. In 2002, Vernon L. Smith and Daniel F. Kahneman were the joint recipients of the Nobel Prize in Economics. Smith was thus acknowledged as one of the founders of experimental economics and as someone who contributed to establishing it as a conclusive method. The main justification for the award was the introduction of the methodology per se (they received the prize 'for having established laboratory experiments as a tool in empirical economic analysis, especially in the study of alternative market mechanisms'). In terms of contributions, the field is seen as interdisciplinary in nature, with Kahneman receiving the prize 'for having integrated insights from psychological research into economic science, especially concerning human judgement and decision-making under uncertainty'. Ten years later, another renowned experimentalist, Alvin Roth, was also granted the

Nobel Prize. But this time, the co-winner was Lloyd Shapley, a pure theorist. Together they were recognised 'for the theory of stable allocations and the *practice* of market design'. It goes without saying that the Smith and Kahneman contributions are of major importance to the discipline, and that these three Nobel Prizes in themselves are convincing proof that experiments have been widely accepted as part of the field. But there is an interesting change in nature between the two prizes: while the first Nobel Prize was awarded for the methodological advance itself, the acknowledgement of Roth's contribution was based on actual laboratory results using the toolbox of experimental economics and applied to research issues that are at the core of economic theory. This is further evidence of the wide acceptance of experimental economics by the academic community. Last, Richard Thaler was awarded in 2017 for having incorporated 'psychologically realistic assumptions into analyses of economic decision-making'. Richard Thaler showed how experimental methods are particularly meaningful for uncovering deep psychological phenomena such as mental processes, self-control behaviour and social preferences. The award also underlines his contribution to public policies based on nudges (see Chapter 9). This is further evidence of the wide acceptance of experimental economics by the academic community, with results from the laboratory now being seen as useful in order to better design choice architectures.

In contrast with the quotes that opened this section, in which experiments were regarded with substantial scepticism, there is now substantial evidence that experimental economics has become a well-established and widely accepted empirical method. One may wonder how an entire new field has managed to surface in such a short period of time. As a first step towards a better understanding of how this change came about, we will show in the next section that this, in fact, was not the case at all: experiments in economics have existed for a long time, producing results that are much in line with the works that appear nowadays in leading publications. It appears that the reason for the lack of experiments in economics comes not so much from their practical impossibility, but rather from the main focus of academic research at the time. Since then, a change in focus occurred towards questions that are closer and closer to the kind of issue that experiments are well suited to investigate.

1.2   Why Such a Change: Two Early Examples

The two examples below are among the best known of the early experiments. They illustrate the state of infancy of experimental economics at the time, although they are now regarded as important and insightful contributions to economic knowledge.

1.2.1   How Do Competitive Markets Work?

In 1948, Harvard Professor Edward Chamberlin organised a game with his students. The aim was to replicate the functioning of a market in perfect competition with rational agents as closely as possible. Students were randomly assigned a card, which made each student either a seller or a buyer. In addition, the card displayed a price for a hypothetical good to be sold or bought. For students playing as sellers, this price referred to the minimum price at which they were ready to sell. For the buyers, this price indicated the maximum price they were willing to pay to obtain the (hypothetical) good. Afterwards, the students walked freely in the classroom and bargained with their colleagues to either buy or sell the good. Once a deal had been made, the students came to Chamberlin's desk to report the price at which the good had been sold.

In this framework, economic theory predicts outcomes according to the two curves depicted in Figure 1.2, where the supply and demand curves were drawn based on the prices distributed to students – i.e. how many students were willing to buy or sell at each possible price that appears on their card: a 'induced values' design. The game is a textbook example of a market: the demand curve is decreasing in price, whereas the supply curve is increasing. The market equilibrium determines the actual price that should arise from strategic interactions, as well as the resulting quantities exchanged on the market; the unique stable price is the one that clears the market, in such a way that demand meets supply. This point is an equilibrium not only because the two sides happen to be equal, but more importantly because it is the only state of the market in which everyone agrees to stay – there is no possibility of doing better at the individual level by moving out of this situation. For any other price, there is either excess supply or excess demand, in which case either suppliers (sellers) or consumers (buyers) can be in a better situation by moving to another price level. There are thus strong reasons to believe that the equilibrium should result from real interactions in this particular environment.

Surprisingly enough, Chamberlin obtained the results reported in Figure 1.3 based on the actual behaviour of his students. The dashed line depicts the average price at which students traded their goods during the experiment: it is far below the straight line, or the competitive equilibrium price. There was also a huge variation in the actual prices,

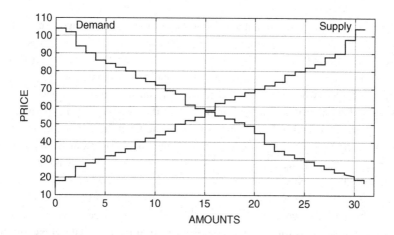

Figure 1.2 Market equilibrium in the Chamberlin (1948) experiment

Note. The figure shows the theoretical equilibrium of the market implemented in the laboratory – at the intersection of the (increasing) supply function and the (decreasing) demand function.

Source: Chamberlin (1948, p. 97, Figure 1).

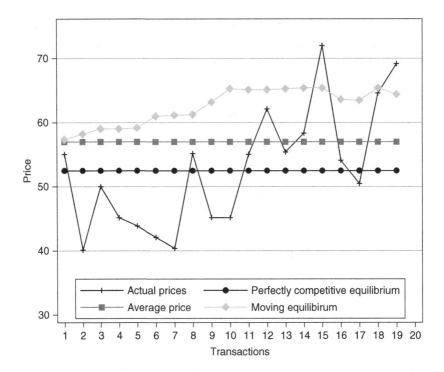

Figure 1.3 Observed behaviour in the Chamberlin (1948) experiment
Note. For each transaction in abscissa, the figure shows the actual price observed in the experiment as well as a recall of the theoretical equilibrium described in Figure 1.2.
Source: Chamberlin (1948, p. 101, Figure 3).

which are represented by the curving line. In addition, the equilibrium volume of trade is higher than what the theory would have predicted. Actual behaviour in this environment thus strongly departs from what economic theory expects, leading Chamberlin to conclude, 'Perhaps it is the assumption of a perfect market which is "strange" in the first place' (and interpret this as a support for his monopolistic competition model). This result is not, however, the end of the experimental story of markets.

Vernon Smith (who, as mentioned above, was subsequently awarded a Nobel Prize) was one of Chamberlin's students and participated in his classroom experiment. Around fifteen years later, in 1962, he decided to replicate Chamberlin's experiment, but with various changes in the environment – aimed at replicating what Smith thought were important actual driving forces of a competitive market. As in Chamberlin's experiment, each student received a card, making him either a buyer or a seller. This card also gave the student a reservation price: the price above which a buyer would not buy, and below which a seller would not sell. The changes implemented as compared to the seminal experiment are as follows. First of all, instead of having bilateral bargaining (or, at most, discussions in small groups) between students, the announcements of offers and demands become public, meaning that buyers and sellers could call out their offers in the room so that everybody could hear. This is aimed to make the information on prices public, so as to mimic what is achieved by an auctioneer receiving and distributing all

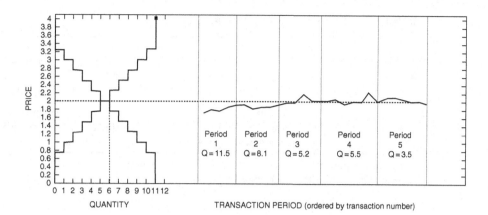

Figure 1.4 Predicted and observed behaviour in the Smith (1962) replication

Note. The left-hand side shows the theoretical market equilibrium – at the intersection of the (increasing) supply function and the (decreasing) demand function. The right-hand side shows the price and number of transactions in each market period.

Source: Smith (1962, p. 113, Figure 1).

offers. Second, the market experiment was repeated over several periods, and allowed the students to better understand the functioning of the market, hence getting closer to market behaviour of professional market traders.

Figure 1.4 reports the observed behaviour and theoretical predictions of the Smith experiment. The theoretical market plotted on the left-hand side shares the same features as the one implemented by Chamberlin. The curve on the right-hand side shows the prices at which market clears for five market periods. The contrast with the previous results is drastic: the observed prices smoothly converge towards the equilibrium price, and the number of transactions (reported on the bottom part of the graph) converges to the equilibrium quantity equal to 6.

Beyond the seminal insights about how the market works, these series of experiments help to describe the methodological issues behind experimental results. Both experiments aim to replicate competitive markets, but with different implementation choices. The best environment to describe markets is a matter of judgement, and the theoretical conclusion drawn will be entirely different whether one or the other experiment is believed to best capture the important features of the economic phenomenon. At the same time, the implementation differences between the two experiments also inform about the key features that explain behaviour in a market situation: the extent of information buyers and sellers receive, for instance, seems to be a critical driving force. Beyond rejection/support of the prediction, the experiment thus informs theory by highlighting the salient dimension to be taken into account. Lastly, as the Smith experiment clearly shows, it is not always the case that the theory is necessarily wrong or that experiments are designed expressly to reject the behavioural assumptions behind the theoretical results (as is sometimes taught, mainly by some academics who view experiment results with scepticism): in this case, experiments serve more to identify the circumstances under which these assumptions are actually accurate.

Table 1.1 The choice sequence of the Allais paradox

	Option A	Option B
A or B?	100% chance of winning 1 million	10% chance of winning 5 million 89% chance of winning 1 million 1% chance of winning nothing
	Option C	Option D
C or D?	11% chance of winning 1 million 89% chance of winning nothing	10% chance of winning 5 million 90% chance of winning nothing

Note. Each respondent was asked to make both choices in turn.
Source: Allais (1953, implemented in 1952).

1.2.2   Choice Consistency in Risky Decisions

The second example focuses on individual decision-making, rather than on strategic situations. During the annual conference of the American Economic Society held in New York City in 1953, Maurice Allais presented the economics professors attending the conference – especially those specialised in game theory and decision theory – with two binary choices. Respondents were shown Table 1.1 and asked to choose either A or B, and then either C or D.

Based on the axiomatic framework of decision theory, the first choice and the second choices are strongly related – although the choice between the two options per se is a matter of preferences that nobody can predict. To understand the link between the two decisions, let us first put aside the 89% probability of winning one million – in situations A and B – or nothing – in situations C and D. Apart from this 89% probability, both situations A and C have the same probability (11%) of winning one million. Similarly, situations B and D offer the same expected outcome: nothing with a probability equal to 1%, and five million with a probability of 10%. As a result, still disregarding this 89% probability, an individual who prefers A over B (B over A) should also prefer C over D (D over C). You can note that the outcome that results from the 89% probability is exactly the same for A and B on the one hand, and C and D on the other. Consequently, it only comes down to the addition of an identical outcome for each pair of situations: one million for A and B, nothing for C and D. It sounds reasonable to assume that this should not affect the preference ordering of consistent decision-makers.[1] Because of this very clever feature in the way situations are built, elicited choices provide a test of consistency: depending on individuals' unknown preferences, either A and C, or B and D, should be picked together; no other combination can be rationalised with classical decision theory. Using these choice situations, Allais was successful at tricking the economists at the conference. As he expected, 45% of the leading theorists (including Savage, one of the leading researchers in the field) to whom Allais submitted the choice

---

[1] This property of preferences is named the "independence axiom" in decision theory, which implies that if there are two different gambles and one is preferred to the other, then mixing them with another identical gamble should not alter the order of the preferences. This axiom is the one violated by the results of this experiment, which is now known as the common consequence or Allais paradox.

opted for A against B, but D against C. Almost half of the respondents, who were all well versed in economic and decision theory, and some specialised in decision theory, failed to pass the consistency test associated with the two successive choices. A key feature of this experiment is that it is designed in such a way that there is a unique relationship between one, clearly identified, theoretical assumption driving the predictions and the choices available. Therefore, observed behaviour challenges not only theory, but, more importantly, the specific feature of theory that fails to describe behaviour. Beyond simple rejection (which is unambiguous given the magnitude of the result and the sample pool from which it was obtained) it provides a guide to the particular assumptions that have to be reworked so that they correspond to the real driving forces behind behaviour. In the Allais paradox, two features of the available options are of particular interest. On the one hand, certainty generates a strong attractiveness for option A. On the other, the change in probabilities appears to be quite small between options C and D. These two features of behaviour under uncertainty are central in theories that rationalise behaviour in the Allais paradox (Quiggin, 1982; Kahneman and Tversky, 1979).

1.2.3   Why Was There Such a Fast and Sudden Change?

These early experiments marked the beginning of a new field, which has made rapid gains in terms of both acceptance and popularity over the last decade. But many years went by between the time of those first experiments and the time when the economic community truly started paying attention to them. Until recently, experimental economics was thought of as unworkable or of no meaningful importance. What was it, then, that suddenly made the experimental method so widely accepted?

As shown by the two previous examples, this was not a matter of feasibility. Both experiments were published in very good journals and existed when some of the quotes opening this chapter were written. Experimentation was thus already a possibility. In fact, it has always been quite straightforward to test results from decision theory or game theory in an experimental setting. It simply amounts to having people make choices within a simple set of rules describing the decision-making environment. The most drastic change was in fact the change in the kind of questions, which in the 1970s and 1980s economics began to focus on, with a growing importance put on these two theoretical tools.[2] In the middle of the twentieth century, economics was set in the context of a beautiful model of how the entire economy worked and how all the agents in the economy, as a group, made decisions in the present and for the future. This environment was so complex and all-encompassing that the empirical relevance of behavioural assumptions was obviously not a primary concern. But as economics moved away from this representation, more and more attention began to be given to the forces behind individual and strategic decision-making. Microeconomics became one core focus of economic analysis, making an intensive use of game and decision theory. What were considered revolutionary issues at the time have now become orthodox, and the rise of experimental economics was concurrent with the fall of general equilibrium theory. The reinforcing of

---

[2] See Fontaine and Leonard (2005), in particular Chapter 3, for an insightful review of these trends.

the economic representation of human behaviour, along with clear-cut definitions of the environment, has now made the long-held dream of testing economics in the laboratory an achievable goal.

The role of experiments in the history of economics helps better understand what experimental economics is all about. First, experiments and economic theory go hand in hand: experiments are about assessing the empirical relevance of the behavioural content of economic models. They are not in contradiction with economic theory, but rather serve as a complement to it. Economic theory provides a deep and subtle understanding of how the economy works when decisions are taken by the *homo œconomicus*. Experiments rather involve a *Homer œconomicus*: the ordinary Joe, endowed with an average level of cognitive and social skills – rather than unlimited computational abilities – under the influence of psychological and environmental factors – rather than driven by a well-defined preference functional.[3] They thus allow us to measure whether *homo œconomicus* and *Homer œconomicus* lead to similar or substantially different outcomes in a given economic situation. Second, as the two examples cited above show, these two kinds of people, the *homo œconomicus* and 'real' human beings, are not strangers to one another: they sometimes behave differently, calling for a different theory (rather than different people), but there are also many important situations in which the two behave as if they were one and the same. Why and when they do is one of the key questions that remains to be answered.

1.3   The Research Programme: Three Examples

We conclude this quick overview of the recent history of experiments in economics with three examples drawn from a more recent literature. Although chosen at random (with bias) among many other similar studies, these examples clearly illustrate the current state of the art in the experimental field, and the way it helps elucidate what human beings and economic theory – *Homer œconomicus* and *Homo œconomicus* – have in common, and how they differ. To a large extent, the current answer is similar to the main lesson we learned from the early examples described above.

We first present the prisoners' dilemma (PD), a well-known example of the discrepancy between game-theoretic results in a simple environment, and the behavioural patterns actually observed. This example also shows that, while game theory alone has trouble explaining behaviour – typically, without reference to more general factors related to economic agents' social environment – it is in fact quite effective in predicting changes in behaviour. The second example shows that experimental economics can help significantly in this aspect as it can easily address difficult questions about the basics of economic rationality. The centipede game is a typical example of a simple experiment that calls into question some common principles of rationality. Lastly, we proceed to a more complicated game, a zero-sum game with incomplete information, in which one would expect the gap between economic theory and observed behaviour to be larger

---

[3] The terminology is due to Hall (2005); see e.g. Beggs (2013); Hall (2014) for a full statement of the parallel between economics and the Simpsons.

than in any other context. The example shows that this foregone conclusion is defini-
tively not applicable in this case. These three examples serve as a tour of the type of
research question addressed thanks to experiments in economics and of the variety of
answers it offers.

1.3.1 Nash Equilibrium and Pareto Efficiency

The first example is that of a *non-cooperative game*: a game in which outcomes are
determined by the decentralised and independent actions of players. Figure 1.5 presents
the payoffs each of the two players gets according to the actions they choose. It is a
simultaneous-move game, as each player decides without knowing what the other one is
doing. This type of representation of a game will be used often in this book. For readers
who might not be fully familiar with it, we will take the opportunity here to describe it
step by step.

According to the normal form representation in Figure 1.5, each player can choose
between two actions. Player 1 is the row decision-maker, and Player 2 is the column
decision-maker. Player 1 chooses either Top or Bottom, Player 2 either Left or Right.
Together, both players' actions determine the outcome of the game: the state of the world
resulting from all the players' actions. The numbers in the matrix show the payoffs
linked to each of the four possible outcomes for each player. In each cell, the number
on the left is the payoff Player 1 gets in this particular outcome, and the one on the right
the payoff Player 2 gets. For example, if Player 1 plays Top and Player 2 chooses Right,
then Player 1 loses 10 and Player 2 earns 10.

A quick inspection of Figure 1.5 shows that one outcome seems intuitively preferable: if the players choose Top of Left, they reach an outcome that maximises what
they collectively get. It is a Pareto-dominant outcome: that particular outcome makes it
impossible for one agent to improve his lot by unilaterally modifying his action without making the other player worse off. However, this outcome is not sustainable when
the actions are decentralised and non-coordinated. This is so because, given the Pareto-
dominant situation, both agents have an incentive to deviate: given the action of Player 2,
Player 1 can earn more by playing Bottom than Top against Left, and similarly Player 2
can earn more by playing Right against Top rather than Left. Because of these individual
incentives to move away from the Pareto-dominant outcome, the equilibrium coincides
with the worst outcome of the game: that which occurs when Player 1 chooses Bottom
and Player 2 chooses Right. This is a Nash equilibrium because there is no longer any

	Left	Right
Top	5; 5	−10; 10
Bottom	10; −10	−5; −5

Figure 1.5 Table of payoffs in a non-cooperative game

individual incentive to deviate – none of the players can be better off by moving away from the equilibrium strategy when the others are playing it.

The Nash equilibrium of the game, Bottom–Right, is the outcome that is predicted to occur from uncoordinated simultaneous decisions. Because it does not coincide with the Pareto-dominant situation, this game is a textbook example of the failure to reach an efficient outcome via non-cooperative decisions. It is often called the prisoners' dilemma game, in which case the moves are 'to denounce' or 'not to denounce' for two prisoners who are separately offered leniency if they provide information about the crime they committed together. This strategic framework can be applied to a great many economic situations. Collusion between firms on markets is a typical example of the dilemma of cooperation and defection (which will be studied in length in Chapter 4, Section 4.4.2). Collusion occurs when firms agree to set the market price to a level higher than its competitive value. All firms prefer the collusive outcome, as profits are higher. But each firm has a strong temptation to slightly decrease its price so as to make even higher profits, at the expense of others. This incentive to deviate from the collusion agreement is a natural force against the ability to sustain a non-competitive equilibrium. Another example of non-cooperation when cooperation would be optimal is the Kyoto Protocol, an international agreement which aims to commit countries to reducing their greenhouse gases. A Pareto-optimal outcome would be that all countries sign the agreement. Nonetheless, countries have an incentive to let the other countries sign and to free-ride, thus benefiting from the reduction in greenhouse gases without having to pay the price of the treaty.

Hundreds, if not thousands, of experiments have been run to assess the empirical relevance of this analysis. As an example, Figure 1.6 presents the results of one of the earliest experiments of this type, conducted by Cooper et al. (1996). The x-axis represents each of the ten different periods of the game, while the y-axis depicts the frequency of the cooperative play (i.e. when the collectively optimal, but not individually rational, actions are chosen) when the action leading to the efficient outcome is chosen. The upper curve represents the frequency of cooperative play in the case of a prisoners' dilemma game with repeated interactions, where the same two players play together ten times. The lower curve represents the outcome with different partners for ten periods, each game being a one-shot game. Both curves show a departure from theoretical predictions. Theory predicts a 0% rate of cooperation in the game. It is far from the observed patterns not only in the repeated games – which do not, in the strict sense, implement the model – but also in the one-shot games. For example, in the first period, about 60% of the subjects decided to cooperate in the case of finitely repeated games, but around 35% of the people did so in one-shot games. At the same time, it is not true that these results fit with a view of human behaviour only driven by the well-being of everybody and disregarding self-interest. Free-riding behaviour, based on the temptation to increase one's payoffs at the expense of the other players, accurately describes the results in 70–50% of observed outcomes. Because these two kinds of behaviour (cooperation and deviation) are widespread, both should be accounted for by any accurate theoretical representation. As a result, neither the Nash equilibrium, nor alternative motives leading to full cooperation, are enough to account alone for the observed behaviour in the prisoners' dilemma game.

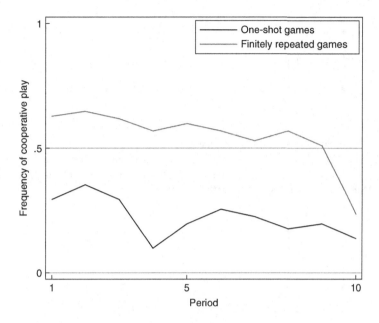

Figure 1.6 Empirical behaviour in prisoners' dilemma games
Note. The figure reports the share of participants who decide to cooperate in each of the ten periods of the game.
Source: Cooper et al. (1996, p. 199, Figure 1).

1.3.2 A Simple Two-Player Sequential Game

The previous example focused on a simultaneous-move game, in which the players decide without knowing what the others will be doing. Another branch of game theory studies behaviour in sequential-move games, in which the players decide one after the other. The big change in terms of strategic interaction is that each player now observes what the other did before choosing an action. Figure 1.7 provides a well-known example of such a game, introduced by Rosenthal (1981) as the *centipede* game. The structure of the game is quite simple. Two players alternately get a chance to take the larger portion of a continually increasing pile of money – the number on each node indicates which of the two players has to decide, with the two payoffs being those experienced by each of the two players respectively if the game ends at this point. For Player 1 payoffs are given in the first row, for Player 2 payoffs are given on the second row. The amount keeps increasing as long as the players continue to play (denoted P in Figure 1.7 and Figure 1.8). But as soon as one of the two players decides to take (denoted T in Figure 1.7 and Figure 1.8), they get a larger portion of the pile while the other gets the smaller part. The trade-off is not easy to resolve from an intuitive point of view: conditional on the game continuing, it is always better to go as far as possible along the tree (the original form had 100 nodes, hence the name centipede), but at the same time each player wants to be the one who stops the game. The question that remains open, then, is when the players will stop and at which stage.

The way game theory resolves this trade-off is, in a sense, even less intuitive than this simple explanation suggests. The key point to note is that the number of steps in the

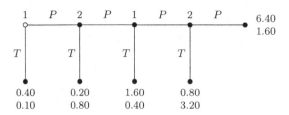

Figure 1.7 A simple four-moves sequential game

Note. Each of the two players (1 or 2) decides in turn at each node to either Pass or Take. For each state, the payoffs of Player 1 appear on the first row, the payoffs of Player 2 on the second row. *Source*: McKelvey and Palfrey (1992, p. 806, Figure 1).

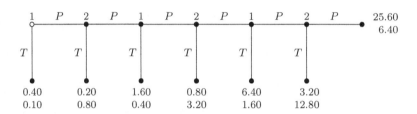

Figure 1.8 A six-moves centipede game

Note. Each of the two players (1 or 2) decides in turn at each node to either Pass or Take. For each state, the payoffs of Player 1 appear on the first row, the payoffs of Player 2 on the second row. *Source*: McKelvey and Palfrey (1992, p. 806, Figure 2).

game (four in the example) is known for sure from the beginning. The usual approach to this type of situation is to predict that the players will play in such a way that actions in each sub-game (i.e. the sub-tree that extends from any node to the end) is a Nash equilibrium. Because of this property, the equilibrium can be elicited through backward induction. Starting from the terminal node of the game, the equilibrium behaviour is relatively straightforward: the last player will decide to take, because it earns more than to pass and there is no point in waiting. For Player 1, in the node just before, it means that the decision actually faced is between taking now or having Player 2 take at the last stage. But then the best thing to do is to take at this node so as to avoid letting the other player take at the following one. And this reasoning applies to all the steps leading backward taken one after the other. The result of this reasoning would be the *sub-game perfect equilibrium*, where the first mover takes at the very first node and the game stops. What is startling in this result is that the outcome is not predicted to depend on either the rate at which the pie grows from one step to the other, or on the number of steps – as long as the number is known right from the beginning.[4]

This striking prediction was first tested against actual behaviour by McKelvey and Palfrey (1992). When the participants in their experiment were asked to play the four-move game described in Figure 1.7, only 7% of them actually played according to the sub-game perfect equilibrium, stopping at the very first node. The top part of Table 1.2

---

[4] See Reny (1993); Aumann (1995); Ben-Porath (1997); Aumann (1998) for theoretical attempts to weaken this paradoxical result, and Chapter 4, Section 4.4.2, for a more detailed discussion of finite- and infinite-horizon games.

Table 1.2 Observed continuation decisions in centipede games

		Session	N	f_1	f_2	f_3	f_4	f_5	f_6	f_7
Four	1	(PCC)	100	.06	.26	.44	.20	.04		
Move	2	(PCC)	81	.10	.38	.40	.11	.01		
	3	(CIT)	100	.06	.43	.28	.14	.09		
	Total	1-3	281	.07	.36	.37	.15	.05		
High Payoff	4	(High-CIT)	100	.15	.37	.32	.11	.05		
Six	5	(CIT)	100	.02	.09	.39	.28	.20	.01	.01
Move	6	(PCC)	81	.00	.02	.04	.46	.35	.11	.02
	7	(PCC)	100	.00	.07	.14	.43	.23	.12	.01
	Total	5-7	281	.01	.06	.20	.38	.25	.08	.01

Note. Actual behaviour in the four-move (upper part) and six-move (bottom part) centipede game. *N* denotes the number of subjects, each column f_t provides the share of subjects who decide to take at the tth node.
Source: McKelvey and Palfrey (1992, p. 808, Table IIA).

shows the full distribution of the share of subjects who stopped at each node of the game (denoted f_t for the tth decision stage). While it is true that the subjects were not anyway near to playing the sub-game perfect equilibrium, at the same time few of them reached the last stage of the game – less than 5% did. From this evidence, the question remains open: what is it that makes subjects decide to stop or go on?

To help answer this question, McKelvey and Palfrey (1992) consider a second experiment that implements the six-move centipede game displayed in Figure 1.8. The results are displayed in the bottom part of Table 1.7. From 7% in the four-moves game, the share of subjects who play the sub-game perfect equilibrium is now almost 0 – only two subjects out of 281 do so. But again, the distribution of subjects according to the node at which they decide to stop is not concentrated at the end. Half the subjects rather decide instead to stop at node 5 or 6, two steps before the last stage.

From these two examples, it appears that sub-game perfectness clearly fails to predict behaviour in the extremes. But at the same time, this theory accurately mirrors the trade-off people face in this type of situation: as subjects reach a node closer and closer to the end, it becomes more and more difficult for them to maintain a decision to pass, and more and more likely that the decision they will take as the game proceeds is to stop a few rounds (two to four) before the end.

1.3.3   The Use of Private Information

The first two examples were simple games whose results challenge theory in one way or another. As a third example, we will move on to another quite different environment in which both the rules and the strategies are far more complicated. Its full name is a zero-sum repeated game with incomplete information – each part is explained in turn below. Figure 1.9 shows the stage games of two different versions of the game. We first focus on the non-revealing (NR) version of the game – the difference with the fully revealing (FR) version will be described later.

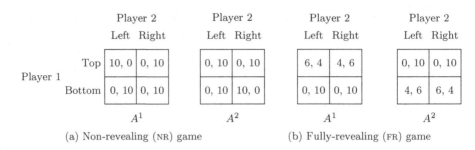

Figure 1.9 Payoff matrices of two zero-sum games

It is a zero-sum game because the payoffs are such that everything that is won by one player is lost by the other – as opposed, e.g., to the prisoners' dilemma game – so that concerns about the situation of other players have no influence over the results. All stage games shown in Figure 1.9 involve two players and two actions. Player 1 chooses either Top or Bottom, and Player 2 chooses either Left or Right – both players decide simultaneously. The numbers in the matrix represent the payoffs of both players after they have chosen their move. In matrix A^1 of Figure 1.9.a, for instance, '10, 0' indicates that Player 1 gets 10 and Player 2 receives 0 if Top/Bottom is played.[5] Inspecting the payoff tables, the game is straightforward to play for both players, because they both have a dominant strategy, i.e. an action which is preferable whatever the action chosen by the other player. For instance, in this matrix A^1, Player 1 does better by playing Top rather than Bottom, and Player 2 by playing Right rather than Left – whatever the decision of the other player. Similarly, in matrix A^2, choosing Bottom is a dominant action for Player 1 and Left is a dominant action for Player 2.

The information structure of the game makes it more interesting than a complete-information zero-sum game. In fact, a random draw (with equal probability) decides on the 'state of the world' before any decision is made. This state of the world is the payoff matrix, either A^1 or A^2, that players are facing. There is incomplete information (on one side) because players are asymmetrically informed about the result of this draw: only Player 1 is given this information. First consider the situation in which the stage game is played only once. Player 1 is privately informed of the consequence of each action and can thus pick up the dominant action of the matrix that has been drawn. Player 2, by contrast, needs to decide without being aware of the state of the world, and will thus randomise between Left and Right. But this information structure in fact becomes interesting when the game is repeated – players face the stage game together several times, and the state of the world is drawn once for all at the beginning. In this context, Player 2 can infer some information about the state of the world from the observed decisions of Player 1.

To see it more clearly, suppose you are Player 1 facing the stage games of Figure 1.9.a and knowing which state of the world you, and the other player, are in. You have to

---

[5] The sum of players' payoff is positive rather than equal to 0, but since the sum is constant across decisions, it is conceptually equivalent to a zero-sum game.

Table 1.3 Theoretical predictions in the non-revealing and fully revealing games

	Value of the game, v_t if t is						Optimal use of information
	1	2	3	4	5	∞	
FR	5.00	4.50	4.33	4.25	4.20	4	Fully revealing
NR	5.00	3.75	3.33	3.21	3.07	2.50	Non-revealing

Note. Theoretical predictions on behaviour in the NR and FR games.
Source: Jacquemet and Koessler (2013, p. 110, Table 1).

choose between Top and Bottom and you know the game will be repeated. You also know that Player 2 would like to play Right in A_1 and Left in A_2. First imagine that you decide to use your dominant action: you play Top if A_1 is drawn and Bottom if it is A_2. If this is an equilibrium strategy, then Player 2 knows this is how you react to the draw: observing Top delivers perfect information to Player 2 that A_1 has been drawn. At the next stage, Player 2 will thus play Right. But the combination Top, Right is clearly not in your interest, since you get 0: by revealing your information you no longer benefit from it. The other options for you are either not to use your information at all (deciding with equal probability between the two decisions as if you did not receive the information about the draw) or to use it only slightly, by playing the dominant action a bit more often than the other. The game thus features a trade-off in the way private information is used by Player 1, and how beneficial it is to hold such private information (the only exception is the last stage of the game, when the dominant action will always be chosen, because there is no longer any possibility to exploit the signal contained in your choices). This kind of game thus allows one to study the extent of the use of information, and the value of private information, i.e. how much more the informed player is able to earn.

The equilibrium strategies depend on two crucial features of the game: the length, denoted T, which is the number of stages during which both players play in the same matrix, and the structure of payoffs. The payoff structure we just described (the one shown in Figure 1.9.a) is called a non-revealing game, because the optimal strategy for Player 1 is to not reveal their private information in all stages but the last one: at equilibrium, it is best for Player 1 to behave as if the information were not available and the randomly drawn matrix were unknown. In the payoff structure shown in Figure 1.9.b, the prediction is exactly the opposite: the optimal strategy is for Player 1 to actually reveal private information about the true state of the world, by going straight for the stage game dominant action despite the loss incurred through sharing this information with Player 2. These theoretical predictions are summarised for different lengths of the game in Table 1.3. Is is worth noting that this change in the predictions is entirely due to the change in the payoffs. Before turning to empirical evidence on this game, you should try to think of each of the two matrix pairs, and ask yourself whether the way you will play the game will change so dramatically with the payoff structure.

A last theoretical prediction about this kind of game is that the expected payoff of Player 1 (known as the 'value of the game') is bounded above by the value of the infinitely repeated game (shown in the last column of the left-hand side of Table 1.3), and bounded below by the value of the average game. These theoretical predictions have

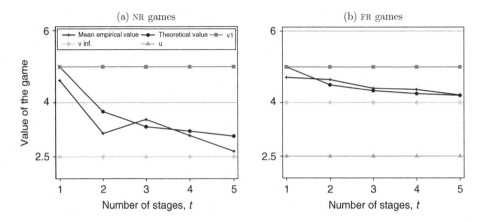

Figure 1.10 Empirical value functions

Note. Observed average payoff in the NR and FR games, along with the theoretical upper (v_1) and lower (∞) bounds.

Source: Jacquemet and Koessler (2013, p. 112, Figure 8).

been tested by Jacquemet and Koessler (2013) in an experiment in which participants play either the NR game or the FR game.

Figure 1.10 provides an overview of a comparison between the average observed values of the games in the experiment (measured as the average payoff earned by Player 1), and the predicted values as presented in Table 1.3. The empirical value functions confirm the theoretical bounds discussed above: the empirical value in both games lies between the value of the infinitely repeated game and the value of the average game. The empirical value is decreasing and smoothly converges towards its lower bound. This provides support for the theoretical analysis of the game. But the most challenging prediction is about the individual strategies, and their change according to the payoff structure.

Figure 1.11 provides information in that regard, through a summary of how information is used in each treatment. Remember that all the treatments have one prediction in common: Player 1, who knows which matrix has been drawn, has nothing to lose by using their private information (i.e. playing the stage-dominant action) at the last stage of the game. The figures are thus separated according to the stage within each game: the last stage of all games is reported on the left-hand side and the intermediate stages of all repeated games (in stages $t = 1$ to $t = T - 1$ for all $T > 1$) are reported on the right-hand side. From both the left-hand figure and the frequency of the stage-dominant action observed in the FR and NR games, experimental subjects unambiguously use information whenever it is worthwhile to do so. The relative frequency of the dominant action in the FR games is always higher than 90% and is much the same as in the last stage of the NR games. This frequency is much lower during intermediate stages of NR games, and is lower and lower as the overall duration of the game increases – when the revelation of information becomes more and more costly. Thus experimental subjects adjust their use of information not only as a reaction to experimental treatments, but also according to the decisions taken during the different stages of a given game.

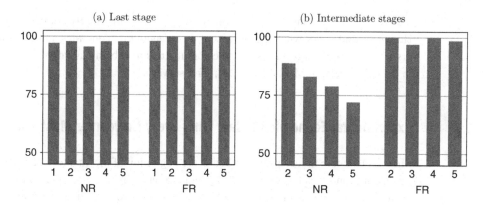

Figure 1.11 The actual use of information: informed players' behaviour
Note. For each treatment and each length, the figures display the mean share of the informed player's decisions that are the current stage-dominant action, in the final stage (*left-hand side*) and in intermediate stages (*right-hand side*).
Source: Jacquemet and Koessler (2013, p. 116, Figure 10).

Overall, empirical behaviour is relatively consistent with theoretical predictions in this environment, in sharp contrast with the two previous examples. This shows that complexity – in the game structure, but also in the theoretical predictions it induces – does not necessarily induce a larger gap between theory and empirical behaviour. The reasons for this consistency, in sharp contrast with the previous examples, is still a largely open question.

1.3.4 Beyond the Examples: Experimental Economics and Behaviour

These examples are not meant to provide a complete picture of the state of the art. But they do offer several important insights as to how experiments can help us better understand decision-makers. First, they show that experiments and economic theory are closely related. Empirical questions and the way data can be most usefully analysed are all based on a theoretical understanding of the situation. Second, and perhaps more importantly, the results described above shows a wide range of conclusions regarding the empirical relevance of theoretical results. Theory seems to accurately predict the outcomes in some games, and fails to do so in others based on similar behavioural assumptions. But the empirical relevance of theory goes beyond predicting outcomes. In particular, it accurately identifies the trade-offs and incentives people face, and how they are likely to resolve these issues. The above examples show that theory is often empirically influential in achieving this goal.

At the same time, it is also true that many behaviours and observed outcomes differ radically from theoretical expectations. Over the years, observations of this type have led specialists to enlarge the scope of the driving forces behind behaviour, to include psychological and sociological motives (this is the aim of behavioural economics). As the examples illustrate, the behaviour observed in economic experiments is related to theory in a complicated way: at times the *homo œconomicus* and human beings act as if they were perfect strangers, and at other times they are surprisingly close to one another. How, why and under what circumstances do behavioural economics and economic theory converge or diverge? These are the core matters now being taken into consideration in the field (see, e.g. McFadden, 1999, for a survey).

1.4   Experimental Economics Today: What Every Newcomer Must Know

Since its tentative first steps, described at the beginning of the chapter, the use of experiments in economics has grown rapidly and dramatically. A very large number of contributions in economics nowadays rely on assumptions on individual decision-making, about which experiments definitely have something to say. What every newcomer must know in order to become familiar with experimental economics is so vast that no single work could possibly cover the whole field. This book is no exception. Instead, the following section offers an overview of the must-knows of experimental economics. Each of the items listed below corresponds to an index entry (see p. 441) that will refer the reader to sections of the book that discuss or illustrate this particular aspect. The section concludes the outline of the book, describing the must-knows this book will focus on.

1.4.1   Must-know 1: Microeconomic Theory and Decision Sciences

As explained above, experimental economics has grown together with game theory and decision theory. As a consequence, an important part of experimental economics focuses on assessing the empirical content of theories of behaviour. This requires familiarity with a vast number of topics from microeconomic theory. The most important of them are as follows.

- **Decision theory**. This strand of literature tries to better understand how individuals make decisions under risk and uncertainty, what role time-preferences and discounting of the future play and what leads to choice inconsistencies.
- **Game theory**. Agents in an economy interact with one another; their behaviour is directly influenced by the decisions of other agents and, in particular, by the beliefs they may hold about future behaviour of these other agents. Such considerations lead to strategic decision-making, which is a major topic in experimental economics.
- **Non-standard preferences**. The focus on the driving forces of individual behaviour led to challenging the standard way of looking at preferences. Alternative views of behaviour have been developed and are now part of the economists' toolbox. This includes non-standard decision models, such as prospect theory, where contingent states of the world influence decisions; and social and other-regarding preferences, according to which people's preferences not only are defined by consequences for themselves, but also account for the situations of others.
- **Aggregation**. Society has to make decisions, and thus needs to aggregate in one way or another individual tastes. This is the focus of auction theory, the analysis of markets and studies of collective decision-making, such as voting.

- **Psychology of behaviour**. The focus on individual decision-making makes it natural to borrow much from psychology. A large part of this literature is devoted to exploring the systematic deviations from rational decision-making, associated with several well-documented biases such as anchoring and status quo bias, endowment effect, confirmation bias, conjunction fallacy, framing effect, illusion of control, loss aversion.
- **Neuroeconomics**. The analysis of individual behaviour also borrowed in recent years from decision theory in medical sciences, leading to the field of neuroeconomics, which uses physiological measures to relate behaviour to its physiological driving forces.

1.4.2   Must-Know 2: Games and Decision-Making Frameworks

The implementation in a laboratory of the theoretical frameworks described above often makes use of environments, procedures and rules of particular types. They are tools designed to study different aspects of individual behaviour. They are nowadays considered part of the standard toolbox of anyone working in the field.

- **Elicitation procedures** are mechanisms that force agents to reveal something about themselves, such as risk or intertemporal preferences, or beliefs about what others will do.
- **Experimental games** are games structured with specific theoretical properties that are widely used and studied in experimental economics. These key games include the prisoners' dilemma, the trust game, the stag hunt game, the dictator game, the guessing game, the ultimatum bargaining game, the voluntary-contribution mechanism, the minimum effort game and many others.
- **Psychological questionnaires** can be used to gather data on how people think through their decisions and how they consider different situations. Psychometric questionnaires include, for instance, measures of cognitive and non-cognitive skills, personality traits or emotions.

1.4.3   Must-Know 3: Fields and Applications

The insights from (micro)economics that are implemented in the laboratory can be applied to a wide range of field applications. As a result, there is a growing literature of experiments contributing to a better understanding of issues related to the various fields of interest to economics. Among them, the most important are:

- **Labour economics**, which focuses on the effects of labour market policies, the trade-off between consumption and leisure, the education production function, etc.
- **Personel economics** focuses on how people behave in firms, dealing with questions such as how people choose jobs and the reasons why they choose these jobs, how much people work and how they respond to monetary and non-monetary incentives.
- **Industrial organisation** focuses on how firms interact with one another under decision variables of different kinds, such as volumes, prices or levels of advertisement,

and different market structures, such as auctions, oligopoly or perfectly competitive markets.

- **Environmental economics** studies the policies designed to discipline behaviours that are detrimental to the environment, dealing with problems such as greenhouse gas emissions, air pollution, water quality, toxic waste or global warming. The issue of collective decision-making and the problem of free-riding are of critical importance in this domain.
- **Health economics** is a field concerned with the health of individuals, the health care market, the supply of health services or the public health system in general. Preventive health care is an important behavioural issue, for example, and the supply of health care services by physicians raises intriguing questions about incentive design and payment schemes.
- **Law and economics** tries to understand how individuals react to different sets of legal rules. The focus is on circumstances that make people comply with the law, and how the law changes social norms and equilibria.

1.4.4   Must Know 4: Methodological Issues: Outline of the Book

Lastly, laboratory experiments are a very precise way of gathering data and providing an empirical counterfactual to microeconomic theory. This comes with drawbacks and advantages, with several constraints on how experiments are run, and with questions regarding what they tell us about relevant economic issues. The aim of this book is to provide a review of the current answers to this strand of questions.

Chapter 2 is an introduction to the field, by describing step by step what an experiment looks like from the point of view of a participant, before turning to the analysis of the same experiment. This is a critical starting phase in becoming an experimenter, as running experiments is all about understanding how people behave, and avoiding any misunderstanding they may have about the environment. The best way to deal with this issue is to imagine how you would act if you were a participant in an experiment. The second important lesson from this introductory chapter is that experiments involve many unusual procedures and implementation rules, which may not appear quite appealing at first glance. The last part of the chapter describes the reasons why each of these features is required to make an experiment convincing – and will discuss what *convincing* means for an experiment.

This book is divided into four parts. As is explained above, Part I provides an overview of what experiments are. Part II explains why experiments in economics are needed and to what extent they are useful for empirical research in economic science. Each chapter provides a specific answer to this question. In Chapter 3, we describe how experimental economics is related to other empirical methods in economics. Basically, experiments provide a way to choose the data-generating process, enhancing the ability to measure unknown quantities relevant to economic analysis. Chapter 4 turns to the relationships between experiments and economic theory. We will see that experiments serve three different purposes: testing theory in a controlled environment, searching for facts and whispering in the ears of princes. Theory and experiments share a dynamic of mutually informing each other in this process.

Part III describes how laboratory experiments can achieve these goals. Each chapter explains how to produce experimental results, one step after the other. Chapter 5 focuses on how to design an experiment such that observed behaviour can be related to the institutions under study – i.e. which is internally valid. Chapter 6 covers all the practical aspects required for running an experiment. These practical aspects include all the phases, from building a laboratory well upstream to the final laboratory session. Last, in Chapter 7, we review the main statistical methods that are commonly used to analyse experimental data.

The focus of Part IV is to assess the relevance of what laboratory experiments tell us. Each of the chapters presents an overview of areas in which experimental results are able to shed additional light on existing knowledge. Chapter 8 begins with a question called the 'external validity' of experiments: what do decisions taken in the artificial framework of a laboratory tell us about real life? When an experiment satisfies the conditions so as to be both internally and externally valid, then the experimental results can be used by economic theory and public policy. This opens the way to a more general discussion on the possibility of inductive reasoning in economics, an issue covered in the first section of Chapter 9. This discussion will also show that observed behaviour in the lab has drastically changed the way economists think of institutions and how to organise collective decisions. This point will be the focus of the last sections of this chapter, on the design of public policies thanks to the lessons drawn from the laboratory.

Summary

This introductory chapter presented the field of experimental economics from a general perspective. Originally, experiments in the social sciences and in economics, in particular, were thought to be impossible. The first experiments beginning in the second half of the twentieth century showed otherwise. However, experimental economics did not truly break through until the focus of economics changed with the fall of general equilibrium as the central theory and the questions started to turn more towards issues related to human behaviour. To illustrate the current state of the art, we reviewed three examples from the experimental literature testing behavioural insights from game theory: the prisoners' dilemma, the centipede game and a repeated zero-sum game with incomplete information. Observed behaviour and theoretical predictions may not match up perfectly but they are not perfect strangers to each other either. This summarises the current state of the art in the field: the core issue at stake in ongoing experimental research is identifying situations where theory goes wrong and where it performs well. Since experimental economics has developed together with the use of decision and game theory in economics, the range of topics to which experiments are applied is now far too wide to be reviewed in a single book. This book focuses on experiments as an empirical methodology to inform economic science.

2   A Laboratory Experiment: Overview

The goal of this chapter is to introduce the methods used in experimental economics to study people's behaviour. This book will subsequently focus on how to design laboratory experiments, how they allow measurement of interesting and relevant parameters and how to interpret the empirical conclusions drawn from the experiments. Chapter 6, in particular, will describe the practicalities related to the implementation of laboratory experiments. Before getting to this material, we would like you, the reader, to learn what a laboratory experiment looks like from the inside. To that end, you will see things from the point of view of what we will call a *subject* or *participant*: you will be a person who comes to the laboratory to be involved in an 'experiment in economics, hence contributing to scientific researches' (this is more or less the kind of general statement one finds in the advertisements used by experimental laboratories across the world to recruit subjects).[1]

To be sure anyone reading this book will actually go through this preliminary step, let us add a few words about why we believe that to truly learn about laboratory experiments it is essential to do so from the inside at least once in your life (it goes without saying that such an experience will be best achieved by being involved in an actual experiment in a department close to your location, if such an option is available). The first reason is that, as an economist, you will certainly have your doubts about the value of the results generated by laboratory experiments. A great many experimental results seem either wonderful, trivial or silly at first glance. Once you have made the effort to mentally represent how you would have behaved in a given situation, we think you will be well prepared to better understand and use experimental economics' method and results.

A second, even more important, reason is that a good part of this book will be devoted to explaining how to carefully design laboratory experiments. The term *carefully* will mean *in such a way that observed behaviour delivers general lessons about the properties of the decision-making environment*. The first thing you should learn about laboratory experiments is that observed behaviour comes from real human beings to whom you are describing the environment. Consequently, you, as an experimenter, are the one responsible for everything participants get, everything they miss and everything they misunderstand or get confused about. An important skill in order to achieve this goal is your ability to put yourself in a participant's shoes.

---

[1] The remaining describes the proceedings of a typical experiment based on the ones we know best, which is how they are run in our own departments. There are, of course, many location-specific variations: our aim is not to describe best practices, but to provide one detailed example of how experiments are run.

Lastly, as you will see in the paragraphs ahead, the methodology of laboratory experiments means that subjects will be involved in what they may find to be some very surprising procedures. The reasoning behind these procedures is not always obvious to the participants. Again, you may understand the issue more clearly if you are able to remember how you yourself felt as a participant. In this chapter you will be exposed for the first time, without any prior knowledge about the method, to this strange sequence of events called an experiment (the rationale of which will be described in Chapter 5).

Now try to imagine that you have signed up on a website to participate in an experiment. Soon after you register, you will receive an e-mail asking you if you would like to come on *HOUR, DAY-MONTH-YEAR* for an experimental session to take place at *ADDRESS*. You agree to participate and confirm your participation in the given experimental session.

2.1 The Experiment

When you arrive at the building, you will be welcomed by someone with the full list of people who have confirmed. You will then be asked to show an ID and once your identity is confirmed you will be given a form similar to the one shown in Figure 2.1. You will have to sign the form in order to participate in the experiment. Once the appointed time is reached, all the people waiting in the hall will be asked to go through the university building to the door of a lab room.

In front of that door, the same person who has welcomed you will explain the following:

You will enter one by one into the room behind me, which is the laboratory where I will explain everything you need to know to participate in this experiment. Before going in, I will ask for the consent form you signed, and have you take a sheet of paper. The name written on this sheet is the name or number of your computer, where you will sit once you are in the room. Once everybody has entered, we will all start the experiment together as a group. Meanwhile, please wait quietly; thank you for your patience.

Before you begin the experiment, you will be informed about the way it will proceed. To that end, you are given a sheet of paper with the following text, the *instructions for the experiment*. The experimenter reads it aloud and encourages you to carefully follow on your own paper – that is yours for the entire duration of the experiment. Let's read it together.

Instructions for the experiment

You are participating in an experiment in which you can earn money. The amount you earn will depend on your own decisions as well as the decisions of the other participants. Before starting the experiment, we will ask you to answer a few questions in order to get to know you better (your age, gender, occupation, etc.). **All this information will remain anonymous and confidential.**

CONSENT FORM TO PARTICIPATE IN
A LABORATORY EXPERIMENT

Theme: 'XXX' ; Research project n° XXX

Name, Surname:...

Address : :...

(below denominated 'the participant')

The participant freely consents to be involved in the experimental sessions.
Date of the experiment : ....
Maximum duration : ....

The amount of compensation obtained at the end of the session by the participant will depend on the outcomes of the experiment. The amount will fall in a range between…XX.. € (Euros) and a maximum of…XXX.. € (Euros).

Done in XXX, the same day.

Signature of the contracting participant

Figure 2.1 Consent form

Procedures for the experiment

At the beginning of the experiment, **two groups, each involving 9 participants**, will be formed. **Each participant belongs to the same group during the whole experiment**.

Overview. You will be participating in an auction in which you are the buyer. The currency unit used in the auction is the ECU (Experimental Currency Unit). Its value in euros is described at the end of the instructions. You will submit a bid in ECU to acquire one unit of the good which the experiment monitor then will reacquire from you. There will be several rounds of bidding. The outcome of the auction in each round directly influences how much you will be paid at the end of the experiment.

Procedures for each round

Each round has 8 steps.

Step 1. Each bidder looks at his or her **resale value** on their screen. We label **resale value** the price in ECU that the monitor will pay to buy back a unit of the good that is purchased in the auction. **The resale values of different participants in a group can be different**. Once you have looked at your resale value, press the OK button.

Step 2. Each bidder then submits a bid in ECU to buy one unit of the good. To do this, move the scroll bar up or down until you see the price you want to submit. Then press the OK button below the scroll bar to confirm your choice.

Step 3.   The monitor will rank the bids from highest to lowest. For instance:

n° 1   fs.l ECU   **Highest bid**
n° 2   df.g ECU
n° 3   za.f ECU
n° 4   sc.d ECU
n° 5   qs.a ECU
n° 6   nj.h ECU
n° 7   hh.m ECU
n° 8   ht.t ECU
n° 9   ky.l ECU   **Lowest bid**

Step 4.   The second-highest bid (bid n^o2) determines the **market price**. In the above example, if the second-highest bid is df.g ECU then the market price would be df.g ECU:

n° 1   fs.l ECU

———————————————————

n° 2   df.g ECU   **Second-highest bid: market price**

———————————————————

n° 3   za.f ECU
n° 4   sc.d ECU
n° 5   qs.a ECU
n° 6   nj.h ECU
n° 7   hh.m ECU
n° 8   ht.t ECU
n° 9   ky.l ECU

Step 5.   The buyer who bids the highest price (the buyer ranked n^o1) purchases one unit of the good at the market price. In the above example the buyer who bid fs.l ECU purchases one unit of the good that costs df.g ECU.

Step 6.   Buyer n^o1 then sells the unit back to the monitor. The price of this transaction is the resale value listed on the screen for that round. The profit in ECU that bidder n^o1 earns for that round is the difference between the resale value and the market price:

$$\text{profit} = \text{resale value} - \text{market price}$$

Important remark. Your profits can also be negative: if you buy a unit of the good and the resale value is less than the market price, your profits will be negative.

Step 7.   All bidders at or below the market price (buyers n^o2 to n^o9) do not buy anything, **so they make zero profit for that round**.

Step 8.   End of the round. Your profit in ECU in that round appears on your screen. Press the OK button once you have noted it. Your screen will then indicate whether a new round is about to begin or the experiment is over.

How will you take your decisions?

Your screen is divided into three areas:

All the information you need to take your decisions will be displayed in the upper part of the screen.

You then take your decisions by pressing on the buttons displayed in the middle part of the screen.

The bottom part will show you your past decisions and profits.

Payment of your earnings

At the end of the experiment, we will compute the sum of your profits in ECU across rounds. If your profit in a given round is negative, the total decreases; if your profit in a given round is positive, the total increases. This total is converted into euros according to the rate 3 ECU = 1€. A fixed fee equal to **10 €** is added to this payoff. You will be paid the corresponding monetary payoff in cash privately at the end of the experiment.

Please do not talk and try not to communicate with any other subject during the experiment. If you communicate, you will be asked to leave and forfeit any money earned. It is essential that you understand the instructions correctly. If you have any questions, please raise your hand and someone will come and answer them. Please be sure to follow these instructions.

Thank you for participating.

If you have any questions about the instructions, you will be able to quietly raise your hand. The experimenter will then come over to you to answer your question(s) in private. Obviously, in this textbook experiment you cannot raise your hand to ask questions. So please take the time you need to read and reread the above text, until it is perfectly clear in your mind how the experiment will be conducted and what happens depending on what you and the others do ...

Good. Now let's go through the last stage: a short questionnaire to check that everything in the instructions is crystal clear for you. The answers provided on the questionnaire will not influence your earnings or participation in the experiment in any way: its only aim is to help you be sure everything is clear to you. Please fill in the questionnaire.

Pre-experiment questionnaire

1. New groups are formed after each round.

   ☐ YES   ☐ NO

2. Each group includes _____ participants.

3. At the beginning of each round, all the participants in my group are attributed the same resale value.

   ☐ YES   ☐ NO

4. When I make a bid, I can bid any amount I want.

   ☐ YES   ☐ NO

5. The market price is set by the bid of the second-highest bidder in my group.

   ☐ YES   ☐ NO

6. If my bid is the highest bid and is equal to rr.u ECU and the second-highest bid in my group is gg.k ECU, then I buy the unit of the good.

   ☐ YES   ☐ NO

   If YES, I pay: _____ for the good.

7. If I purchase a unit of the good and my resale value is greater than the market price, I will make positive profits.

☐ YES   ☐ NO

8. The monetary payoff I will be paid at the end of the experiment depends on the amount of ECU I earned during the auction.

☐ YES   ☐ NO

Now that you are done, let's go through the questionnaire together, and stress the answers that accurately describe how the experiment will proceed.

Q1 *'New groups are formed after each round'*. The answer is **No**. The groups remain the same during the entire experiment.

Q2 *'Each group includes 9 bidders'*.

Q3 *'At the beginning of each round all the participants in my group are attributed the same resale value'*. The answer is **No**. The resale value of the various participants in your group can be different.

Q4 *'When I make a bid, I can bid any amount I want'*. The answer is **Yes**. There is no constraint imposed on the price you choose.

Q5 *'The market price is set by the bid of the second-highest bidder in my group'*. The answer is **Yes**, the market price is the second-highest one among all bids chosen in your group.

Q6 *'If my bid is the highest bid and is equal to rr.u ECU and the second-highest bid in my group is gg.k ECU, then, I buy the unit of the good and I pay gg.k, i.e. the market price.'* The answer is **Yes**.

Q7 *'If I purchase a unit of the good and my resale value is greater than the market price, I will make positive profits'*. The answer is **Yes**, since your profit will be computed as your resale value minus the market price.

Q8 *'The monetary payoff I will be paid at the end of the experiment depends on the amount of ECU I earned during the auction.'* The answer is **Yes**.

If you are surprised by any of these answers, please read again the instructions sheet carefully before returning to the question you had doubts about.

Now that all the written material has been read, the experiment can start. The first step is illustrated in the screen capture in Figure 2.2. The display has three frames. The top frame gives you information about the current round. The middle frame is devoted to your own decisions. The bottom frame provides a reminder about previous rounds. The information provided here includes the round number and three key elements: your resale price, the price you have chosen and your profit in each round. The first display, on the top of the screen, gives you a resale value for the good (24 ECU). All you have to do is to click on the OK button to proceed.

Once you have clicked on the OK button, a second screen appears as shown in Figure 2.3. This second display asks you to choose a price for the good. To choose the price

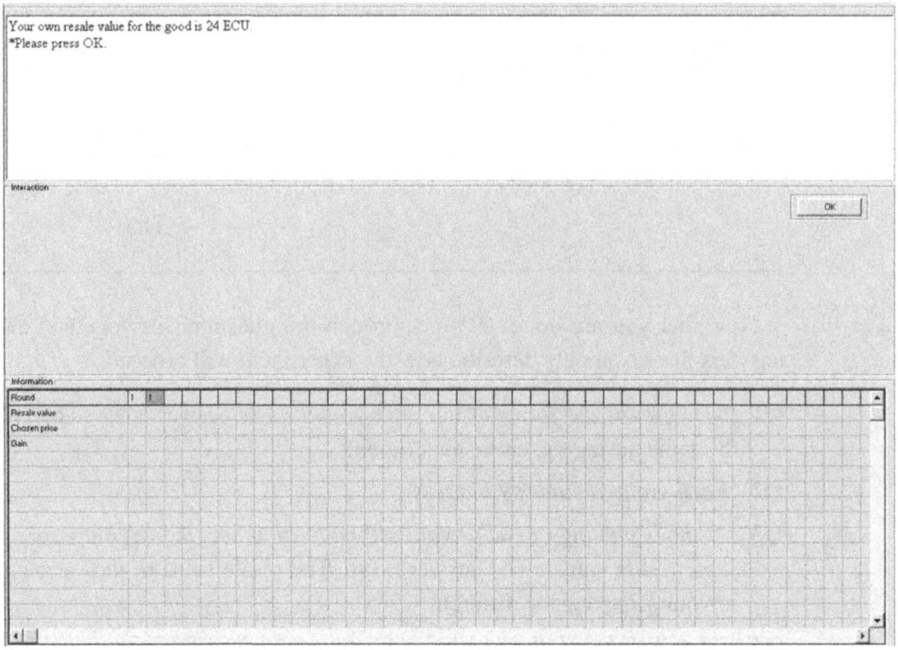

Figure 2.2 First screen: resale value in the first round

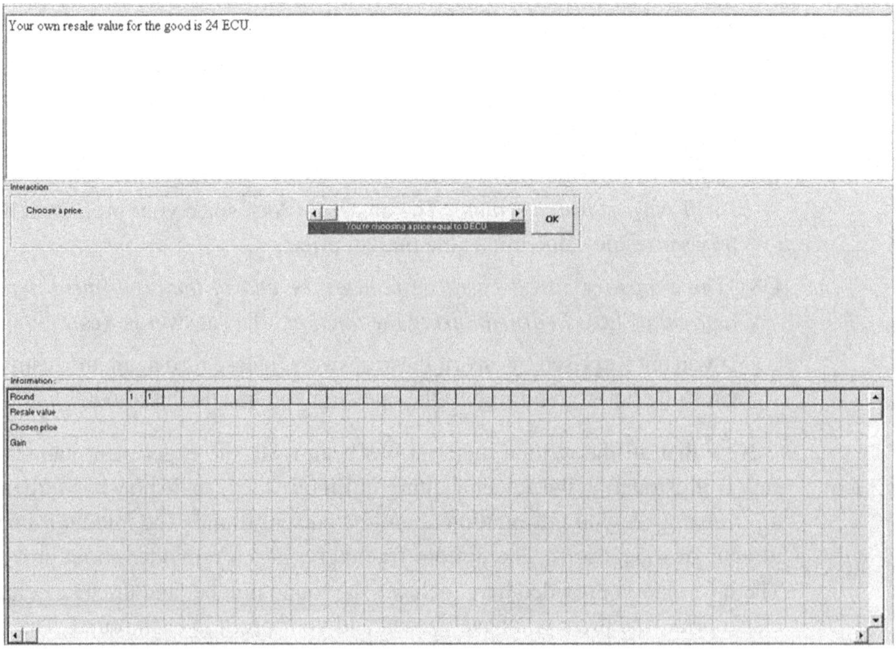

Figure 2.3 Second screen: bid in the first round of play

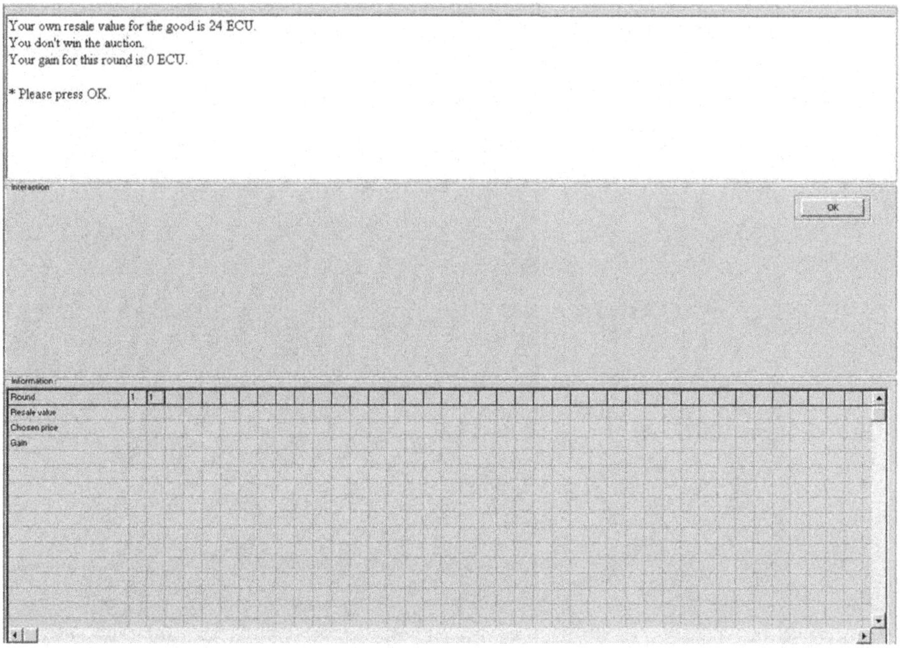

Your own resale value for the good is 24 ECU.
You don't win the auction.
Your gain for this round is 0 ECU.

* Please press OK.

Figure 2.4 Third screen: results of the first round

you are willing to bid you have access to a scrollbar in the middle frame. Once you have chosen the price you want to bid, click on OK to proceed. Let us say, for the sake of the example, that you chose a price of 37 ECU for that round. The third display in Figure 2.4 shows you the result of the auction. The information about whether or not you won the auction appears on your screen, saying you didn't win the auction. Your resale value for the good and the profit you gain from that round (0 here) is also reported in the top frame. Click on OK to proceed and a second round will start.

Let us skip the subsequent rounds, and jump to round 6. The display you get at this stage is shown in Figure 2.5. The bottom frame shows the past experiences you have had with the auction. In round 1, your resale price was 24 ECU, your chosen price was 37 ECU and your profit was 0 ECU. In round 2, your resale value was 84 ECU, your chosen price was 86 and your profit was equal to 8 ECU. From this you can infer that the second price was equal to 76 ECU. In rounds 3 to 5, you gain nothing from the auctions. Now, in round 6, the top frame assigns you a resale value for the good equal to 65 ECU. As before, you have access to a scrollbar in the middle frame to choose the price you want to bid. Once you have chosen the price you are willing to bid, click on OK to proceed. Let us state that you are willing to bid 88 ECU for the good. As shown in Figure 2.5, your bid was high enough to win the auction and the profit you made is equal to −19 ECU. On the screen, you can also see the second price you paid for the purchased good. This price is equal to $65 + 19 = 84$ ECU. Click on OK to proceed and a new round will start.

Once you have finished with all the scheduled rounds, the screen shows a summary of all rounds and the resulting monetary gain you earn from the experiment. All participants

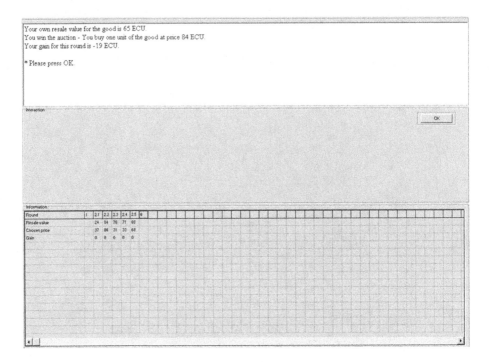

Your own resale value for the good is 65 ECU.
You win the auction - You buy one unit of the good at price 84 ECU.
Your gain for this round is -19 ECU.

* Please press OK.

Figure 2.5 The sixth round of the experiment: screen captures

come one by one to a separate room inside the lab, and get paid in cash according to this amount. You are then thanked for your participation, and you can leave the room where the experiment was run.

2.2   The Experimenter's Role: The Game under Study

If you belong to the same population as the students that usually come to experimental economics laboratories, then you probably did not recognise the rules of the mechanism described above. Otherwise, you probably have already guessed that these instructions are meant to put subjects into a second-price auction.

Before getting to a description of the experiment from the experimenter's point of view – what is called *the design of the experiment* or *experimental design* – you need to become familiar with the questions answered thanks to experiments of this type in empirical research in economics. These answers come from the extremely powerful properties of such mechanisms according to economic theory, as shown in detail in the next section.

2.2.1   Theoretical Properties of Second-Price Auctions with Private Values

The above experiment considered a market with one single seller and n buyers. Only one unit of the good was to be sold on that market. Here, we are not concerned by the seller's behaviour, so we can assume the good is worth 0. In that case, the seller agrees to sell the good at any positive price.[2] The main aim of economic theory in such a context is to find the equilibrium. The equilibrium here signifies who buys the good and what price is paid for it, given economic agents' preferences.

Let us start by formalising the buyer's preferences. We denote v_i the monetary equivalent of the buyer's i utility of obtaining the good, aka the *private value* of the good. The value is private because different people, i, are allowed to have different values. Moreover, an individual i does not know the others' value (i.e. values v_j for $j \neq i$). This utility of owning the good is a measure of the buyer's willingness to pay because if the buyer trades a monetary loss equal to v_i against the consumption good, their situation remains exactly the same. If q is the price to be paid for consuming the good, the buyer's benefit is thus exactly equal to $v_i - q$. The seller's profit is equal to $\pi = q - 0 = q$. Thus, in moving from the seller's hand to the buyer's hand, the good generates a value equal to v_i. The higher the buyer's private value, the higher the amount of wealth created in the way the available scarce resource (one unit of the good) is allocated. This observation highlights the first important property of an allocation mechanism: its efficiency. Efficiency is measured here as the ability of the allocation mechanism to allocate the good to the agent who attributes the highest value to it, to achieve the highest possible level of wealth.[3]

An examination of the payoff functions of the two agents clearly shows that the price is not relevant to efficiency. A change in price is a zero-sum transfer between the buyer and the seller, leaving unchanged the total amount of wealth. The price only decides on how the surplus is shared between the two economic agents. However, buyers will not agree to pay just any price, because they would incur a loss were they to pay a higher price than their private value v_i to acquire the good. This means that the price the buyer announces in the auction (what we called a *bid*) is correlated with their privately known valuation v_i. As a result, the bid becomes an observable signal of the buyer's own preferences. This points to the second important property of an allocation mechanism: its revelation property, measured as the informativeness of the bid regarding the underlying true preference.

How a given allocation mechanism performs on both these levels depends on the bidding behaviour it induces. The second-price auction implements the following allocation rule: the buyer with the highest bid wins the auction, but the price paid for acquiring the good is the second-highest bid. In order to elicit what a given buyer i can best do in such a context, let us denote their bid b_i and B_i the highest bid chosen from among the other $n - 1$ bidders.[4] Since values are private, buyer i knows nothing about B_i. What they know for sure, though, is that they will win the auction by choosing a bid b_i higher than

---

[2] One possible rationale for this assumption is that the good is already produced and has no consumption value for the seller.

[3] An alternative view is that efficiency also exhausts all possibilities of trade: if the mechanism allocates the good to an agent whose value is lower than that of another, then the two could find a mutually beneficial agreement to trade the good – since another agent in the economy is willing to pay more for the good than what it is worth for its current owner. This applies for as long as the final allocation remains sub-efficient.

[4] Formally, $B_i = max_{j \neq i} b_j$, which can also be denoted $B_i = maxb_{-i}$, with $-i$ denoting all the bidders except i

B_i, whatever B_i. And that, in this case, B_i will be the price they will pay for the good. Thus, buyer i (weakly) prefers to win the auction if $v_i \geq B_i$ (so that $v_i - B_i \geq 0$) and prefers to lose it otherwise (if $v_i - B_i < 0$). Consider each possible state of the world in turn.

If, on the one hand, B_i is strictly higher than v_i, then buyer i prefers to lose the auction – because winning it would mean a decrease in wealth. There is one choice which guarantees that the buyer is sure to lose the auction in all instances such that $v_i - B_i < 0$: the bid b_i simply should never be higher than the private value v_i. If, on the other hand, B_i is lower than v_i, buyer i will want to win the auction. You might have already noted that the outcome of the auction stays the same whatever the bid b_i is, as long as it is higher than B_i. In a second-price auction, the price q to be paid will always equal B_i and buyer i will remain the winner. For any bid b_i chosen in such circumstances, moving to a higher bid increases the probability of winning the auction without changing the price to be paid, provided that such a bid remains compatible with this particular state of the world. The threshold separating the two states of the world is reached when the bid b_i reaches the private value v_i. At that point, the chances of winning the auction against a B_i higher than v_i become positive.

As a result, the optimal bidding strategy for buyer i in this environment is to choose a bid b_i exactly equal to their private valuation $b_i^* = v_i$ as it provides the highest possible likelihood of winning the auction when and only if it is desirable. This strategy is followed by all bidders on the market, leading to the two main theoretical properties of the second-price auction. First, the ranking of equilibrium bids is exactly the same as the ranking of valuations: the winner of the auction will thus be the one with the highest private value, so that the mechanism achieves an optimal allocation. Second, the equilibrium bidding behaviour induced by the auction is *perfectly revealing*: each bid is a perfect signal of the buyer's underlying true preference. For daily-life goods, either market ones like a pen or a coffee or non-market ones like those described in Focus 2.1, these preferences are privately known by their holder, and unobservable. In such contexts, the auction can be used as a revelation mechanism – a way to better know what the distribution of individual preferences is.[5]

2.2.2   Why Experimental Auctions Are Important

The above-mentioned properties of second-price auctions are all the more impressive given the observational context of the model's assumption. While each buyer is the only

---

[5] This last property is the main difference from the behaviour induced by the first-price auction mechanism. In first-price auctions the winner's bid is also the market price. There, the bid determines both who wins and the price the winner will pay. A unique instrument is used to select the winner and to offer the winner's prize. The second-price auction, by contrast, relies on two instruments each serving only one objective: the winner's bid determines the winner while the second-highest bid determines the profits. The optimal strategy in first-price auctions thus resolves the trade-off between winning the auction on the one hand, and maximising profit in the event of winning on the other. This results in an equilibrium bid slightly lower than the private value, so that the mechanism is not perfectly revealing. But the allocation achieved is still efficient, as all bidders will adjust their strategy in this way and the ranking of bids will perfectly match the ranking of private values.

Focus 2.1
Preference elicitation and policy-making: the hypothetical bias

Most non-market goods – such as environmental protection, new medicines or amenities like a park in a city – are publicly funded. When it comes to deciding on how much to invest in one particular good of this type, it is necessary to run a cost–benefit analysis. In particular, decision-makers have to assess the benefits of the investment. One key aspect of these benefits is how desirable the good is for the target population. The desirability of the good is central not only because it is a measure of how much welfare the investment generates but also because it measures the willingness to pay for the good of the people who will consume it. Obtaining such a measure amounts to eliciting people's true – unobservable – preferences for the good. To that end, the most commonly used method is to conduct surveys requesting respondents to state how much they would like to pay to have the good produced. But a widely recognised challenge of such an elicitation method is that people may declare a higher amount than they are actually willing to pay for the good, because the question is asked in a hypothetical context without real economic commitments or consequences (Arrow et al., 1993). Of course, relying on such stated preferences if hypothetical bias does exist leads to many inefficient investment decisions. Revelation mechanisms, such as the second-price auction, are thus studied experimentally in order both to study the phenomenon, and to find settings that overcome the bias.

---

one to know their own individual preferences, and knows only that, one merely has to ask each buyer for a simple bid. Beforehand, though, each buyer has to be warned that the allocation of the good will follow the rules of a second-price auction. Based on these very simple market rules, the outcome of the mechanism is to allocate the good to the buyer everyone would have chosen based on a perfect knowledge of the full demand function (in the aim of achieving the highest possible level of wealth from the available resources). Moreover, an inspection of the individual bids even provides perfect knowledge of the underlying individual preferences. Focus 2.1 describes the consequences of this property for policy design. The remarkable properties of second-price auctions remain theoretical, however. In other words, all of this is conditional on the empirical relevance of the bidding behaviour predicted by the model.

These are the kinds of question that laboratory experiments are particularly good at answering. This is so for two reasons. First, the experimental context provides more control over the setting in which behaviour is analysed. Second, an experimental context provides more measures of what happens in different circumstances. We will detail these two reasons in turn.

First, note that the experiment we described in Section 2.1 is the exact empirical counterpart of the model. The allocation rule is the same, but even the payoff functions driving individual preferences parallel those embedded in the model. The resale values v_i, in particular, play the same role in the empirical world provided by the experiment as the private values do in the world described by the model. This means that the experimenter 'chooses' or induces the participants' preferences; for that reason, this kind of setting is called an *induced value* experiment – as the experimenter chooses, induces, the individual preferences according to which people in the experiment are making decisions (see Section 5.3.1).

At the same time as they are induced – hence controlled – individual preferences are also perfectly observed by the experimenter. This represents a huge added value compared to what is generally available when one is working on data from the real world. Such an observation is crucial as theoretical predictions are all about the relationships between the outcome of the auction (the list of bids, the identity of the winner, the market price, the winner's profit) and the underlying factors driving such outcomes, namely preferences. As a matter of fact, the experimental context allows one to observe not only the market price but also the complete list of all the prices proposed for each bidder and each auction. Again, this is not the case in most observational data available from real-world auctions (where one typically observes only the winning bid). These features make the empirical outcomes from experiments highly reliable, as will be explained in Chapter 3.

As a result of this combination of strong control capabilities and wide observation opportunities, the experiment in which you have just participated provides much information on the theory of second-price auctions. First, one can test the efficiency of the allocation rule by comparing the private value of the winner to the highest private value present in the market. If the winner is the participant with the highest value in the market, then the allocation rule was empirically efficient. Second, the revelation properties of the mechanism can be empirically assessed. This assessment is based on the comparison between individuals' bids b_i and their private values v_i. If the bids correspond to the private values then the second-price auction is an accurate preference revelation mechanism. It is worth noting, on a final note, that theory serves as a benchmark for the empirical observations delivered by the experiment – the way data are analysed is framed and driven by the theoretical understanding of the environment. Chapter 4 will feature a more detailed discussion of this important aspect.

2.3   Experimental Second-Price Auction with Private Values

It is now time to move from the front stage to the backstage of the experiment and look at it from the point of view of the researchers rather than the participants. There are always some features of an experiment that are not visible to participants (hence not described in the instructions presented in Section 2.1) but are very important to know in order to fully understand the results. In the case of a second-price Vickrey auction, a significant part of the design lies in the way the resale values (the experimental equivalent of the private values v_i) are chosen. In the example opening the chapter, the second-price auction experiment involves nine bidders and nine bidding rounds. For the nine bidders, the list of induced values is $\{84; 76; 71; 68; 65; 63; 53; 38; 24\}$ and is kept constant during the experiment. From the point of view of the experimenter, $\{84; 76; 71; 68; 65; 63; 53; 38; 24\}$ is the induced demand curve. Each value in the list is allocated to exactly one bidder in each round. From one round to the next, each bidder's value changes as they pick up another

Table 2.1 Empirical revelation properties of a second-price auction

Induced value	24		38	53	63	65	68	71	76	84	All
Aggregate demand (AD)											
($v_i \times 18$)	432		684	954	1134	1170	1224	1278	1368	1512	9756
Revealed AD	492		678	816	1145	1121	1229	1260	1406	1490	9637
in % of AD	114		99	85	101	96	100	99	103	98	99
Round	1		2	3	4	5	6	7	8	9	
Aggregate demand (AD)											
($2\sum_i v_i$)	1084		1084	1084	1084	1084	1084	1084	1084	1084	9756
Revealed AD	895		1045	1141	1065	1174	1143	1116	1045	1013	9637
in% of AD	83		96	105	98	108	105	103	96	93	99

Note. The table reports the revealed demand in the experiment, i.e. the sum of bids posted by all bidders defined in columns. The upper part groups bidders according to their induced value; the lower part provides round-by-round data.
Source: Jacquemet et al. (2009, p. 38, Table 1).

one in the list which they have not yet tested. Since there are exactly nine bidding rounds (note that the instructions only say that there will be several rounds; the reason for this choice is to avoid *end-game effects*), such a rotating bidders-value matching puts into practice all possible permutations of the constant aggregate demand curve.

Table 2.1 shows the baseline results obtained by Jacquemet et al. (2009).[6] The behaviour displayed in the table stems from 18 subjects, resulting in two markets of nine subjects each in the experiment. Each subject participated in one of the two nine-person markets, with nine repetitions, each with different induced values. The experiment provides 2 (markets) × 9 (subjects) × 9 (repetitions) = 162 observations of bidding behaviour (which are not independent, however, as is often the case with experimental data: Chapter 7 describes the statistical tools used to address such specificities). Table 2.1 is made up of two main parts. The upper part classifies the answers to each of the induced values proposed to the participants (remember that each induced value is proposed to each subject once, and only once, at some point of the nine repetitions of the second-price auction). The lower part classifies the answers with respect to the rounds in which the bids were revealed. Before we turn to commenting on observed behaviour of the participants in the experiment, try to recall how you decided to behave in the experiment and, in particular, whether any of the theoretical insights of Section 2.2 came to mind when you decided on a bidding strategy ...

In the upper part of Table 2.1, the second row reports the corresponding induced aggregate demand (*AD*) for each induced value in column (24, 38 ...). For each induced

[6] This design was first implemented by Cherry et al. (2004). The primary focus of Jacquemet et al. (2009) is to assess the influence of the origin of the experimental endowment on bidding behaviour. To that end, a preliminary step is added to the design presented in Section 2.1. Before participating in the auction, subjects answer a 20-item quiz in which the right answers are remunerated. These subjects thus enter the auction with an amount of money they consider as their own (because it was 'earned') rather than 'windfall'.

value, the aggregate demand is equal to 18 times the induced value. For example, when the induced value is equal to 24, the aggregate demand for the 18 subjects is equal to $24 \times 18 = 432$. As each induced value is allocated to exactly one subject in each auction round, the aggregate demand for a given induced value pools together participants irrespective of the order in which they obtained that value. For example, when the induced value was equal to 24, the aggregate demand pools subjects who acquired this value in first, second, ..., nth position. A consequence of this is that aggregate demand smooths out the effect of learning or experience (see Section 5.5 for a detailed discussion).

What subjects actually did is displayed in the third row of the upper part. The empirical counterpart of the aggregate demand, called revealed aggregate demand (*revealed AD*), is shown here. The revealed aggregate demand is the sum of the bids chosen by all the subjects who have experienced the induced values provided in a given column. For example, the sum of the bids of subjects with an induced value of 24 is equal to $2 \times \sum_{i|v_i = 24} b_i = 492$. An empirically perfectly revealing auction should equalise aggregate demand and revealed aggregate demand. To make the comparison easier, the fourth row presents the ratio between the revealed aggregate demand and the aggregate demand. This ratio is called the revelation ratio, i.e. the share of the induced demand which is stated through the bids. For (almost) all induced values the average revelation rate is remarkably close to 100%; and it is true all along the demand curve, i.e. along the whole distribution of induced values. These results suggest that the second-price auction performs remarkably well in terms of demand revelation.

The picture is quite different in terms of the second theoretical property of the mechanism, namely its ability to implement an efficient allocation. Strictly speaking, efficiency can be fully assessed from the induced value of the winner in each round. In this experiment, the winner should always be the bidder with the maximum induced value, which is equal to 84. This actually happened in 61.1% of all cases, which is far from what theory predicts. The experiment also allows measurement of the extent of the loss associated with such sub-efficient outcomes: this can be measured by the share of the potential wealth that is actually realised in the experiment. The data reveal that the average induced value of the winner over the 18 auctions is 77.5 in the experiment, so that 92% of the potential efficiency is actually achieved at the aggregate level – the cost of the loss in efficiency is thus rather small in this context.

Lastly, in order to assess whether these results are related in any way to repetition-based learning, the bottom part of the table presents the data in terms of round-by-round behaviour. In each column, the second row aggregates all the bids posted by all the subjects in the round, the third row shows the revealed aggregate demand and the fourth row displays the revelation ratio. Each of these subjects has different induced values because the full demand curve is induced in each round, making the induced aggregate demand the same in each column (AD = 1084). The table reveals a small effect of learning on bidding behaviour, which occurs only at the very beginning of the experiment. The revelation ratio rises from 83% to 96% between the first two rounds and remains stable after that. This result illustrates the importance of practice questions in the beginning of the experiment. The result also shows that learning is not a major issue in this setting.

To sum up, the induced-value context allows us to test both theoretical properties of second-price auctions: efficiency and preference revelation. The mechanism performs worse on the first dimension than on the second, although the cost of the loss remains small. The revelation property, by contrast, is very accurately replicated by empirical behaviour. For this reason, second-price auctions have been extensively used as a mechanism to study preference revelation in the laboratory. It is worth noting that this property occurs even though most subjects were very likely to behave in the same way as those of you who had never heard about auction theory before. All these subjects might have been using rules of thumb to make up their mind, and they might also have misinterpreted the instructions. None of these behavioural elements are related to the behaviour described by theory. The main lesson is thus that the rationality assumptions that lie behind the equilibrium predictions accurately describe the outcome resulting from the environment, even though actual rationality might well not be what is behind such an observation. This (likely) discrepancy between the theoretical representation of behaviour and its actual driving forces is irrelevant in the context of this particular institution, because the institutions drive people's choices in such a way that they behave *as if* theory were descriptively right.

2.4   *Case Study*: Experimentally Designed Devices to Reduce Hypothetical Bias

Hypothetical bias in stated-preference work challenges the credibility of stated-preference methods as a tool for measuring economic values in a credible way. As Illustration 2.1 shows, hypothetical bias is best studied in the context of the elicitation of real-world goods rather than the artificial setting of induced preferences – otherwise, there is little to no difference in elicited preferences according to the monetary consequences of respondents' answers. It thus seems important to consider an elicitation context that is closer to the real-world situation of a cost–benefit analysis. This enhances what one is able to learn about the real-world behaviour thanks to the experiment – a question that will be discussed in length in Chapter 8.

One of the most common stated-preference methods used in economics is contingent valuation. This methodology uses surveys that request respondents to make decisions regarding a non-market good. Experimental researchers have tried to adapt the survey design to undermine the risk of hypothetical bias. A first possibility is to adjust, or calibrate, the answers to the valuation tasks *ex post*. An alternative is to frame the context of the individual choice to correct the hypothetical bias *ex ante*. This section will describe each of these two methods in turn. Among the *ex ante* methods, cheap talk scripts have garnered substantial attention. As such, they will be the object of a special subsection. The aim of all this research is to improve the design of preference elicitation surveys, in such a way that responses deliver a more reliable measure of true preferences in the population. They thus exemplify how experiments help public policy decision-making, which will be more systematically discussed in Chapter 9.

Illustration 2.1

Second-price auctions as a preference revelation mechanism: home-grown and induced values

An important question about the hypothetical bias phenomenon, described in Focus 2.1, is whether it actually arises as a consequence either of the mechanism itself, or of the preference revelation exercise. To study this question, Jacquemet et al. (2011) implement two sets of second-price auctions. The first one is the induced-values design described in Section 2.1. The second set of second-price auctions uses a real good: a donation to the WWF, by adopting a dolphin. In this kind of context, subjects enter the laboratory with their unknown private preferences for the good, which remains unobserved to the experimenter – hence called a *home-grown* value good. It also means that, in contrast with an induced-value design, subjects need to elicit their own preferences before answering the question. For both kinds of good, the rules of the auction remain as similar as possible – to ease comparison – but the auction is performed under two different sets of rules. In the first, subjects' earnings from the experiment are directly affected by the outcome of the auction. This condition is called the REAL treatment. In the second condition subjects are asked to behave *as if* they were directly affected by the outcome of the auction, but without any monetary consequence – hence labelled HYPOTHETICAL. The difference in revealed preferences in REAL as compared to HYPOTHETICAL measures the hypothetical bias. The results are twofold. First, there is no evidence of hypothetical bias in the induced-value context: the bids in HYPOTHETICAL are very similar to those displayed in Table 2.1. Second, the difference in revealed demand between the HYPOTHETICAL and REAL in the home-grown auction is huge. These results are in line with existing evidence reported by, e.g., Taylor et al. (2001); Vossler and McKee (2006); Murphy et al. (2010) in various experimental designs. Such results suggest that hypothetical bias is more a matter of preference formation (how subjects elicit their own preferences) rather than of preference revelation (whether self-reported preferences match the true ones). The challenge is thus to find survey designs that lead subjects to think about their true underlying preferences in the hypothetical context as seriously and deeply as they would if there were actual monetary consequences.

2.4.1   *Ex post* Methods

A famous *ex post* technique consists in calibrating down hypothetical responses – in such a way that the post-calibration values of hypothetical answers match the answers one would elicit with actual monetary incentives. Of course, the main question here is the amount of the scaling of the hypothetical responses. Many surveys in the stated-preferences literature have attempted to calculate the size of the hypothetical bias for calibration purposes. The general conclusion is that there is no golden rule for calibration. Diamond and Hausman (1994) predicted that proper calibration stipulates dividing hypothetical estimates by anywhere from 1.5 to 10. List and Gallet (2001) ran a meta-analysis on 29 studies from the literature. They found that on average subjects overstate their preferences by a factor of about three in hypothetical settings. Moreover, the amount of over-revelation appears to be good-specific and context-specific (also see Fox et al., 1998). List and Gallet (2001) found that the hypothetical bias is less important for private goods (as compared to public goods) and for willingnesses to pay (as compared to willingnesses to accept). A possible lower bound for calibration is about 1.3, which is very close to the Diamond and Hausman (1994) lower bound.

A similar attempt at *ex post* adjustment is the use of follow-up certainty questions (Champ et al., 1997). This procedure adds a question to the survey, where respondents are asked their level of confidence in the truthfulness or accuracy of their answer to the preference elicitation survey. A threshold is then chosen, and only preferences revealed with a high enough degree of certainty, or confidence, are actually accounted for in the analysis.

2.4.2   *Ex ante* Methods

The *ex ante* methods try to build on the reasons why hypothetical bias appears to change revelation before it occurs.

A first possible reason for the poor revelation performance of hypothetical questions is that, because they are based on a hypothetical scenario, subjects do not take the valuation exercise seriously enough. Consequential procedures aim to address this issue. The procedure consists of improving the realism of the scenario (Carson et al., 2000; Cummings and Taylor, 1998). The improvement in the elicitation procedure is usually made by giving subjects the probability that their own choice in the experiment will become real. The frame underlines the fact that the participant's choice might actually impact the policy. Earlier experiments provide contrasting results on consequential procedures. Cummings and Taylor (1998) show that probabilities have to be high (greater than 0.75) to produce an effect, while Carson et al. (2002) find a coincidence with preferences elicited in the real context starting at a probability level of 0.2, which is still substantially higher than the probability level any reasonable person would assume.

In any case, even if subjects take the exercise seriously, they can still lack experience with the elicitation mechanism, or with the good to be valued. This lack of experience might lead to misconceptions, even in the case of a truthful answer to the hypothetical question. It has led some researchers to teach the valuation exercise to subjects *ex ante*, either by training them in the use of the mechanism or by increasing their knowledge of the good. In an attempt to address this last issue, Carlsson and Martinsson (2006) elicit the willingness to pay (WTP) to avoid power outages in Sweden. The WTP was expressed in an open-ended survey before and after the subjects experienced the negative consequences of the power outages. In this particular case, the WTP referred to a protection good, i.e. the right to access power without outages in the event of a hurricane. Carlsson and Martinsson (2006) obtained a somewhat paradoxical result. First, informed subjects tend to propose a 0 WTP more often than non-informed subjects. On the other hand, the answers in the subset of positive offers remain unaffected by the experience of a power outage. This paradoxical result could be explained by the fact that subjects who experienced a power outage became aware of their right to get power for free when such an event occurs. As a consequence, having faced the event of a power outage might have provided information that changes respondents' private valuation.

Focus 2.2
Preference elicitation: auctions, referenda and BDM mechanisms

While the revelation properties of the second-price auction are very attractive both empirically and theoretically, a recurrent critic against its actual use in contingent valuation surveys is its complexity. In the seminal report commissioned by the NOAA (National Oceanic and Atmospheric Administration), the panel suggests using a binary voting referendum which respondents might find more familiar and realistic. In a referendum, subjects are asked to vote for or against the funding of a public good. If a majority votes in favour, then everybody will contribute, and the public good will be provided. On the contrary, if only a minority votes in favour of the public good, then nobody will pay for the good and it will not be provided. A second attractive feature of the referendum voting procedure is that it is strategy-proof (there is no way to manipulate the outcome by distorting one's own preferences). Another popular preference elicitation tool is the Becker–DeGroot–Marschak (Becker and Brownson, 1964, BDM) mechanism. In its more standard version, a subject is asked to post a bid to buy the good. The bid is then compared to a price determined by a random-number generator. If the bid is lower than the price, the subject pays nothing and receives nothing. If the bid is greater than the price, the subject pays the randomly drawn price and receives the good. Because of this property, the equilibrium bidding strategy in the BDM mechanism is similar to what happens in a Vickrey auction: the bid affects the likelihood to buy the good but leaves unchanged the price actually paid in that case. The mechanism is thus incentive-compatible, and perfectly revealing. Noussair et al. (2004) compare the BDM mechanism and the Vickrey auction to reveal willingness-to-pay information for individual customers. For standard private goods, their results show the Vickrey auction outperforms the BDM mechanism, with fewer biases, lower dispersion of bids and faster convergence to truthful revelation.

Regarding subjects' attitudes towards the mechanism, Bjornstad et al. (1997) show that experience with contingent valuation procedure eliminates the bias. Here, experience was gained through a sequence of referenda in which participants had to vote on a proposal stating a WTP for a non-market good (see Focus 2.2 for a description of the most often used elicitation mechanisms, referenda in particular). If more than 50% of the participants voted for a given proposition, then the proposal was accepted. The good was provided and all the participants were supposed to pay the WTP. Bjornstad et al. (1997) show that a learning phase on the mechanism using real incentives strongly reduces the hypothetical bias. List (2001) studies the impact of experience by comparing experienced and non-experienced subjects. His study compared the preference elicited in a second-price auction depending on whether the card dealers were professional or not. The subjects familiar with both the good and the mechanism revealed preferences that were significantly different from those of the other subjects. The demand for professional dealers was higher than that for non-professionals: when positive, their bids were higher and their number of zero bids lower. However, experience did not succeed in overcoming the discrepancy induced by the change in the incentives context, and the hypothetical bias remained present.

Another possible problem with the hypothetical context is that subjects may face a dissonance between two competing wills. On the one hand, participants want to provide their true preferences. On the other, they want to show their support for the provision of the good to be valued. In a hypothetical context, the sending of such a message is a cost-free procedure. The dissonance minimisation (DM) procedure, introduced by Blamey et al. (1999), consists in separating the revelation of preference from the provision of support messages. The DM procedure is based on an additional response category in the survey in which subjects are explicitly asked to express their attitude towards the good. More specifically, these additional response categories clearly dissociate the respondents' support for the programme and their willingness to pay for it. For example, Blamey et al. (1999) provided respondents with the following extra response categories: 'I support the [programme] ... but it's not worth $50 to me', 'I support the [programme] ... but I cannot afford $50', and 'I support the [programme] but not if it requires a [fee] of any amount'. The initial study by Blamey et al. (1999) showed that DM questions elicit steeper demand functions, but they do not contrast their result obtained in a real setting.

2.4.3   Cheap-Talk Scripts

A last strand of *ex ante* methods tries to warn subjects about the hypothetical issue. In one of the first manifestations of this procedure, Bohm (1972) warns subjects involved in a public good game to avoid strategic behaviour. In a seminal contribution to the more specific field of preference valuation, the National Oceanic and Atmospheric Administration (NOAA) recommended reminding subjects of their actual budget constraint (Arrow et al., 1993). Loomis et al. (1994) tested the effectiveness of reminding subjects of their budget constraints and substitute goods, prior to elicitation. In a mail survey asking people to value old-growth forests in Oregon, they found that the effect of a reminder of this type was insignificant. Neill et al. (1994) found a similar result: the fact of reminding subjects of the value of alternative environmental goods did not change the response rates; and a similar result was found by Loomis et al. (1994). However, replications of this experiment by Kotchen and Reiling (1999) and Whitehead and Blomquist (1995, 1999) showed that this led to narrower intervals of estimated preferences when it was applied to goods with which subjects were less familiar. This approach has been systematised through the use of 'cheap-talk scripts'. A cheap-talk script provides 'persuasive' information within a social context to realign a person's behavioural expectations through communication. These scripts set the social context by explicitly revealing that people tend to overbid in hypothetical surveys (Cummings et al., 1995).

Ajzen et al. (2004) showed that the introduction of cheap-talk scripts before the decision modified the disposition of the subjects by realigning beliefs, attitudes and intentions with those in the real context. Moreover, the answers collected after a cheap-talk script are good predictors of real behaviour. However, while cheap-talk design is effective under some conditions, it is not a panacea for hypothetical bias. Evidence from the literature suggests that the length of the script is of considerable importance. For example, Aadland and Caplan (2006) found that if the cheap-talk script is short,

---

Illustration 2.2
An experimental comparison of correction methods

Morrison and Brown (2009) provide an experimental test of the effectiveness of the three known methods to reduce hypothetical bias: certainty scales, cheap talk and dissonance min-imisation. In this experiment, students participate in a referendum where they have to decide whether the group should give a certain amount of money to the Red Cross Breakfast Club, described as an initiative to provide meals to children. Each student is given 20 Australian dollars (A$) for participation, and the amount of money to be sent to the Red Cross varies across sessions. Participants are told that if a majority votes yes, all of them will have to give the proposed amount to the Red Cross (including those having voted no). Four treatments are implemented. The first treatment is the only one with ACTUAL PAYMENTS. The three oth-ers are hypothetical so that in those treatments, students know they would keep their A$20. These three conditions are the main treatments of interest, in which preference elicitation is coupled, respectively, with CERTAINTY SCALES, CHEAP TALK and DISSONANCE MINIMISA-TION methods. Answers given in CERTAINTY-SCALE before the certainty question are used as the results for hypothetical estimate without correction. Certainty questions are implemented as a ten-point scale from 'very uncertain' to 'very certain'. The CHEAP-TALK treatment uses a modified version of Cummings and Taylor (1999). Finally, DISSONANCE MINIMISATION introduces four more answers, allowing students to express their support for the goal of the Red Cross Breakfast Club even if they vote against the contribution. The main results are displayed in the table below (from Table 3 in Morrison and Brown, 2009, p. 315).

Bid level (A$)	Treatment				
	ACTUAL PAYMENT	HYPOTHETICAL	CERTAINTY SCALES (limit = 7)	CHEAP TALK	DISSONANCE MINIMISATION
10	49	74	49	39	45
15	46	57	43	36	41
20	44	53	40	27	43
All	46	61	44	35	43

The experiment provides evidence of hypothetical bias: as expected, the percentage of students voting yes is greater in the HYPOTHETICAL (61%) as compared to the referendum with actual payments (46%). Dissonance minimisation appears rather efficient at correcting hypothetical bias. If calibrated at 7, the certainty scale also gives results close to ACTUAL PAYMENT. Those two methods give results which are on average 3 and 2 points away from the actual payment situation. On the other hand, the cheap-talk method produces an underestimate of the actual willingness to give. All results are more than 10 points below the actual payment. Interestingly, when asked for feedback, students report that the cheap-talk script reads as an inappropriate persuasion to vote no: 'If you're not saying no you're not being honest'.

---

it can actually make the hypothetical bias worse. Here, accumulated evidence favours the conclusion that a short cheap-talk script does not help to eliminate the hypothetical bias (Cummings et al., 1995; Poe et al., 2002). On the contrary, long and informative cheap-talk scripts have proven to be more valuable (Cummings and Taylor, 1999).

This success does not come without its limitations, however. In the above-mentioned experiment in which people were asked to state their willingness to pay for sports cards, List (2001) found that cheap talk did not effectively decrease the hypothetical bias for professional dealers (i.e. for agents who were well informed about the good being valued). Similarly, Lusk (2003) found that a cheap-talk script is effective in attenuating hypothetical bias only for certain classes of subject – those with less market experience or less knowledge of the good being valued. This suggests cheap talk can work as a learning booster, if the researcher provides subjects with information that under normal circumstances could only be acquired through a costly trial-and-error process. In addition, Brown et al. (2003) and Murphy et al. (2005) found that cheap-talk scripts that are long and directional work only for higher levels of provision. Carlsson and Martinsson (2006), by contrast, observe that the only effect of cheap talk is to decrease the number of zero offers, while leaving the mean value among positive offers unchanged.[7] Aadland et al. (2007) suggest that cheap talk is nothing more than an informative signal, which interacts with the anchoring effect produced by the threshold provided in dichotomous choice formats. Interestingly, this interaction results in making cheap talk drive down preferences in favour of low values but drive up preferences against high values. Based on accumulated evidence, cheap-talk scripts have to be long and detailed enough to shave the preferences towards truth revelation elicited in a hypothetical context.

Summary

The main lessons from this chapter are twofold. On the one hand, it aims to make it easier to think about the design of the experiment from the point of view of a participant – how the rules and procedures will be understood by the subjects. To that end, the chapter has shown, step by step, how an experiment proceeds from the point of view of people coming to a laboratory. This particular experiment described a second-price auction, a preference revelation mechanism with very attractive theoretical properties. First, it is perfectly revealing in theory, because the optimal strategy is to bid one's own private value for the good. Second, it succeeds in achieving the efficient allocation. On the other hand, the chapter also addresses the issue of the empirical relevance of these properties, tested through the behaviour observed in an experimental setting. The results show that the revelation properties of the mechanism are of generally good quality, while the quality of the efficiency property is more mixed. Lastly, the chapter concludes with an important policy application of the results drawn from the literature: the elicitation of preferences for non-market goods, and the design of preference elicitation mechanisms that can eliminate hypothetical bias, the main problem that arises in this context.

In reviewing this material, the chapter has also illustrated the main strengths of controlled experiments: they provide observations and control over dimensions that are otherwise (in particular, based on observational data) either or both hard to observe

---

[7] Ami et al. (2011) show that a neutral and short cheap-talk script can even increase the number of protest responses.

and impossible to control. The next part turns to the question of why such distinguishing features make experiments a relevant empirical method in economics. First, the point of view of the added value of experiments as compared to other empirical methods is discussed in Chapter 3. Second, Chapter 4 takes a broader perspective and relates experiments to economic theory, naturally occurring economic phenomena and the relationships between the two.

Part II

Why? The Need for Experiments in Economics

3 The Need for Controlled Experiments in Empirical Economics

As shown in Part I, experiments both widen the scope of what can be observed in an empirical situation, and are 'controlled' because the decision-making environment is built on purpose according to the objectives of the research question. In designing an experiment, and having people make decisions according to rules and with pieces of information that have all been decided on purpose, experimenters decide on what econometricians call the *data-generating process* (DGP). The aim of this chapter is to describe the consequence of this very special feature of experiments.

In a nutshell, this makes experiments well suited to help address the main challenges facing empirical economics. Empirical works in economics aim to draw general lessons from the casual evidence available in the data; e.g. what does price-sensitivity of consumers tell us about the shape of their utility function? What do differences in wages across gender tell us about discrimination? And so on. Econometrics have been developed to address questions of this kind, called inference issues. The general answer, described in Section 3.1, relies on the consistency between two sets of assumptions about the data-generating process: one about the mechanisms producing what is observed, the other about the informativeness of the statistics computed from the data. This principle is operationalised through identifying assumptions, i.e. hypotheses about how data are generated that make particular statistical treatments informative about the underlying mechanisms. The usual challenge faced in empirical economics is thus to find out the set of assumptions that best fits the unknown data-generating process inherited from the real world. Experiments reverse this challenge: they allow the data-generating process to be chosen in accordance with the empirical question to be answered.

Thanks to this property, what stand as identifying assumptions in econometrics provide a guide about how best to design experiments depending on what is to be learned from the data. An insightful source for such guidelines comes from a well-known ancestor to experimental methods in economics. Although the relevance of experiments was acknowledged only in recent decades in economic thinking, as empirical research shifted increasingly towards microeconomic-oriented works (see Section 1.2.3), a number of works have studied data very similar to experimental data for some time now. This literature focused on so-called 'quasi-experiments' (Campbell, 1969), now most often referred to as 'natural experiments'. The distinguishing feature of the econometrics of natural experiments, described in Section 3.2, is to use spontaneous changes in the institutional rules as a (quasi-)experiment. Such changes are, for instance, induced

---

> ### Illustration 3.1
> ### Labour market effects of the minimum wage: a natural experiment
>
> Whether the minimum wage is detrimental to employment (and if so, to what extent) is a long-standing question in labour economics. The theoretical context is such that, in a world of perfect competition in the labour market, workers are paid their marginal marginal productivity at work. A higher minimum wage thus crowds out from employment workers whose marginal marginal productivity is below the minimum wage. This is only one side of the story, though. The reason why most developed countries implement minimum wages is because many labour markets are far from perfect competition. If firms would rather have market power in the labour market, then the equilibrium outcome is sub-optimal: wages are lower than under perfect competition, as is employment. Whether the minimum wage efficiently restores a balance in bargaining power between workers and firms, or crowds out productive occupations from the labour market, is thus an empirical question.
>
> The answer to this depends entirely on the particular labour market and economy under study. In one of the most influential empirical studies on that topic, Card and Krueger (1994) exploit New Jersey's 1992 decision to amplify the federal increase in minimum wage that was adopted in the US in 1990. This decision is used as a natural experiment: it induces an idiosyncratic shock in the level of the minimum wage relative to other states, the causal effect of which can be inferred from labour market outcomes in this state compared to other states.

by modifications or new implementations of public policies (see Illustration 3.1 for an example). This literature has developed by defining identifying assumptions that are appropriate to analyse the effect of changes in the decision environment. Reviewing these identification strategies in Section 3.4 will help us think about how experimental variations must be implemented depending on the research question.

Lastly, this ability to choose the data-generating process is common to all kinds of (actual) experiments. Section 3.5 reviews the many kinds of experimental methods available in economics, often compared based on how close they are to the social situation the experiment aims to replicate. This criterion is also associated with varying abilities to actually control the data-generating process, hence giving rise to different empirical properties.

3.1   The Econometric Approach to Data Analysis

A major aim of econometrics is to inform about causal relationships between variables. To make things more concrete, our running example in this chapter will be the effect of compensation schemes on performance at work. Empirical analysis focusing on this question seeks to know what is the change in performance of workers resulting from a switch in their compensation – typically, from a fixed wage to a piece rate. To that end, econometrics makes use of statistics, but it does not reduce to it. The difference between the two is not obvious to understand. Why is it that empirical analysis in economics needs a specific set of tools, called econometrics? The answer is that structural relationships generally are not directly observable in the data. Examples abound,[1] but to quote some of the most popular ones: the likelihood of death and the time spent at hospital are strongly positively related in any population; do such data inform us about how dangerous hospitals are for health? The number of policemen in a geographic area is often positively correlated to crime rates; does it mean one should reduce police forces to contain crime? Unemployed people who receive more help from public placement agencies generally experience lower likelihood of finding a job; do placement agencies hurt the labour market potential of job-seekers?

What these examples show is that observed relationships between variables cannot generally be trusted as a measure of their structural counterpart – correlation is not causation. Empirical correlations lie about the mechanisms generating them. In each of the above examples, there do exist forces behind the observed co-variations but these forces are not quite what simple inspection of the data suggests. Similarly, it will often be the case that higher performance is observed in firms paying a piece rate rather than a fixed wage. But without any further tool, it is impossible to know if it is so because piece rates induce higher performance, or just the reverse: that firms with a piece rate compensation scheme attract higher-performance workers (a phenomenon that could well be in operation, as explained in Focus 3.3). This discussion does not mean that data are useless, but rather that one needs to apply particular methods and reasoning to them, so as to be able to understand what is behind the observed patterns. This section summarises the framework used in econometrics to answer such questions, and highlights how it differs from statistics.

3.1.1   The Two Inferential Problems of Data Analysis

Data analysis relies on observations on a subset of the population of interest, called a *sample*. In our example, the population would include all workers of a particular kind (defined by characteristics of the workplace, specifics of the task, etc.), of which the employees of particular firms observed during a given time span are a sample. To formalise, we denote $(\mathbf{y}, \mathbf{X})$ the information available in the sample, where $\mathbf{y}$ will stand for a column vector of n individual observations on the outcome variable (e.g. the performance at work of sample employees), and $\mathbf{X}$ a matrix of n individual observations (in a row) about m input variables (in a column, such as the compensation scheme or individual observable characteristics like age or gender). A formal representation of $(\mathbf{y}, \mathbf{X})$ is the following:

$$\mathbf{y} = \begin{bmatrix} y_1 \\ y_2 \\ \vdots \\ y_n \end{bmatrix}, \text{ and } \mathbf{X} = \begin{bmatrix} x_{11} & ; x_{12} & ; \cdots & ; x_{1m} \\ x_{21} & ; x_{22} & ; \cdots & ; x_{2m} \\ \vdots & ; \vdots & ; \ddots & ; \vdots \\ x_{n1} & ; x_{n2} & ; \cdots & ; x_{nm} \end{bmatrix}$$

Descriptive statistics are tools used to summarise the information available in the sample. The sample mean, for instance, summarises the central tendency of each variable, while covariance allows measurement of the empirical joint variations between

---

[1] Many additional examples of such spurious correlations can be found at www.tylervigen.com/ spurious-correlations.

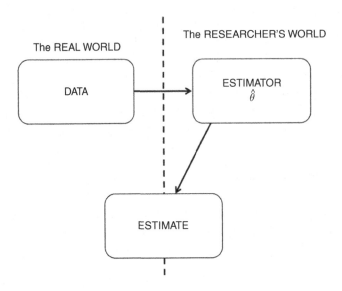

Figure 3.1 The challenge of data analysis

two variables. These are all sample quantities, which inform about the content of the variables for those individuals actually observed.

But the aim of statistics goes well beyond this objective. The main purpose is to use the information available in the sample to draw conclusions about the population characteristics. It is not the performance of those workers that actually appears in the sample that we want to understand and quantitatively characterise; but rather the behaviour of *any* worker belonging to the same population (provided the population is properly defined, something we did not do above!). This exercise is called *inference*, as the casual information available in the sample is used to infer knowledge about the population as a whole.

As an example, denote μ the mean performance at work in the target population of workers. This is something we do not observe, but we want to use sample information so as to quantify it. To that end, statistics defines *estimators*, which are procedures defined on the information available in the sample, and related to the true population parameter. For instance, the sample average of $\mathbf{y}$ defined as the procedure associated with $\bar{y} = \frac{\sum_{i=1}^{n} y_i}{n}$ in a sample of $i = 1, \ldots, n$ observations is the estimator frequently used to inform about the mean μ. Figure 3.1 illustrates such an approach to data analysis. Data are part of the real world. Estimators, denoted $\hat{\theta}$, are defined by researchers in an effort to understand it as a whole – in such a way that the estimate can be considered as a representation of the real world as seen through the prism of the researcher's world.

An important thing to note is that such an estimator is defined for any possible sample of size n, randomly drawn from the population. From one sample to another, the particular observed values contained in $(\mathbf{y}, \mathbf{X})$ will change, because the observation units will be different as a result of the sampling mechanism. This means one can see the sample observations as n draws in the population variables. As a result, the observations contained in $(\mathbf{y}, \mathbf{X})$ are random variables, of which each particular sample giving rise to a data set is a realisation – a particular draw in the variables' distributions. The crucial point here is that estimators are defined over sample values: as functions of random variables, they are thus random variables themselves. The application of the estimator to the actual numbers available in a given sample is called an 'estimate' or an 'estimation', and should be seen as realisations, draws, from the estimators' distribution.

These definitions allow us to state more precisely the two inference problems faced when relying on sample quantities to acquire knowledge about population quantities. The first inference problem is how the sample quantity itself is related to the population parameter of interest, i.e. what is the relationship between what we observe or compute on the data, and what we seek to measure. Imagine, for instance, that you are interested in knowing the level of income of people living in a given city. To gather this information, you stand at the entrance of a golf course nearby. You will obviously gather information that is not a relevant measure of what you are interested in. And this empirical mistake has nothing to do with the size of your sample (the number of people you will be able to meet): even if you stay long enough, your measure will never approach what you expect – because the level of income among members of a golf club is biased upwards as compared to the average income in a typical city. This first issue is a matter of **identification**: what are the relationships between the sample quantity and the true underlying parameter one seeks to measure?

But because of sample variations, what we observe will always differ from what we want to measure, notwithstanding the identification properties. It is so because, as explained above, when we compute estimations, the value of the estimator in the observed data, we work with realisations of a random variable. This question is a matter of **statistical inference**. For instance, the sample average is known to converge to the population mean if sample observations are drawn independently (in application of the law of large numbers, the probability that the sample average differs from the population mean is closer and closer to 0 as the sample size increases). The sample average will never (or barely) coincide with the population mean in any sample, whatever its (finite) size, but the higher the sample size, the closer the two will be. Using properties like this one, sample realisations can be used to characterise their population equivalent.

This two-sided inference problem is at the core of econometrics. Each side raises specific challenges. In the words of Manski (1999, p. 4), 'studies of identification seek to characterise the conclusions that could be drawn if one could use the sampling process to obtain an unlimited number of observations', while 'studies of statistical inference seek to characterise the generally weaker conclusions that can be drawn from a finite number of observations'.

3.1.2   How Econometrics Faces the Challenges: The Idea of Data-Generating Processes

To address these two challenges, econometrics goes even further in the distinction made in Figure 3.1 between the real world and the researcher world, as illustrated in Figure 3.2. The main novelty introduced in this figure is the inclusion of the data-generating process. There are two such data-generating processes in the figure. First,

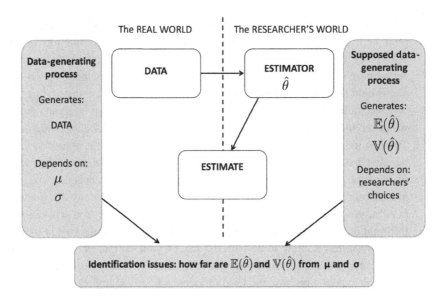

Figure 3.2 The econometric approach to data analysis

the 'true' data-generating process is the one actually producing the data observed in the real world. This includes everything that is behind the actual content of the sample: the sampling mechanism (how the decision to include a given observation from the population is made), the availability of the information (whether, for instance, variables are observed as classes, or as discrete variables, etc.), and last, all the causal mechanisms relating the variables together. By its very definition, this true data-generating process is unknown to the researcher – and impossible to observe; this is precisely the reason why empirical evidence is needed.

It is approached through the **supposed** (sometimes also labelled *assumed*) data-generating process, which gathers all assumptions made about the observed data: the functional form of the model, the assumed sampling rule, etc. It is from this supposed data-generating process that identification and statistical-inference properties of the estimator are deduced: in our running example of the estimation of the mean from a sample average, the estimator converges towards the population mean if observations are randomly drawn (i.e. the likelihood that an individual observation is included in the sample does not depend on any of his relevant characteristics). This way, the supposed data-generating process can be seen as a device to make explicit those features of the data-generating process that guarantee some particular inference properties of the estimation techniques – e.g. that observations are sampled at random, for the consistency of the sample mean.

This leads us to the main take-home lesson of this broad overview: estimators' properties are deduced from the consistency between the true data-generating process and the supposed data-generating process. Applied econometrics, from that point of view, is the art of selecting the assumed data-generating process that best fits the true one, based on one's own understanding of what it actually is. By definition, this is not an empirical question (as any empirical analysis relies on estimators, the properties of which depend again on the consistency between their own assumed data-generating process and the true data-generating process), but rather a theoretical one: the answers will not come from the data, but from one's own understanding of the actual mechanisms at stake.

When using observational data, the true data-generating process is given, and econometric analysis of the data aims to fit for the best its main properties in order to accurately use the information available in the sample. Here lies the key difference between observational data and experiments. When designing an experiment, one actually decides on the true data-generating process: how observations are selected, how some variables are related together, what information is available and when, etc. Econometric theory thus provides the main guidelines on how to build experiments giving rise to conclusive measures. Before moving to this discussion, we illustrate the point made in this section through an application to the OLS estimator.

3.1.3   Illustration: Inference Properties of the OLS Estimator

The classical linear model linearly relates an outcome variable y to m covariates X according to:

$$y_i = \sum_i \theta_k x_{ik} + \varepsilon_i, \forall i \leftrightarrow \mathbf{y} = \mathbf{X}\theta + \boldsymbol{\varepsilon}$$

This equation is a data-generating model. From the point of view of econometrics, it literally means that $\mathbf{y}$, the outcome, is generated by a set of explanatory variables $\mathbf{X}$ combined according to the unknown parameters θ. This first component is named *the measurable* – or deterministic – part of the model, as it is made of observable variables. The way they are combined to produce outcome depends on θ, a column vector of m unknown parameters:

$$\theta = \begin{bmatrix} \theta_1 \\ \theta_2 \\ \vdots \\ \theta_m \end{bmatrix}$$

The term $\boldsymbol{\varepsilon}$ is an error, in the sense that it recovers all the variations in the actual level of $\mathbf{y}$ that are induced by mechanisms beyond the effect of $\mathbf{X}$. As a matter of fact, the equation implies that $\boldsymbol{\varepsilon} = \mathbf{y} - \mathbf{X}\theta$: the error term regroups everything that makes $\mathbf{y}$ vary and does not go through the effect of the $\mathbf{X}$s. By construction, this part of the model is *unobserved*. The error term $\boldsymbol{\varepsilon}$ is a column vector of individual error terms:

$$\boldsymbol{\varepsilon} = \begin{bmatrix} \varepsilon_1 \\ \varepsilon_2 \\ \vdots \\ \varepsilon_n \end{bmatrix}$$

where each ε_i is defined as:

$$\varepsilon_i = y_i - \begin{bmatrix} x_{i1} & ; x_{i2} & ; \cdots & ; x_{im} \end{bmatrix} \times \begin{bmatrix} \theta_1 \\ \theta_2 \\ \vdots \\ \theta_m \end{bmatrix} = y_i - \sum_{k=1}^{m} \theta_k x_{ik}$$

In a sample, one can observe the value taken by $\mathbf{y}$ and $\mathbf{X}$ for a given set of n individuals. These covariations can be used to characterise the unknown parameters θ. The most famous and widely used way of doing it is to use the ordinary least squares (OLS) estimator, $\hat{\theta}_{\text{OLS}}$. It is derived from minimising the error of the model $\boldsymbol{\varepsilon} = \mathbf{y} - \mathbf{X}\theta$ (we denote z' the transpose matrix of z):

$$\boldsymbol{\varepsilon}'\boldsymbol{\varepsilon} = (\mathbf{y} - \mathbf{X}\theta)'(\mathbf{y} - \mathbf{X}\theta) = \mathbf{y}'\mathbf{y} - 2\mathbf{y}'\mathbf{X}\theta - \theta'\mathbf{X}'\mathbf{X}\theta$$

From the first-order condition of minimising the sum of squared errors,

$$\frac{\partial \boldsymbol{\varepsilon}'\boldsymbol{\varepsilon}}{\partial \theta} = 2\mathbf{X}'\mathbf{y} - 2\mathbf{X}'\mathbf{X}\theta = 0$$

the functional form of the estimator results as:

$$\hat{\theta}_{\text{OLS}} = (\mathbf{X}'\mathbf{X})^{-1}\mathbf{X}'\mathbf{y}$$

As such, the estimator is nothing more than an algebraic manipulation that maximises the fit of the model, as measured, for instance, by the R^2 – i.e. the coincidence between the observed value of $\mathbf{y}$ and the predicted value $\mathbf{X}\hat{\theta}_{\text{OLS}}$.[2]

The properties of this estimator, in terms of identification and statistical inference, result from additional assumptions on the data-generating process. To highlight them, we use the assumed relationships between the variables, $\mathbf{y} = \mathbf{X}\theta + \boldsymbol{\varepsilon}$, to write the estimator as:

$$\hat{\theta}_{\text{OLS}} = (\mathbf{X}'\mathbf{X})^{-1}\mathbf{X}'(\mathbf{X}\theta + \boldsymbol{\varepsilon}) = \theta + (\mathbf{X}'\mathbf{X})^{-1}\mathbf{X}'\boldsymbol{\varepsilon}$$

According to this expression, the estimator fluctuates around the true value, θ, according to $(\mathbf{X}'\mathbf{X})^{-1}\mathbf{X}'\boldsymbol{\varepsilon}$. If $\mathbb{E}(\varepsilon_i|\mathbf{X}) = 0$, $\forall i$, these fluctuations induce no systematic difference between the estimation and the true underlying parameter in such a way that $\mathbb{E}(\hat{\theta}_{\text{OLS}}) = \theta$. This defines an important identification property, called unbiasedness. Otherwise, if any correlation exists between the error term, ε, and the explanatory variables, $\mathbf{X}$, i.e. $\mathbb{E}(\varepsilon_i|\mathbf{X}) \neq 0$, then $\mathbb{E}(\hat{\theta}_{\text{OLS}}|\mathbf{X}) - \theta = (\mathbf{X}'\mathbf{X})^{-1}\mathbf{X}'\mathbb{E}(\boldsymbol{\varepsilon}|\mathbf{X}) \neq 0$. This distance between the expected value of the estimator and the true parameter is called a 'bias', a systematic difference between the target and the empirical measure. Under such circumstances, the application of the OLS algebra to observed data will not deliver an evaluation of the true parameters θ combining the $\mathbf{X}$s to generate $\mathbf{y}$. The intuitive reason for the bias is that there are some variations in $\mathbf{X}$ that are simultaneous with those in $\mathbf{y}$ (through ε), not because of the causal effect of $\mathbf{X}$ on $\mathbf{y}$, however, but rather because something unobserved, hence in ε, makes $\mathbf{X}$ and $\mathbf{y}$ vary at the same time. Such a phenomenon is said to be confounding: an unobserved mechanism that makes $\mathbf{X}$ and $\mathbf{y}$ vary at the same

---

[2] The coefficient of determination R^2 is the percentage of the response variable variation that is explained by the linear model. Formally, it is defined as $R^2 = 1 - \frac{\text{sum of squares of residuals}}{\text{total sum of squares}} = 1 - \frac{\boldsymbol{\varepsilon}'\boldsymbol{\varepsilon}}{\sum_i (y_i - \bar{y})^2}$.

time is spuriously attributed to a causal effect of $\mathbf{X}$ on $\mathbf{y}$, leading to wrong conclusions and inferences.

Statistical inference, on the other hand, is deduced from the distribution properties of the n random variables ε_i in $\boldsymbol{\varepsilon}$. If these variables are identically $- \mathbb{E}(\varepsilon_i^2|\mathbf{X}) = \sigma^2 \forall i$ – and independently $- \mathbb{E}(\varepsilon_i \varepsilon_j|\mathbf{X}) = 0 \forall i \neq j$ – distributed, then it can be shown that: $\mathbb{V}(\hat{\theta}_{\text{OLS}}|\mathbf{X}) = \sigma^2(\mathbf{X}'\mathbf{X})^{-1}$.[3] This quantity is the true variance of the estimator: it thus gives information on the magnitude of the variations of the realised value as compared to the expectation of the estimator, which happens to be the true value of interest if the above identification assumption is fulfilled. From one sample to another, the value taken by the estimator will vary and none of these values will coincide with the true value θ, but the range of such variations around θ is given by $\sigma^2(\mathbf{X}'\mathbf{X})^{-1}$. Under the same set of assumptions, this level of precision is even the highest achievable precision among all unbiased estimators of θ (by the efficiency of the OLS): based on the available data, the OLS delivers the most informative measure of the parameter.

As this example illustrates, both identification and statistical-inference properties depend on the nature of the true data-generating process: these properties of the estimator are met only if the unobserved components gathered in $\boldsymbol{\varepsilon}$ that produce $\mathbf{y}$ actually fulfil the three conditions above. Applied to experiments, these conditions become guidelines into best practices so as to provide conclusive measures. The independence condition $\mathbb{E}(\varepsilon_i \varepsilon_j|\mathbf{X}) = 0$, $\forall i \neq j$, for instance, means that the unobserved components applying to any two observations should not be related together in any systematic manner. This condition is met in experiments if people make only one decision; but will fail (by design) if participants are asked to make several decisions one after the other. In this case, there exist several observations for which decisions are made by the same individual. All characteristics that are unobserved and specific to this person, and that belong to the decision-making process (being hungry or angry the day of the experiment, having experienced trouble getting to the laboratory, etc.), will apply to all decisions made by this person during the experiment: the unobserved components producing the outcome of several such decisions will be systematically correlated – challenging the statistical-inference properties of the statistical tools applied to these data.[4] The same reasoning applies to the identification condition, $\mathbb{E}(\varepsilon_i|\mathbf{X}) = 0$, which is the main focus of this chapter.

3.2   Estimating Causal Effects of Treatments

Among the two issues that have to be solved in order to draw solid conclusions from observed behaviour, identification is the first-order question one must address in designing any empirical research. Statistical inference is just meaningless if identification has not been worked out, as it amounts to characterising the sample properties of the estimator as regards some unspecified parameter.

---

[3] For formal proofs and further discussions of the material reviewed in this section, we refer the reader to standard econometrics textbooks, such as Wooldridge (2002); Dougherty (2006).

[4] The statistical analysis of experimental data will be covered in Chapter 7.

To ease the discussion of identification issues in the context of experiments, we will rely on the so-called causal evaluation framework. This will help, in particular, to formalise the properties of the data-generating process (hence the features of experimental designs) that are crucial for achieving identification. The evaluation framework aims to measure the causal effect of a change in the decision environment on relevant outcomes. To formalise it, we frame such an empirical problem by considering two possible states of the world: $T = 0$ will be the benchmark situation, while $T = 1$ refers to exactly the same world except for one of its dimensions. We can think of these two states of the world as a world without a 'treatment' $(T = 0)$ and a world with a treatment $(T = 1)$, where the '*treatment*' stands for any change in the environment of which we want to measure the effect.[5] Illustration 3.2 provides an example of the kind of empirical problem this approach aims to solve. The outcome is denoted μ_{i0} in the world without a treatment and μ_{i1} in the world with the treatment. Both correspond to the true parameters of the underlying data-generating process. If the empirical question is to know the performance at work induced by different compensation schemes, μ_{i0} would be the performance under, say, a fixed wage, and μ_{i1} the performance under a piece rate. These quantities are outcomes in the sense that they are endogenous to the situation: they result from a decision or an aggregation of behaviours that is induced by an individual's reactions to the environment.

3.2.1   The Causal Effect of the Change

In this framework, the main challenge is to measure the causal effect of the treatment: the change in outcome induced by switching from world $T = 0$ to $T = 1$ – as discussed in Focus 3.1, this is the empirical equivalent of comparative statics in theoretical analysis. This exercise would be very easy if one could observe both μ_{i0} and μ_{i1} at the same time. It should, however, be clear from our definitions that it can hardly be the case in empirical work, as this amounts to observing the same sample unit (individual, firm, country) in both states, at the same time period, in the same sequence of events – put otherwise: both in world $T = 0$ and $T = 1$. As a result, if $y_i(1) = y_i(T = 1)$ denotes the potential outcome individual i obtains when receiving the treatment and $y_i(0) = y_i(T = 0)$ denotes the potential outcome individual i obtains when receiving the control; it is impossible to observe both $y_i(1)$ and $y_i(0)$ at the same time. A consequence is that it is impossible to measure $y_i(1) - y_i(0)$, the causal effect of the treatment, on individual i. This defines the so-called evaluation problem.

A prototypical example of this problem is the effect of education on labour market outcomes. One can observe the outcomes of different people with differing levels of education, but it is impossible to observe the outcome for one and the same individual with two different levels of education concurrently. Another example is the impact of an individual's gender on labour market outcomes, where the problem is straightforward:

---

[5] This formalisation is known as the Rubin (1974) causal model, from whom we borrow the title of this section. The terminology is inherited from the metaphor of experiments used in medical field: $T = 1$ is a treatment tested as a cure to some illness. In that case, $T = 0$ is a control, i.e. a world with no medical treatment, which refers to how patients would feel without the help of the medication in question.

Illustration 3.2
Incentives and performance: a 'natural' experiment

The aim of piece-rate schemes is to reconcile the diverging interests of the agent (or the employee) and the principal (the employer): effort at work is a cost for the agent (who cares about consumption) but benefits the principal. Piece-rate schemes achieve their goal by connecting employees' consumption to their performance at work, hence the amount of effort. This is the main reason why economic theory predicts an increased performance by switching from a fixed wage to a piece rate. Lazear (2000) relies on a natural experiment to investigate the causal impact of such a change in payment schemes on performance within a firm. The natural experiment occurred at the Safelite Glass Corporation, specialsing in automobile glass installation. Following the introduction of a new management team, the firm changed its payment scheme from hourly wages ($T = 0$) to a piece rate ($T = 1$). The outcome of interest is performance at work, measured by the number of glass installations carried out by an employee in a given period of time. The causal effect of interest is the change in performance induced for any given employee when work is compensated using a piece rate rather than a fixed wage.

The figure (from Figure 3, p. 1357) shows the density of performance in the firm both before and after the change in the compensation scheme. The average change in performance amounts to a rise in output of about 44% following the change. The crucial question is: does this change in performance measure the variation in output one can expect from switching an employee from one compensation scheme to the other, i.e. is this outcome a measure of a causal effect?

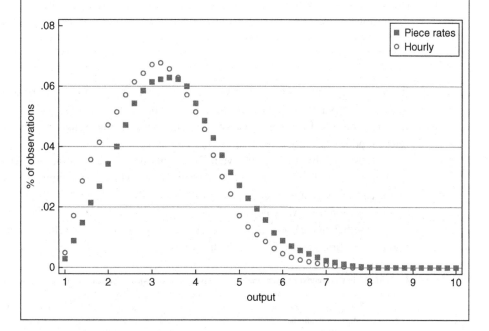

> ## Focus 3.1
> ## Causal effects in theoretical analysis and empirical works
>
> The aim of measuring the effect of treatment variables in empirical economics is strongly grounded in economic theory. Theoretical analysis in economics consists of two complementary approaches. First, equilibrium analysis is intended to predict the state of the world that should result from a given set of circumstances, and should hence be observed in real-life situations happening under the same circumstances. *Equilibrium analysis* is based on three pillars: the existence of an equilibrium, its uniqueness and its stability. In case of multiplicity, the relevant equilibrium is the stable point around which the outcomes would converge, if all conditions remained the same. The empirical counterpart of such an approach only requires observation of the behaviour induced by a given environment replicating in the best possible way the circumstances of the model. This allows comparison of observed behaviour with the equilibrium prediction from theory – for instance: are returns to scale in the production process actually not increasing, as expected in a competitive market? The second kind of approach explicitly involves changes in the decision environment. *Comparative statics* characterise changes in the equilibrium induced by changes in the relevant circumstances. This corresponds to a systematic operationalisation of the classical *ceteris paribus* clause introduced by Marshall (1890). Comparative statics identify the relationships between variables, and the impact a change in one variable has on the outcome variable, in terms of both sign and amplitude. The econometrics of causal effects mimics the comparative-statics approach: a causal effect is nothing but a variation in behaviour induced by a change in another variable, called a treatment, in which other factors are held constant (Heckman, 2010). In measuring the change in the outcome variable before and after a change in one of the exogenous variables, the aim is to compare two different equilibrium states. This replicates the *ceteris paribus* reasoning only if the observed change is induced by the change in the exogenous variable. Anything that makes the exogenous variable change at the same time as the outcome is thus confounding, leading to biased estimation.

it is obviously impossible to observe a labour market income for one person according to whether this person is either a man or a woman – but the causal effect of gender, i.e. what are the differences in market outcomes between males and females, is a highly relevant policy question.[6]

As a result of this lack of observation opportunities, the evaluation problem consists in finding counterfactuals, i.e. empirical observations which convincingly measure what the researcher does not observe. In most instances, this is what would have happened to the observation units y_i, which we observe in the new world $T = 1$, were units instead still in the benchmark world $T = 0$. The accuracy of the counterfactual depends on two critical dimensions. The first is the ways in which the counterfactual observations

---

[6] Similarly, in the context of experiments in medical science, once the medication has been administered to the patient ($T = 1$), the researcher cannot observe what would have happened to the same patient with $T = 0$. Therefore the researcher can never be sure if any change in the patient's condition stems from the medication, or from another circumstance that may have changed at the same time as the prescription. This applies to the labour market in just the same way as it does to medical research.

Table 3.1 Individuals, treatments and observations

i	T_i	$y_i(0)$	$y_i(1)$
1	1	–	10
2	0	2	–
3	1	–	3
...	...	...	...
n	0	5	–

resemble the observations of interest. The second dimension is, of course, the kind of causal effect the researcher is seeking to identify. Before discussing each dimension in turn, we more formally specify the identification issue raised by observational data.

3.2.2 The Content of Observational Data

Observational data from natural experiments typically deliver cross-sectional information on two kinds of individuals: people who behaved in an environment where the treatment was absent (state $T = 0$), and people who behaved in an environment where the treatment has been implemented (state $T = 1$). In both cases, it is possible to identify those individuals who 'received the treatment' (individuals i for whom $T_i = 1$) and those who didn't (individuals i for whom $T_i = 0$). The observed outcome $\mathbf{y}$ in the whole sample results from the combination of the implementation of the treatment (state $T = 0$ or $T = 1$) and the status of the individual (treated or not). Table 3.1 shows an example of observational data for one outcome, n individuals and one treatment. Due to the outcomes delivered by the sample, the vectors of potential outcomes $\mathbf{y}(0)$ and $\mathbf{y}(1)$ are incomplete. Individuals with $T_i = 1$ are missing in the former case; individuals with $T_i = 0$ are missing in the latter case.

If one could observe all individuals i in a world without treatment, the model would be:

$$\mathbf{y}(0) = \boldsymbol{\mu}_0 + \boldsymbol{\varepsilon}(0)$$

where the first element, $\boldsymbol{\mu}_0$, is the vector of true parameters – or outputs – specific to this state of the world, and the second element, $\boldsymbol{\varepsilon}(0)$, is, as usual, the unobserved heterogeneity of the observational units. Similarly, if one could observe all individuals in the state of the world with $T = 1$, the outcome would result from the model:

$$\mathbf{y}(1) = \boldsymbol{\mu}_1 + \boldsymbol{\varepsilon}(1)$$

Again $\boldsymbol{\mu}_1$ is the actual true parameter, while $\boldsymbol{\varepsilon}(1)$ is the measurement error due to heterogeneity. These two equations stand for the data-generating process of the outcomes in each state of the world. As mentioned above, the disturbances $\boldsymbol{\varepsilon}(0)$ or $\boldsymbol{\varepsilon}(1)$ stand by definition for any unmeasured aspect of each outcome (the whole model could be rewritten by adding explanatory variables $\mathbf{X}$, without changing the main point of the discussion: $\boldsymbol{\varepsilon}(0), \boldsymbol{\varepsilon}(1)$ will stand for any component that is influential on the outcomes, but is not explicitly measured through the $\mathbf{X}$s).

The important lesson from the discussion in Section 3.1 is that it's not the mere existence of $\varepsilon(0)$ and $\varepsilon(1)$ that challenges identification: there is always noise in the observed relationships between the outcome and the parameter of interest. Noise is not an issue per se, it is a necessary feature of empirical economics. What might lead to identification issues is some specific configurations of the noise, namely if the errors $\varepsilon(0)$ and $\varepsilon(1)$ are correlated with the treatment T. Which kind of correlation is actually confounding entirely depends on what one seeks to measure: identification requires one not only to characterise the properties of an estimator, but first of all to define what this estimator aims to measure, i.e. the causal parameter of interest.

3.2.3   Treatment Effects Parameters

The most natural way of defining a causal effect in the above setting is as the average change in the outcome induced by the treatment for any individual from the population. This is called the average treatment effect in the policy evaluation literature. The most widely used alternative is the average treatment on the treated.[7]

The Average Treatment Effect (ATE)
This parameter measures the impact of the treatment on any individual from the population endowed with individual characteristics $\mathbf{X}$:

$$\Delta^{\text{ATE}} = \mathbb{E}\left(y_i(1) - y_i(0)|\mathbf{X}\right)$$

Intuitively, it provides a measure of the effect of moving a randomly drawn individual from no treatment to treatment, regardless of whether the individual was treated ($T_i = 1$) or not ($T_i = 0$). In the example of the employment effect of the minimum wage (Illustration 3.1), the ATE would be defined as the variation in the probability of employment for any individual in the population that results from a change in the minimum wage. Similarly, the ATE of a change in compensation on performance would be defined for any worker on the market.

The Average Treatment on the Treated (ATT)
The target parameter is restricted to the sub-population who receive the treatment:

$$\Delta^{\text{ATT}} = \mathbb{E}\left[y_i(1) - y_i(0)|\mathbf{X}, T_i = 1\right]$$

The only difference from the previous parameter is its conditioning on the group of treated individuals.[8] The ATT measures the change in outcome for those individuals who are involved in the change. In the minimum-wage example, the ATT would now focus on the employment effects of minimum wage not for all workers, but rather for those workers who actually face a change in wage when the minimum wage changes –

---

[7] Heckman (2010) describes other parameters of interest like the voting criterion or more general welfare criteria. The presentation in this section closely follows the seminal survey of Heckman et al. (1999).

[8] For the sake of notational simplicity $\mathbf{y}(1|\mathbf{X}, T = 1)$ and $\mathbf{y}(0|\mathbf{X}, T = 1)$ will be often denoted $\mathbf{y}(1)|\mathbf{X}, T = 1$ and $\mathbf{y}(0)|\mathbf{X}, T = 1$. The same applies with $T = 0$.

i.e. workers whose wage is just between the level of the minimum wage before and after the rise. In the compensation example, the ATT measures the change in performance induced by using a piece-rate rather than a fixed wage for those individuals who are paid a piece rate.

These two definitions make clear that these two parameters might be the same or not depending on the precise mechanism behind the change in outcome. If the individual response to the treatment is homogeneous in the population – any individual can expect the same change in outcome on average from benefiting from the treatment – then the two parameters will be the same. They are different, however, if the population is heterogeneous in terms of the response to the treatment, and assignation to the treatment is related to such heterogeneity – inducing a systematic difference in the expected effect of the treatment between individuals from the two groups.

Such a difference is driven by the existence of a relationship between the benefit from the treatment (its expected effect on the outcome) and participation in the treatment. Two kinds of implementation typically give rise to this kind of mechanism. It will be the case, for instance, if participation in the treatment is free, and those individuals who expect to benefit the most from it actually decide to get it. In the example of a change in compensation, more productive workers are likely to experience a higher raise in wage from a piece rate – in such a way that their response to higher power incentives is likely to be different from what would be the response of less productive workers. Similarly, the ATE and ATT are different quantities if the treatment targets a particular sub-population (low-wage workers, for instance) and is purposefully designed to change their outcome, rather than to improve the situation of any individual in the population. In the minimum-wage example, for instance, the ATT is likely to differ from the ATE because the labour market is strongly segmented in terms of skills, hence of wages. Individuals who earn more than the minimum wage are likely to face very little change in their employment opportunities, because the minimum wage is non-binding for the kind of job they occupy.

The ATE and the ATT both are true parameters of the distribution of the causal change induced by the treatment under study – see Focus 3.2 for a discussion of the generalisability of these two parameters, and Illustration 3.3 for an application. When they differ, the obvious question is which one we want to know and/or which will best inform on the consequences of the treatment. Unsurprisingly, the answer depends on the research question.

The ATE measures a population parameter. It thus answers questions about the likely change in the economic outcomes if the treatment is to be generalised to the whole population, or parts of the population that do not belong to the treatment group. But if the treatment is specific to those individuals who are treated, then the ATE is not very informative. For instance, a child care programme mainly targets parents with young children, and in no way aims to change the outcomes of people whose children are adults; similarly, training programmes are often designed to improve the labour market position of the long-term unemployed. In both cases, it might well be that the effect of the treatment would differ were it applied to the general population or to the target

---

Focus 3.2
The programme evaluation approach and the structural approach

The policy evaluation literature focuses on identification – how to best use available data to measure causal effects – from policy changes. A growing debate in this literature challenges the nature of the causal effects identified through such a 'experimentalist view of econometrics' (Keane, 2010, p. 3). The main criticism about such an approach (advocated by, e.g., Angrist and Krueger, 1999) is that the parameters identified are specific to the observed change, population, time-period, etc., i.e. they lack generality because they identify a reduced form effect. A different approach is to try to identify the mechanisms behind the causal effect – so as to achieve greater generalisability. Such a *structural* approach to evaluation explicitly specifies the mechanisms underlying individual behaviour based on the preferences, the constraints, the interactions and the sources of heterogeneity leading to a particular individual outcome. As such, the model provides a description of 'hypothetical worlds obtained by varying hypothetically the factors determining outcomes' (Heckman, 2010, p. 360). The first attractive property of this approach is to make explicit the assumptions made about the behaviour of an individual which remain implicit in the reduced-form approach (Rosenzweig and Wolpin, 2000; Keane, 2010). Second, inferences from data are based on the causal model: structural parameters leading to the reduced-form effect are estimated based on the observed variation. Such an approach thus allows one to generalise the policy effect in alternative contexts, in which determinants of behaviour are expected to be the same. The price for this increased generalisability is that the empirical analysis makes more statistical and theoretical assumptions about foundations of behaviour. Each approach thus has its own strengths and weaknesses. It is worth noting that each amounts to different specification choices, through the definition and nature of the parameters to be estimated. In both approaches to the data, though, the identification properties of the estimation depend on the structure of the data-generating process (Blundell, 2010).

---

individuals. But the average treatment effect is just irrelevant; what matters for both policy decision-making and academic research on the topic is the ATT. The estimation strategy must thus be adapted to the true parameter of interest – measuring the ATE without bias is of little help when the two are different and the ATT is what one actually seeks to measure.

The observational requirements of the two parameters are actually quite different. The ATT relies only on the outcomes of the sub-sample of treated individuals: $\Delta^{\text{ATT}} = \mathbb{E}\left[y_i(1)|\mathbf{X}, T_i = 1\right] - \mathbb{E}\left[y_i(0)|\mathbf{X}, T_i = 1\right]$. Beyond the output under treatment for treated individuals, which is generally easy to observe, the ATT thus requires data on the outcomes of treated individuals had the treatment not been implemented – the counterfactual world for treated individuals. In the context of the example given in Table 3.1, measuring the ATT amounts to restricting the analysis to individuals who are treated – those lines in black, for which $T_i = 1$. For those individuals, $\mathbf{y}(1)|\mathbf{X}, T = 1$ is available. The counterfactual problem is to find a way to measure the missing values in these lines, i.e. $\mathbf{y}(0)|\mathbf{X}, T = 1$.

Illustration 3.3
The need for assumptions on the data-generating process to achieve inference (even) from experimental evidence

To illustrate the lack of generalisability of experimental evidence without assumptions about the data-generating process, Manski (1999) insightfully revisits the results from the famous Perry preschool project. This natural experiment was implemented in Michigan starting in 1962. A random sample of disadvantaged black students is provided intensive educational services, while students from another random sample are used to build a control group, with no particular service. A key outcome from this experiment is that 67% of students in the treatment group were high-school graduates at age 19, while the proportion was 49% in the control group. Denote X the covariates of children who participated in the experiment (disadvantaged black children), $\mu_1 (= 1$ if high-school graduate by age 19, 0 otherwise) the true outcome of a child when assigned to the treatment and μ_0 the similarly defined outcome when a child does not receives the treatment. What this experiment identifies is that: $\Pr[\mu_1 = 1|X] = 0.67$ and $\Pr[\mu_0 = 1|X] = 0.49$. Two kinds of questions can be asked based on these results: (i) what do we learn about the effect of the programme? (ii) What would be the effect of the same programme implemented using an alternative treatment policy? The main issue in addressing the first question is that the answer not only involves the marginal distributions delivered by the experiment, but also depends on the joint distribution of the outcomes. For the sake of the illustration, consider the following joint distribution (according to which the outcomes are strongly negatively correlated):

$$\Pr[\mu_1 = 0, \mu_0 = 0|X] = .00; \quad \Pr[\mu_1 = 0, \mu_0 = 1|X] = .33$$
$$\Pr[\mu_1 = 1, \mu_0 = 0|X] = .51; \quad \Pr[\mu_1 = 1, \mu_0 = 1|X] = .16$$

This is consistent with the experimental evidence, as $\Pr[\mu_1 = 1|X] = \Pr[\mu_1 = 1, \mu_0 = 1|X] + \Pr[\mu_1 = 1, \mu_0 = 0|X] = 0.67$ and $\Pr[\mu_0 = 1|X] = \Pr[\mu_1 = 0, \mu_0 = 1|X] + \Pr[\mu_1 = 1, \mu_0 = 1|X] = 0.49$, and leads to graduation rates ranging between 0.16 and 1 depending on who receives the treatment. As a result, very little can be said about this question if nothing is known or assumed on the joint distribution of outcomes. This is also needed to answer the second question, i.e. to characterise the distribution of the outcome that results from policies j providing educational services to some children and not to others: $\Pr[\mu_j|X]$. In this case, the answer also depends on prior information on the treatment policy that would be implemented. Manski (1999) shows that depending on the prior information used, the range of possible values compatible with the observed outcomes from the experiment is as large as [0.16; 1]. The table below (from Table 3.1 in Manski, 1999, p. 59, the computations are nothing but straightforward and we refer the interested reader to Manski, 1999, pp. 60–72) for more details) shows how prior information can be used to narrow the range, and infer more informative values about the outcome of interest.

Prior information	$\Pr[\mu_j|x]$
No prior information	[0.16; 1]
Ordered outcomes ($\mu_1 \geq \mu_0$)	[0.49; 0.67]
Independent outcomes	[0.33; 0.83]
9/10 of the population receives the treatment	[0.57; 0.77]

In particular, the target probability lies between the two observed outcomes only if the joint distribution of the outcomes is such that the outcomes are perfectly ordered, or if the treatment is independent of the outcomes.

The counterfactual requirement for measuring the ATE is even stronger. Denoting $p = \Pr[T = 1]$ the probability of being treated,[9] the ATE is defined as:

$$\Delta^{\text{ATE}} = p\,\mathbb{E}\left[y_i(1) - y_i(0)\,|\mathbf{X}, T_i = 1\right] + (1 - p)\,\mathbb{E}\left[y_i(1) - y_i(0)\,|\mathbf{X}, T_i = 0\right]$$

The requirement for the empirical evaluation of this parameter is more demanding than for the ATT, as non-treated individuals are now included as well. In the example given in Table 3.1, this amounts to having access not only to the missing numbers for black lines where $T_i = 1$, but also to the missing numbers in grey lines with $T_i = 0$. On top of the observed behaviour of non-treated individuals, one also needs to find a counterfactual for the outcome of non-treated individuals had they been treated.

3.3   Identification Based on Observational Data

The formal definition of the treatment effects of interest now allows us to state more precisely the identification assumption that observational data must fulfil depending on the target parameter.

3.3.1   The Cross-section Estimator

The cross-section estimator compares the mean outcomes of treated and untreated individuals within a single period of time. The outcomes in each group are $\mathbf{y}(1)\,|\mathbf{X}, T = 1$ for those who received the treatment (corresponding to the available observations in column $y_i(1)$ in Table 3.1) and $\mathbf{y}(0)\,|\mathbf{X}, T = 0$ for those who did not (corresponding to available observations in column $y_i(0)$ in Table 3.1).The cross-section estimator seeks to measure the effect of the treatment based on:

$$\widehat{\Delta}^{Cross} = \frac{1}{n}\sum_{i=1}^{n} y_i(1) - \frac{1}{n}\sum_{i=1}^{n} y_i(0)$$

This expression makes clear that the estimator uses the outcome in the control group as a counterfactual to the outcome of the treated group, i.e. the estimator measures a relevant parameter only if $\mathbf{y}(0)\,|\mathbf{X}, T = 0$ is an accurate measure of what the treated individual's

---

[9] We omit in this presentation the possible dependency of this probability on the covariates $\Pr[T = 1|\mathbf{X}]$ as it is irrelevant for our discussion. This probability is also sometimes called the propensity score – the likelihood of being treated.

outcome would have been without the treatment. Formally, what the estimator delivers depends on the data-generating process according to:

$$
\begin{aligned}
\mathbb{E}(\widehat{\Delta}^{Cross}|\mathbf{X}) &= \mathbb{E}[y_i(1)|\mathbf{X}, T_i = 1] - \mathbb{E}[y_i(0)|\mathbf{X}, T_i = 0] \\
&= \mathbb{E}[y_i(1)|\mathbf{X}, T_i = 1] + \mathbb{E}\big[y_i(0)|\mathbf{X}, T_i = 1] - \mathbb{E}[y_i(0)|\mathbf{X}, T_i = 1\big] \\
&\qquad - \mathbb{E}[y_i(0)|\mathbf{X}, T_i = 0] \\
&= \mathbb{E}[y_i(0)|\mathbf{X}, T_i = 1] - \mathbb{E}[y_i(0)|\mathbf{X}, T_i = 0] \\
&\qquad + \underbrace{\mathbb{E}[y_i(1)|\mathbf{X}, T_i = 1] - \mathbb{E}[y_i(0)|\mathbf{X}, T_i = 1]}_{\Delta^{ATT}}
\end{aligned}
$$

The cross-section estimator thus contains the ATT – the average treatment effect on those individuals actually treated. But it contains more, as

$$
\mathbf{B}^S = \mathbb{E}[y_i(0)|\mathbf{X}, T_i = 1] - \mathbb{E}[y_i(0)|\mathbf{X}, T_i = 0] = \mathbb{E}[\varepsilon_i(0)|\mathbf{X}, T_i = 1] - \mathbb{E}[\varepsilon_i(0)|\mathbf{X}, T_i = 0]
$$

also contributes to the value taken by the comparison. This quantity measures the difference in outcome that would occur without the treatment between the two groups of individuals. If this term is non-zero, it implies that people belonging to the control group ($\forall i$ s.t. $T_i = 0$) and those in the treatment group ($\forall i$ s.t. $T_i = 1$) are characterised by different mechanisms producing the outcome – the data-generating process is not the same in both sub-samples. For this reason, the control group does not provide an accurate counterfactual to the treatment group outcome. As compared to the ATT, the cross-section estimator is biased with a magnitude measured by $\mathbf{B}^S$. Since this is a measure of the difference in outcome between the two groups of individuals depending on whether they will benefit from the treatment or not, this is a called a selection effect. Any such selection induces a bias in the estimation of the ATT based on the cross-section estimator.

It is worth noting that this selection effect amounts to a violation of the identification assumption because $\mathbf{B}^S = \mathbb{E}[\varepsilon_i(0)|\mathbf{X}, T_i = 1] - \mathbb{E}[\varepsilon_i(0)|\mathbf{X}, T_i = 0] \neq 0$ implies that unobserved heterogeneity is correlated with the treatment: its distribution is different in the sub-population of individuals who will subsequently receive the treatment, and those who do not. This is typically induced by endogenous selection in the treatment, due, for instance, to the fact that programmes are targeted on people whose need for a 'treatment' is higher – resulting in lower unobserved heterogeneity as compared to those who will not receive the treatment. Focus 3.3 shows how the very same issue can arise from spontaneous choices to be treated on the part of economic agents – because people who expect the most from being treated will opt in if offered the choice.

3.3.2   Identifying Assumptions of the Cross-section Estimator

A joint product of the above result is that identification of the ATT based on cross-section comparisons will be unbiased if the data-generating process is built in such a way that there is no selection:

$$
\mathbb{E}[y_i(0)|\mathbf{X}, T_i = 1] = \mathbb{E}[y_i(0)|\mathbf{X}, T_i = 0] \Rightarrow \mathbb{E}[\widehat{\Delta}^{Cross}|\mathbf{X}] = \Delta^{ATT}
$$

Focus 3.3
Incentives and performance: the confounding effect of self-selection

The figure below illustrates the choice of a worker (individual A), whose preferences are defined over effort (the inverse of leisure, on the x-axis) and income (y-axis). There is a trade-off between the two, as income can only be raised by increased effort, reducing the amount of leisure. Utility thus increases towards the north-west.

    The graph illustrates the effect of switching to higher power incentives. The two straight lines are two different budget constraints induced by different compensation schemes. The first one, CB, only weakly correlates income to effort (reduced leisure), while the second one, CB$'$, is a pure piece-rate scheme offering higher power incentives. Switching between the two moves individual A's optimal choice (the tangency between A's indifference curves and each budget constraint) towards higher levels of effort – what empirical analysis of the performance effect of payment schemes seeks to quantify.

Income

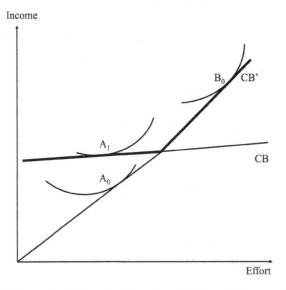

Effort

But more insights can be drawn from the figure. When moving from CB to CB$'$, individual A falls to a lower level of utility, as A_0 is dominated by A_1. This means A will not work under a piece-rate compensation scheme if he can choose the budget constraint – if, for instance, several firms offer the same kind of occupation but opt for different managerial policies, in such a way that the two budget constraints are available on the labour market. The picture is different for individual B, whose preferences are such that moving from CB$'$ to CB would lead to a lower level of utility. Individual B would thus prefer to stay on B_0, hence working in a firm offering a piece-rate scheme. The main difference between A and B is the shape of their preferences: in the trade-off between income and leisure, B puts more weight on income relative to effort than A does. This may be because B experiences a lower cost of effort, or is more efficient such that a given sacrifice of leisure leads to higher performance. The main consequence of this heterogeneity in preferences is that it is very unlikely to observe A, and very likely to observe B, in piece-rate firms. This has two consequences for empirical analysis. First, simple comparison in performance between piece-rate firms and others does not identify any treatment effect: it mixes treatment effects and selection – the difference in performance between individuals due to their heterogeneous preferences. Second, the individual responses of A and B to higher power incentives will systematically differ, and this is related to whether or not they are actually observed in a piece-rate situation. The ATE is thus different from the ATT.

In other words, identification of the ATT by the cross-section estimator requires the affectation to the treatment to be independent of the baseline, without treatment, outcome $\mathbf{y}(0)$. As such, this condition is the identifying assumption of the ATT based on the cross-section estimator. The ATT is the parameter of interest if one seeks to measure the change in outcome experienced by people targeted by the treatment. As discussed above, this might be different from the effect obtained by giving the treatment to an individual randomly drawn from the population – or by generalising the treatment to everyone – an effect that is measured by the ATE.

The above expression is enough to show that the cross-section estimator, even under the identifying assumption of no selection on $\mathbf{y}(0)$, is a biased estimator of the ATE – just because it measures the ATT and will thus miss the ATE as soon as the two differ. The bias can be written more explicitly using the expression for the unconditional outcomes:

$$\mathbb{E}[y_i(1)|\mathbf{X}] = p\,\mathbb{E}[y_i(1)|\mathbf{X}, T_i = 1] + (1-p)\,\mathbb{E}[y_i(1)|\mathbf{X}, T_i = 0]$$

so that:

$$\mathbb{E}[y_i(1)|\mathbf{X}, T_i = 1] = \mathbb{E}[y_i(1)|\mathbf{X}] + (1-p)\,[\mathbb{E}[y_i(1)|\mathbf{X}, T_i = 1] - \mathbb{E}[y_i(1)|\mathbf{X}, T_i = 0]]$$

The same manipulations applied to

$$\mathbb{E}[y_i(0)|\mathbf{X}] = p\,\mathbb{E}[y_i(0)|\mathbf{X}, T_i = 1] + (1-p)\,\mathbb{E}[y_i(0)|\mathbf{X}, T_i = 0]$$

lead to a similar expression for $\mathbb{E}[y_i(0)|\mathbf{X}, T_i = 0]$. The cross-section estimator is then related to the ATE according to:

$$\begin{aligned}
\mathbb{E}(\widehat{\Delta}^{Cross}|\mathbf{X}) &= \mathbb{E}[y_i(1)|\mathbf{X}, T_i = 1] - \mathbb{E}[y_i(0)|\mathbf{X}, T_i = 0] \\
&= \mathbb{E}[y_i(1)|\mathbf{X}] + (1-p)\,[\mathbb{E}[y_i(1)|\mathbf{X}, T_i = 1] - \mathbb{E}[y_i(1)|\mathbf{X}, T_i = 0]] \\
&\quad - \mathbb{E}[y_i(0)|\mathbf{X}] + p[\mathbb{E}[y_i(0)|\mathbf{X}, T_i = 1] - \mathbb{E}[y_i(0)|\mathbf{X}, T_i = 0]] \\
\mathbb{E}(\widehat{\Delta}^{Cross}|\mathbf{X}) &= \underbrace{\mathbb{E}[y_i(1)|\mathbf{X}] - \mathbb{E}[y_i(0)|\mathbf{X}]}_{\Delta^{\mathrm{ATE}}} + \mathbf{B}^{\mathrm{H}}
\end{aligned}$$

where

$$\begin{aligned}
\mathbf{B}^{\mathrm{H}} &= (1-p)\,\big[\mathbb{E}\left[y_i(1)|\mathbf{X}, T_i = 1\right] - \mathbb{E}[y_i(1)|\mathbf{X}, T_i = 0]\big] \\
&\quad + p\ \ [\mathbb{E}[y_i(0)|\mathbf{X}, T_i = 1] - \mathbb{E}[y_i(0)|\mathbf{X}, T_i = 0]]
\end{aligned}$$

Last, simple rearrangement of the expression leads to:

$$\mathbf{B}^{\mathrm{H}} = \underbrace{\mathbb{E}[\,y_i(0)|\,\mathbf{X}, T_i = 1] - \mathbb{E}[\,y_i(0)|\,\mathbf{X}, T_i = 0]}_{\mathbf{B}^{\mathrm{S}}}$$

$$- (1 - p)[\mathbb{E}[\,y_i(1) - y_i(0)|\,\mathbf{X}, T_i = 1] - \mathbb{E}[\,y_i(1) - y_i(0)|\,\mathbf{X}, T_i = 0]]$$

Even if selection on the baseline outcome is not endogenous, in such a way that $\mathbf{B}^{\mathrm{S}} = 0$, the cross-section estimator will deliver a biased measure of the average treatment effect if the second term is different from 0. The magnitude of the bias depends on the relative size of the potential treatment effects in the two groups, i.e. on the extent of the heterogeneity in the treatment effect: the higher the difference in outcomes for treated individuals as compared to the difference for those in the control group, the higher the bias (and the higher the difference between the ATT and the ATE). The only context in which the estimator identifies the ATE is when not only the baseline outcome $\mathbf{y}(0)$, but also the outcome resulting from the treatment $\mathbf{y}(1)$, are distributed independently of the affectation to the treatment – but in this case, the ATE and the ATT do not differ, because the treatment effect is homogeneous.

To illustrate selection bias and heterogeneity in the treatment effect, consider a CV-writing and job interview workshop offered at a university to foster students' success in finding a job. Students are free to choose whether or not to participate. All participants belong to the treatment group and consider that observations are also available for a random sample of non-participants from the university. A measurement strategy could be to follow both groups for a year following the programme in order to record their success in finding employment. However, the problem is that the individuals who choose to participate in the workshop in the first place may be more motivated about getting a job than those who do not. They are more likely to be hard-working students who obtain better results than the non-participants. Therefore using the treatment effect of participating in the workshop to measure how quickly students find a job may be spurious, because those students who participated would have, in any event, found a job faster than those who chose not to participate, even in absence of the workshop. The choice of participating or not is the selection effect based on individual student characteristics, making the two sub-samples difficult to compare (also see Illustration 3.4). In addition to the selection bias there is also the fact that once they have participated, the participants may benefit more from the workshop than the non-participants would have had they participated, because the more motivated participants are more knowledgeable and involved and thus draw a greater benefit from it. This represents the heterogeneity of the treatment effect.

3.4   Inference Based on Controlled Experiments

The main difference between experimental and naturally occurring data is that experiments allow us to decide on the data-generating process. First, the variation of interest is implemented on purpose in line with the research question. This is an important difference from natural experiments, for which any estimation of the treatment effect requires observations i, such that $T_i = 1$, to be available. Controlled experiments, by contrast, allow us to generate any variation T of interest. Second, the participation decision is part of the experimental design. Identifying assumptions that have been developed in

Illustration 3.4
Incentives and performance: selection and incentive effects

The 44% increase in performance observed in the Safelite experiment (Illustration 3.2) mixes incentive effects, and selection effects associated with self-selection of workers in the firm based on their preferences after the switch to a piece-rate scheme. The table below (from Table 4 in Lazear, 2000, p. 1355) displays the differences in turnover between the hourly wage regime and the piece-rate regime (*performance pay plan, PPP*), organised according to the relative performance (decile) of workers.

Decile	Hourly regime			PPP regime			Difference between PPP and hourly separation rates	
	Separation rate	No. of obs.	St. error	Separation rate	No. of obs.	St. error	Difference	St. error
Lowest								
0	0.041	1,641	0.005	0.039	1,285	0.005	−0.002	0.007
1	0.043	1,465	0.005	0.038	1,491	0.005	−0.006	0.007
2	0.042	1,358	0.005	0.037	1,625	0.005	−0.005	0.007
3	0.039	1,245	0.005	0.037	1,691	0.005	−0.002	0.007
4	0.037	1,282	0.005	0.034	1,693	0.004	−0.003	0.007
5	0.038	1,279	0.005	0.04	1,792	0.005	0.002	0.007
6	0.025	1,223	0.004	0.03	1,777	0.004	0.005	0.006
7	0.029	1,135	0.005	0.03	1,879	0.004	0.001	0.006
8	0.03	880	0.006	0.022	2,169	0.003	−0.008	0.007
9	0.033	2,437	0.004	0.027	339	0.009	−0.007	0.009
Highest								
Overall	0.033	13,945	0.002	0.036	15,741	0.002	0.003	0.002

The simple overall effect of the change in payment regime goes from 0.033 to 0.036, but the difference is not statistically significant. The magnitude of the turnover thus remains the same. Selection, however, refers to a differential productivity of workers who leave and enter the firm due to this process. It is possible to look at this concern by focusing on those workers who work in the firm both after and before the change. On this specific sub-sample, the estimated effect is a 22% change in productivity: selection and incentive effects thus account for half the observed aggregate change in performance.

econometrics to better analyse naturally occurring phenomena thus serve as a guide for experimental practices that help identify the treatment effect of interest from the observed behaviour generated by the experiment. From the above discussion, two main devices appear to facilitate identification: one is to break correlations between unobserved components of the outcome and the change in the explanatory variable of interest; the other is to measure and thus eliminate the effect of confounding factors. Both are central to understanding how experimental methods improve the accuracy of empirical identification.

Focus 3.4
Two additional difference estimators and their identifying assumptions

The cross-section estimator uses the current behaviour of untreated individuals as a counter-factual for the treated individuals without the treatment. There exist two other very popular difference estimators, relying on alternative counterfactual assumptions.

The **before–after estimator** is based on longitudinal data – i.e. it applies when repeated observations from the same individuals are available before (at time $t = \underline{t}$) and after (at time $t = \bar{t}$) the treatment occurs. Basically, such an estimator compares the difference in the average outcome for a group of individuals before the treatment and after the treatment:

$$\widehat{\Delta}^{\mathrm{BA}} = \frac{1}{n}\sum_{i=1}^{n} y_{i,\bar{t}}(1) - \frac{1}{n}\sum_{i=1}^{n} y_{i,\underline{t}}(1)$$

This estimator thus uses the past outcome of the treated group as a counterfactual to the outcome of the group being treated at the time. Based on the data-generating process, the identification achieved by the estimator is

$$\mathbb{E}(\widehat{\Delta}^{\mathrm{BA}}|\mathbf{X}) = \mathbb{E}[y_i(1)|\mathbf{X}, T_i = 1, t = \bar{t}] - \mathbb{E}[y_i(0)|\mathbf{X}, T_i = 1, t = \underline{t}]$$
$$= \Delta^{\mathrm{ATT}} + \mathbb{E}[\varepsilon_i(1)|\mathbf{X}, T_i = 1, t = \bar{t}] - \mathbb{E}[\varepsilon_i(1)|\mathbf{X}, T_i = 1, t = \underline{t}]$$

The second term is the variation in unobserved heterogeneity in the group of treated individuals, from before $(\varepsilon(1)_{t=\underline{t}})$ to after $(\varepsilon(1)_{t=\bar{t}})$ the treatment. By construction, any permanent (typically, individual-specific) heterogeneity is eliminated. But any difference occurring over time will not be eliminated, and biases the estimation of the treatment effect – because the treatment variable is then correlated with time-varying unobserved heterogeneity. The identifying assumption of the BA estimator is thus that there is no unobserved change over time inducing a variation in the outcome beyond the treatment itself. Otherwise, the bias comes from the fact that the estimator attributes any change over time in the outcome to the causal effect of the treatment.

The **difference-in-difference estimator** relies on both cross-sectional and longitudinal data, and estimates the treatment effect for a given group of individuals as:

$$\widehat{\Delta}^{\mathrm{DD}} = \left(\frac{1}{n}\sum_{i=1}^{n} y_{i,\bar{t}}(1) - \frac{1}{n}\sum_{i=1}^{n} y_{i,\bar{t}}(0)\right) - \left(\frac{1}{n}\sum_{i=1}^{n} y_{i,\underline{t}}(1) - \frac{1}{n}\sum_{i=1}^{n} y_{i,\underline{t}}(0)\right)$$

It amounts to using the past difference between treated and untreated individuals as a counterfactual of their current difference. The aim of this double difference is to eliminate confounding issues related to problems of both timing (as in the BA estimator) and selection (as in the cross-section estimator):

$$\mathbb{E}(\widehat{\Delta}^{\mathrm{DD}}|\mathbf{X}) = \Delta^{\mathrm{ATT}} + \mathbf{B}_{\bar{t}}^s - \mathbf{B}_{\underline{t}}^s$$

As a result, the identifying assumption of the difference-in-difference estimator is also known as a 'parallel trend assumption': the unobserved difference between individuals from the control and treatment groups should remain unchanged or, put otherwise, the change in outcome in the control group must replicate the change that would have occurred for treated individuals, without the treatment.

3.4.1 Identification through Randomisation

The above discussion of both the OLS estimator and the econometrics of treatment effects points to one crucial condition for identification: the exogeneity of the
explanatory variables, i.e. that there is no correlation between the unobserved component of the outcome and the variables of interest. The most natural way to avoid
correlation is randomisation. It is quite straightforward to see in the identification
condition of the OLS estimator, derived in Section 3.1.3:

$$\mathbb{E}(\varepsilon_i|\mathbf{X}) = 0, \, \forall i \Rightarrow \mathbb{E}(\hat{\theta}_{\text{OLS}}|\mathbf{X}) = \theta$$

Identification is achieved if the distribution of the error is not correlated with the values
taken by the $\mathbf{X}$. In the extreme case, this would obviously be obtained if one can decide
on a purely random basis the value of the explanatory variable for each and every individual. If, for any i, the value taken by $x_{i1}, x_{i2}, \ldots, x_{im}$ results from a random draw then
it is mechanically the case that this value is independent of the unobserved component
of any outcome variable. Think, for instance, of the measurement of gender-specific
behaviour in groups (of which Illustration 3.5 provides an example). The aim of such a
study is to measure the causal effect of the gender composition of a group on male and
female members. The challenge faced when trying to measure such an effect on observational data is the endogeneity of the composition variable: people may decide whether
or not to belong to different groups according to their gender composition based on their
specific ability to accommodate such circumstances. This induces a correlation between
the composition variable and some unobserved component of the outcome of interest.
While gender obviously cannot be randomly chosen (even in an experiment!), the group
composition faced by male and female subjects can easily be randomised. This achieves
identification of the causal effect of interest.

This same principle applies as well to the estimation of treatment effects in the policy
evaluation framework. As shown above, selection bias and heterogeneity of the treatment effect arise when individuals can freely choose their treatment groups, i.e. if people
sort themselves into treatment groups according to their characteristics and preferences.
The way to counteract this phenomenon is again randomisation, applied to the treatment
participation groups. This amounts to choosing randomly whether individuals belong to
the control or to the treatment group. Under this rule (often called random assignment to
the treatment), the value of the treatment variable is decided by a coin toss. By construction, this implements the identifying assumption of the cross-section estimator, i.e. the
average non-participant in the programme $-\mathbb{E}[y_i(0)|\mathbf{X}, T_i = 0]$ – obtains the same non-
treatment outcome as the average participant in the programme $-\mathbb{E}[y_i(0)|\mathbf{X}, T_i = 1]$).
Put otherwise:

$$\mathbb{E}[\varepsilon_i(0)|\mathbf{X}, T_i = 1] = \mathbb{E}[\varepsilon_i(0)|\mathbf{X}, T_i = 0]$$

A simple comparison in outcomes between treated and untreated individuals (based on
the cross-section estimator) is thus enough to measure the ATT (see Illustration 3.6
for a simple application in the field). But randomisation in fact does more: because
participation in the treatment is not at all based on unobserved heterogeneity, it is also
the case that

Illustration 3.5

Gender differences in competitiveness: experimental evidence from exogenously chosen composition of groups

Gender differences in labour market outcomes are well documented facts in most countries. In order to better understand the behavioural reasons behind such differences, Gneezy et al. (2003) experimentally investigate whether competition induces gender-specific behaviour. More specifically, the experiment considers tournaments in which the gender composition of the team is either all females or males, or mixed with exactly half males and half females. The task in the experiment is to solve mazes. The baseline provides a control on possible performance differences between gender, by having the task paid according to a piece rate. A fourth treatment aims to provide a control on the sole effect of the uncertainty about compensation faced in tournaments due to the need to anticipate other members' performance. In this treatment, compensation is individual but uncertain – one individual is randomly chosen to be paid according to the piece rate. The figure below (from Figure 3, p. 1062) displays the main results obtained in the experimental treatments.

For each treatment in abscissa, the figure displays the performance of males and females as well as the gender gap. The gender differences are insignificant in both the piece-rate and the random pay scheme. Both males and females positively react to competition, since both kinds of tournament elicit higher performance. But group composition has a strong effect on the gender gap: females do much worse when competing with males rather than females, while males do slightly better.

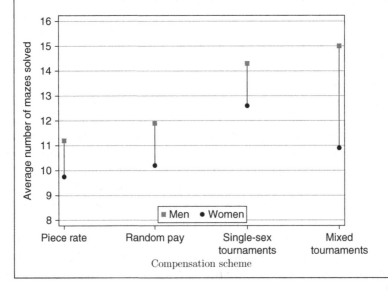

$$\mathbb{E}[\, \varepsilon_i(1)|\, \mathbf{X}, T_i = 1] = \mathbb{E}[\, \varepsilon_i(1)|\, \mathbf{X}, T_i = 0]$$

Randomisation also eliminates any heterogeneity in the treatment effect, in such a way that there is no difference between the ATT and the ATE. Random assignment allows us to measure the expected effect of the treatment on any individual randomly drawn from the population.

Illustration 3.6
Piece rate: a field experiment

Shearer (2004) reports on a field experiment aimed to measure the impact on productivity of piece-rate payment mechanisms. The experiment is implemented in the tree-planting industry in British Columbia (Canada). The industry has a number of characteristics that facilitate the study of interest: daily compensation in the tree-planting industry varies regularly according to the properties of the land area where the work occurs. This makes the sudden change in compensation (from the usual hourly wage to a piece rate) more natural for workers. Productivity is also easy to measure and can be simply computed as the number of trees planted during a given period of time. In order to run the experiment, three areas of varying levels of difficulty were selected, and each is randomly subdivided into two parts. The two parts define compensation regions: one has a fixed wage (FW) announced and paid, while the other part has a piece-rate payment (PR). Nine workers were randomly selected for 120 workings days: each of them is reallocated each day to a land area and a compensation region, in such a way that 60 daily observations are available in each compensation region. The table below (from Table 3, p. 518) provides the descriptive statistics from the experiment for each planter.

Planter	Observations	Total	PR	FW	Difference
1	16	1127.50	1275.00	980.00	295.00
2	12	1098.33	1220.00	976.67	243.33
3	12	1226.67	1430.00	1023.33	406.67
4	16	992.50	1000.00	985.00	15.00
5	12	1163.33	1266.67	1060.00	206.67
6	4	1330.00	1470.00	1190.00	280.00
7	16	1121.25	1165.00	1077.50	87.50
8	16	1157.50	1255.00	1060.00	195.00
9	16	1252.50	1420.00	1085.00	335.00

Thanks to the random allocation to groups, simple comparisons provide an estimate of the average treatment effect. It amounts to a 20% increase in productivity induced by the change in incentive.

It is important to be precise on the definition of the population – and generalise our understanding of the ATT/ATE. The above relations make it clear that identification is specific to the experimental population (from which individuals from both groups are drawn). The estimation is an ATE in the sense that the experiment measures the average expected change for any individual randomly drawn from this population. But it does not mean it is the effect of the treatment on any human being among those who do not participate in the experiment: if such people are likely to react differently to the treatment, then the experiment obviously fails to identify what the treatment effect would be in this specific population. Whether or not such a difference challenges the lessons drawn from experiments depends on the definition of the population on which inference is made. This is a matter of intensive debate in the literature, further discussed in Chapter 8. But in terms of the definitions above, this has nothing to do with a biased estimation of the effect of interest; it is rather a matter of a heterogeneous treatment effect – the experimental ATE is in fact specific to the experimental subject pool. The effect is accurately measured in the experiment, but it might not generalise to other populations because the treatment effect is specific to the experimental population.

3.4.2   Identification through Control Variables

One distinguishing feature of experiments discussed in the previous chapter is their ability to widen the set of available measures – improving the set of research questions that can be addressed based on experimental data. This also plays an important role in the identification properties of experiments, as it widens the set of control variables that can be used to enhance identification. In econometrics, control variables are individual specific information that are accounted for to improve identification, rather than because their effect actually belongs to the research question. Despite this strong difference in nature, concretely speaking they are nothing but additional explanatory variables – typically, age, income, occupation, etc. A typical example of control variables is their use in discontinuity designs. Consider a policy that applies according to a threshold – e.g. additional benefits offered to people whose income is below a target – in a such a way that people who benefit from the policy are selected as regards to the outcome variable. The distance to the threshold is a control variable achieving identification: conditional on being in a close neighbourhood around the threshold, the treatment status can be assumed to be exogenous, i.e. people around the threshold can be assumed to fall below or above for purely random reasons (see Black, 1999, for an application to the measurement of parents' willingness to pay for the quality of schools, based on discontinuities at district borders).

Note that in all previous discussions, the explanatory variables $\mathbf{X}$ enter the identifying assumptions in two different ways. They enter directly in the conditioning, reflecting the fact that their effect cannot be identified unless they are exogenous – uncorrelated with the unobserved components of the outcome. The consequences in terms of identification are the ones discussed above: randomising participation in treatments based on individual specific characteristics is enough to achieve identification.

But individual specific variables also enter indirectly the identifying assumption, through the unobserved component itself. Remember that the noise component of the model, ε, is residual in nature: it stands for the part of the outcome data-generating process that is not accounted for by the measurable part involving $\mathbf{X}$. In the OLS specification, this has been noticed in Section 3.1.3 from a simple rearrangement of the linear equation leading to $\varepsilon = \mathbf{y} - \mathbf{X}\theta$. By construction, any component leading to $\mathbf{y}$ for which an empirical measure is available is thus eliminated from ε as soon as it is included in $\mathbf{X}$. This opens an additional strategy to improve identification. Adding measures to the model will reduce the noise, hence undermining the scope of possible confounding factors in the error term. It is worth insisting again on the fact that such control variables and additional measures do not improve identification just because they reduce the noise. Noise itself is a matter of statistical inference, not of identification. The circumstances in which they improve identification are when unmeasured dimensions that are correlated with the observables of interest become measured. For instance, the case study below (Section 3.4.4) discusses the potentially confounding effect of risk attitudes in the evaluation of alternative compensation schemes. In a study on observational data, such an individual specific characteristic is likely to be unmeasurable and belong to the error ε of a model estimating the determinants of performance at work. The experimental context, by contrast, allows us to collect data on this dimension (using specific elicitation methods which are the topic of the case study presented in Section 7.4). Once a measure of individual risk attitudes is available, its effect on the outcome no longer belongs to the unobserved component of performance. The model involves an error $\tilde{\varepsilon}$ identical to $\tilde{\varepsilon}$ but excluding risk attitude. If risk attitudes are actually confounding in the study, identification is thus recovered thanks to their explicit measure.

3.4.3   Enhanced Inference Thanks to Control

A last possibility to achieve identification is to rule out confounding variations in the noise, by blocking their value to a specified level. The idea is fairly simple: consider a situation with an unobserved component, z, generating endogeneity – hence belonging to the noise ε. In the policy evaluation framework, this means that variations in the value of z induce variations in the value of both y and $\mathcal{T}$ in such a way that $\mathbb{E}[z \in \varepsilon_i(0) | \mathbf{X}, T_i = 1] \neq \mathbb{E}[z \in \varepsilon_i(0) | \mathbf{X}, T_i = 0]$, because $\varepsilon(0)$ contains different values of z when looking at different values of $\mathcal{T}$. Randomisation solves this issue by letting z vary from one individual to another, $z_i \neq z_j$, $i \neq j$; but by breaking the correlation between unknown causes of the outcome and the target variation $\mathcal{T}$, in such a way that $\mathbb{E}[\varepsilon_i(0) | \mathbf{X}, T_i = 1] = \mathbb{E}[\varepsilon_i(0) | \mathbf{X}, T_i = 0]$. Identification is thus achieved thanks to statistical balance in unobserved components between groups: the values of z are different between different individuals, but randomisation makes it more and more likely as the sample size becomes bigger that the distribution of these values in subgroups defined by $\mathcal{T}$ is the same. Consider instead a design holding z constant at a given value: $z_i = z$, $\forall i = 1, \ldots, N$. Because the value of z now is the same for all individuals, there is no longer any difference in the unobserved component of y it induces between the two sub-samples; since there is no variation in z, there is no confounding variation in the data. The big difference is that the sample now is exactly balanced, i.e. $\{z | \mathbf{X}, \mathcal{T} = 1\} = \{z | \mathbf{X}, \mathcal{T} = 0\} = z$.

This property implies that using control as an identification strategy comes with an improvement in statistical inference as compared to randomisation. Remember that statistical inference refers to the uncertainty about the value of the target parameter measured thanks to an estimate, due to variations in the sample. This is again summarised in the noise component of the econometric model: the target parameter is imperfectly measured based on the observed relationship between the outcome variable and the exogenous regressors because this observed relationship is only an imperfect signal of the true relationship going through the unknown parameters. In the context of the linear model of Section 3.1.3, $\mathbf{y} = \mathbf{X}\theta + \varepsilon$ implies that $\hat{\theta}_{\mathrm{OLS}} = (\mathbf{X}'\mathbf{X})^{-1}\mathbf{X}'(\mathbf{X}\theta + \varepsilon) = \theta + (\mathbf{X}'\mathbf{X})^{-1}\mathbf{X}'\varepsilon$: the more noisy the data, the larger the estimator variations around the true parameter. In this example, this results in a precision equal to $\mathbb{V}(\hat{\theta}_{\mathrm{OLS}} | \mathbf{X}) = \sigma^2 (\mathbf{X}'\mathbf{X})^{-1}$, which is increasing in the variance of the noise. The more unobserved dimensions are set to a unique, constant, value, the lower this quantity will be.

For the sake of the illustration, consider again two different components embedded in the noise of this linear model: an unobserved factor z, and everything that remains beyond its effect on y, denoted $\tilde{\varepsilon}$. Writing this noise as $\varepsilon = \theta_z z + \tilde{\varepsilon}$ – i.e. θ_z measures the extent of the variations in y that come from variations in z. Now consider two data-generating processes. In the first, z freely varies from one observation to another. The noise of this empirical model is such that $\sigma_\varepsilon^2 = \theta_z^2 \mathbb{V}(z) + \sigma_{\tilde{\varepsilon}}^2$. Now consider the other extreme, in which z is still unobserved (typically because it is impossible to build a measure of it) but is held constant to a given value, $z_i = \underline{z}$, $\forall i$. In this sample, $\mathbb{V}(z) = 0$ so that $\sigma_{\varepsilon_0}^2 = \sigma_{\tilde{\varepsilon}}^2 < \sigma_\varepsilon^2$: the estimates drawn from such a sample will be closer to the target parameter, hence more informative, because data are less noisy. As a result, the sample quantities delivered by experimental data are more informative the more unobservable dimensions are held constant between observations – which also improves identification as soon as they are possibly confounding.

3.4.4   *Case Study:* The Incentive Effects of Tournaments: Evidence from the Laboratory

The main limitation of the use of piece-rate incentive schemes is that they are not renegotiation-proof when effort is non-verifiable – i.e. when the level of performance cannot be proven based on evidence (Malcomson, 1984). In this kind of situation, the employer always has an incentive to renegotiate the work contract *ex post*, once the performance of the employee becomes known, so as to avoid paying high wages. Tournaments are an alternative compensation scheme that are robust to this issue.

The principle of a tournament (introduced by Lazear and Rosen, 1981) is to rely on relative, rather than absolute, performance. To formalise the comparison between tournaments and piece rate, assume all workers i in a firm have a production function $y_i = g(\ell_i) + \varepsilon_i$, where effort ℓ_i is exerted at cost $c_e(\ell_i)$.[10] If employees work under a piece-rate payment mechanism, denoted w, then the level of incentives is $w.y_i$ so that performance is chosen according to $c_e'(\ell_i^*) = w.g'(\ell_i^*)$. Since the wage is an increasing function of effort at work, the optimal level of effort increases in the piece rate. A tournament relies on different 'prizes', for instance A and a such that $A > a$, that are distributed according to the rank of the employee in the distribution of efforts. For instance, worker i gets A if $y_i > y_j, j \neq i$ but will get a otherwise. In the context of the simple production function above, the tournament provides incentives according to the probability of winning the biggest prize $\pi(\ell_i, \ell_j) = \Pr[\varepsilon_i - \varepsilon_j > g(\ell_j) - g(\ell_i)]$. Based on this probability, it is possible to replicate the optimal effort induced by any piece rate through an appropriate choice of the prizes offered in the tournament. The main difference between the two is that the total amount of the wage bill is determined *ex ante*: there must be a winner who gets the highest prize. The tournament is thus renegotiation-proof.

Whether or not tournaments empirically achieve the same level of incentive as piece rate, however, remains an open question. Bull et al. (1987) provide evidence aimed at comparing the incentive effects of these two incentive schemes. In the tournament treatment, subjects are told that they have been assigned a partner in the room, whose identity

---

[10] $g(\ell_i)$ is assumed to be increasing, continuous and concave in ℓ_i, and $c_e(\ell_i)$ is assumed to be increasing, continuous and convex in ℓ_i.

remains hidden. Subjects are then asked to pick a number between 0 and 100, called the 'decision number', standing for the effort variable. The cost function is set equal to ℓ_i^2/b, where ℓ_i is the subject's chosen number and b a parameter. Rather than asking subjects to do their own computations, subjects are provided with a 'cost list' with the individual cost of each number between 0 and 100. Last, subjects are asked to draw a random integer between $-h$ and $+h$ (0 included) from a box of bingo balls, standing for the noise between performance and effort. The amount of production is set equal to the sum of the two numbers. The experimenter computes each subject's production, and announces and rewards the subject pair with the highest number. The parameter values are chosen in such a way that the equilibrium effort (ℓ^*) in this baseline tournament is equal to 37 for each individual. In a benchmark experiment, the compensation scheme is set to a piece rate tuned in such a way that it replicates the same equilibrium level of effort.

The upper part of Figure 3.3 compares the level of effort observed in the experiment depending on the compensation scheme. On each graph, the straight line represents the

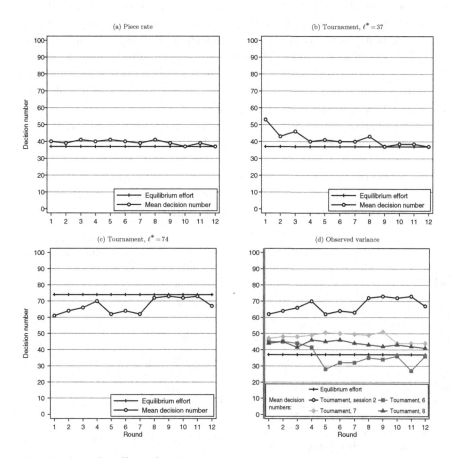

Figure 3.3 Incentive effects of tournaments

Note. Observed effort over time in the piece-rate treatment (a), the tournament treatment with equilibrium effort equal to 37 (b) and the tournament treatment with equilibrium effort equal to 74 (c). d shows the variance in effort observed over time in all treatments.

Source: Bull et al. (1987, p. 17–20, Figures 1–3, 11).

equilibrium effort and the joint dots are the mean decision numbers chosen in each round. First, the results clearly show that tournament and piece rate achieve the same convergence rate towards the equilibrium effort. In order to double check this coincidence between the theoretical prediction and empirical behaviour, a third experiment is implemented in which the tournament is designed to induce an equilibrium effort equal to 74. Observed behaviour further confirms the incentive effect of the tournament scheme: as shown in Figure 3.3.c, the level of effort chosen by the subjects matches the new equilibrium value. In both instances, the rate of convergence, however, seems lower in the tournament treatments as compared to the piece rate. Figure 3.3.d aims to investigate the reasons why it happens: rank-order tournaments exhibit a very high variance in effort between subjects, while piece-rate schemes have a rather small variance.

Such a variance in effort may reflect the need to account for other workers' behaviour: the decision in a tournament is a function both of a worker's preferences and skills and of their co-workers' behaviour – heterogenity in skills and preferences is likely to make coordination at work harder, as shown by Meidinger et al. (2003). This might affect not only the incentive properties of tournaments, as shown above, but also their selection effects. Eriksson et al. (2009) aim to study the determinants of self-selection into tournament schemes. The experiment involves two treatments, a benchmark and a choice design. The benchmark experiment allocates subjects randomly to either piece-rate payment or a tournament, while the second treatment allows subjects to choose *ex ante* how they want to be paid in each period.

Figure 3.4 focuses on the dispersion in effort observed under a tournament compensation scheme: the larger the grey areas, the further are quartiles of the effort distribution from its median. Self-selection is the only difference between the left-hand-side figure and the right-hand-side one: subjects are randomly assigned to the tournament in the benchmark, while they freely opt for it in the choice treatment. Self-selection drastically decreases the variance of effort: half the variance disappears when people self-select

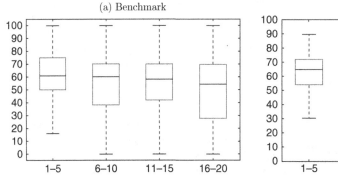
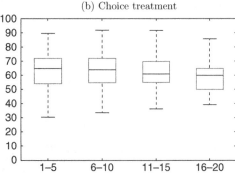

Figure 3.4 Dispersion of efforts in tournaments

Note. Observed effort in the tournament in each treatment, according to the time period in the experiment (in abscissa). The straight line shows the median effort, the box provides the quartiles and the horizontal lines show the adjacent values.

Source: Eriksson et al. (2009, p. 538, Figure 2).

themselves according to their preferences and abilities. Based on additional control variables, the authors also observe that those who select the tournament have particular preferences: it is chosen half the time, by the least risk-averse subjects. Illustration 3.5 shows that the same kind of phenomenon applies according to gender.

3.5   From the Laboratory to the Field: An Overview of Controlled Experiments in Economics

The ability to better achieve identification through control over the data-generating process is common to all (actual) experimental methods. This feature is shared, in particular, by the two types of controlled experiment that are often referred to in the literature: laboratory and field experiments.

3.5.1   The Many Forms of Field Experiment

A field experiment is commonly defined as an experiment that produces observations from (i) a random allocation of individuals to the treatment, but (ii) in a '*natural*' or '*real*' environment (field experiments are also sometimes called 'random controlled trials' in the literature). The latter underscores the main difference between a laboratory experiment, in which social phenomena are observed in highly artificial circumstances – implementing 'the sterility of the laboratory experimental environment' according to Harrison and List (2004, p. 1009) – and a field experiment, in which individual behaviour is observed in its naturally occurring environment. The field is thus characterised by the fact that subjects take decisions in the same social context as they would under normal circumstances; the information they receive makes use of this social context which the experiment reproduces; they are familiar with the rules they are dealing with, etc.; in a nutshell: all features ensure that the environment remains as 'realistic' as possible (see Illustration 3.6).

While the difference in nature between the two kinds of environment is easy to understand, there are many dimensions that make observed decisions close or far from their naturally occurring circumstances. In an attempt to summarise the relevant dimensions, Harrison and List (2004) characterise experiments according to the following six items:

1. the nature of the subject pool,
2. the nature of the information that the subjects bring to the task,
3. the nature of the commodity,
4. the nature of the task or trading rules applied,
5. the nature of the stakes,
6. the nature of the environment that the subject operates in.

Even if one considers that there is a choice between only two options for each of these dimensions, one closer to the naturally occurring environment and the other closer to the sterility of the laboratory, this classification defines $6 * 6 = 36$ different kinds of experiment. Except for the two extreme cases, where all six dimensions are set to either their naturally occurring or their artificial value, none of the remaining 34 'types' of experiment are clearly a field or a laboratory experiment. More recently, Gerber and Green (2012, p. 11) define the 'fieldness' of an experiment based on the following criteria:

1. authenticity of treatments,
2. identity of participants,
3. the nature of the context,
4. the outcome measures.

This narrower classification still leads to at least 16 different kinds of experiment, with varying relationships between the phenomenon of interest and the naturally occurring environment. This points to the fact that 'field' or 'laboratory' is hardly a label one puts on experimental evidence to indicate the main focus of the research. In terms of the content of the experimental design, whether an experiment should be classified as a field or laboratory experiment rather defines a continuum with an increasingly close match between the social situation of interest and the experimental task.

3.5.2   A Guide to Choosing between Lab and Field Experiments

Experiments along the continuum nonetheless feature varying properties in terms of identification and the overall quality of the measures they generate. According to a well-known econ joke, if you ask three economists what they think about an economic issue, you'll get five different opinions. Having a look at experimental papers published in the academic literature, the same reaction seems to apply to the question whether laboratory experiments are superior to field experiments or vice versa. Having recognised that neither laboratory experiments nor field experiments are self-contained methodological categories, it is easier to understand what the answer is: it depends entirely on the research question, hence the social situation and the treatment effect one wants to identify. Along the continuum between field and laboratory experiments, each choice amounts to a trade-off, whose main dimensions are described below.

The first set of trade-offs involves practical aspects and the ease of implementation. Its cost is the most obvious issue. The closer an experiment is to a pure field experiment, the more expensive it is likely to get. Experiments occurring in the field are extremely costly in terms of the resources they consume. They take a lot of planning, time and money before they can be implemented. The first step is to get the agreement of the real-world institution where the experiment will take place, and interact on-site about the details of the experiment. It is also necessary to recruit local research assistants in order to find participants and conduct the experiment. The experiment may run over a very long period of time before the researcher is able to observe and gather data on its outcomes. In addition, the researcher has to ensure that the research design respects local customs and habits. All this can make the implementation of a field experiment a very lengthy and costly process.

Second, the choice between the field and the laboratory implies a number of trade-offs in terms of inference. The closer an experiment is to the field, the closer it is to the actual social-life phenomenon one seeks to study. This amounts to better *external validity*, a methodological challenge to be discussed in Chapter 8. At the same time, the aim to be closer to the field also implies a larger set of 'dimensions' at stake in the experiment, many of which cannot be controlled or randomised. This reduces the ability to provide 'pure' causal evidence, the laboratory becoming a natural place to test-bed causal measures before moving to situations closer to their naturally occurring environment.[11]

A third concern is related to the ability to actually randomise the treatment variable in order to produce the observations needed to estimate the causal effects. The discussion in Section 3.4.1 clearly shows that what one needs to achieve identification are two random samples of individuals: one in which all individuals receive the treatment, one in which nobody does. Two phenomena may typically challenge this requirement in field experiments. The first is *attrition*, i.e. when, for any reason, some subjects drop out of the experiment. If such drop out is purely random, then the consequences are only a matter of sample size as some observations will no longer be available. But a more serious concern arises if dropouts are specific to individuals who carry some specific heterogeneity related to the outcome variable. The dropout is then endogenous, and identification is challenged despite the random assignment. It will typically be the case if people who give up do so because they realise they cannot expect much improvement in their situation thanks to the programme. The second kind of phenomenon restricting the scope of random assignment in the field is *non-compliance*. This refers to the fact that subjects do not behave according to the rules or framework set out in the experiment. This may very well happen, as a field experiment takes place in reality, and the ability to 'constrain' people to follow rules is naturally limited. In terms of identification, it means that some people in the treatment group actually did not receive the treatment, or received a treatment that is different from the one studied. In both cases, the experiment does not deliver the observations on outcomes required to identify the effect of interest (see Deaton, 2010; Greenberg and Barnow, 2014, for more detailed discussions of such limitations to the identification achieved by field experiments).

A last concern is that treatments in the field may have spillover effects: because the change occurs in real life, changes in the situation of treated individuals may have an impact on untreated ones. Crépon et al. (2013), for instance, show that the enhanced probability to be employed of job seekers who benefit from a job placement programme actually comes at the expense of a lower probability of employment among similar job seekers who did not benefit from the programme. A simple comparison in outcomes between the two groups provides a highly biased measure of the treatment, as this effect magnifies the difference in outcomes between individuals from the two groups.

All the limitations listed above, and the many others discussed in the literature, can be addressed by either carefully designed experiments or additional experimental evidence

---

[11] Al-Ubaydli and List (2015) advocate an opposite perspective on this point, based on the ability of field experiments to bypass participant self-selection.

from the field. The main lesson from this comparison is actually not to name the one experimental environment that is best suited to serve research questions. The comparison rather shows the strengths and weaknesses of the two methods. To sum up: laboratory experiments provide strong control over the data-generating process, hence making the measure of causal effects easier and more convincing – how it is achieved is the purpose of Chapter 5. This generally comes at the price of a highly artificial decision environment, leading to strong doubts on their ability to describe what happens in real life. Field experiments, by contrast, provide evidence in their naturally occurring context by running experiments inside 'real life' itself. In this much more realistic context, however, many aspects of the environment are beyond the control of the experimenter, resulting in weaker inference properties.

Summary

Inference based on empirical observations involves two different issues: statistical inference, the relationships between sample observations and their population equivalent, and identification, the ability to measure a well-defined parameter based on available observations. Econometrics adjusts data analysis methods to the specific data and inference issues under study thanks to the elicitation of the data-generating process. Whether the assumed data-generating process in the econometric model matches the properties of the true data-generating process of the data is the key driving force to the ability to achieve proper inference. As regards identification issues, this consistency leads to identifying assumptions – properties of the data-generating process that condition the identification properties of different kinds of estimator. When the econometric model is linear, for instance, the identifying assumption is that the noise in the outcome variable is not correlated with the covariates.

The policy evaluation literature applies these ideas to the identification of a causal effect induced by a spontaneous change in the economy, called natural experiments. This literature provides a discussion of the true parameters of interest in such situations, and identifying assumptions that can be used to estimate them. The average treatment effect (ATE) is the expected causal effect of the change on a randomly drawn individual from the population. The average treatment on the treated (ATT) is the expected causal effect of the change on those individuals who actually face it. In estimating any of these parameters, the challenge is to find counterfactual observations – i.e. observations of what would have happened in situations that are not observed in the data.

Actual experiments differ from other empirical approaches in that they provide control over the data-generating process itself, by means of the design of the experiment and the choice of experimental treatments. Identifying assumptions in econometrics, and more precisely in the policy evaluation literature, thus provide a framework on how to design experiments to achieve proper identification and statistical inference. This leads to several strategies: randomisation, which allows us to break any possible correlation between what is unobserved (the noise) and the covariates of interest; measurement, which develops tools to include in the list of unobservable covariates that could be confounding; and control, which holds constant any source of variation that is possibly confounding. This ability to choose the data-generating process is shared by all kinds of actual experiments along the continuum defined by the many dimensions in which experiments can be close or far from the field situation under study. The choice over the intensity of the 'fieldness' of an experiment implies a trade-off that balances (i) the improved identification offered by the strength of control over the environment in laboratory experiments and (ii) the generalisability of the results when they are observed in their naturally occurring environment.

4 The Need for Experimental Methods in Economic Science

As discussed in Chapter 3, experiments answer a specific need in empirical economics thanks to their ability to provide proper identification of the true parameters embedded in the data-generating process. The nature of such parameters, i.e. the reason why researchers are interested in their empirical identification, still remains an open question. This question is important for a critical assessment of the quality of identification: as shown in Chapter 3, empirical identification always hinges on (untestable) assumptions about the true data-generating process. The set of assumptions achieving identification, on which the interpretation of the results relies, heavily depends on the aim of the empirical study.

In order to answer such questions, this chapter first reviews the commonly recognised objectives of laboratory experiments – testing theory, searching for facts, or informing public policies. Each of the three involves a particular kind of dialogue between economic experiments on the one hand and economic theory and/or reality, on the other hand. To understand how laboratory experiments can serve these goals, it is necessary to clarify the relationships between experiments, theory and reality. These definitions will make clear that each aim comes with specific identification assumptions conditioning the usefulness of the estimated parameters. When testing theory, the first-order question is whether or not the observed behaviour is induced by the decision environment replicating the theoretical model – an issue defined as internal validity in Chapter 3. When searching for facts, by contrast, the main question is whether or not the same behaviour is to be observed outside the laboratory environment – a matter of external validity; while, finally, informing public policies requires both theoretical insights and well-documented facts, so that both internal and external validity are required. This discussion will thus provide the main background of the topic of the remaining parts: how the design of an experiment is adjusted to achieve its goal, and what experiments accordingly tell us about the specific research question stimulating their implementation.

4.1 What Laboratory Experiments Aim For

As all social sciences, economics aims to provide an understanding of social reality – how people behave and why? Can we collectively do better than what we currently do? And if yes, how? Unlike most social sciences, though, the main tool used in economic science to that end is to build formal theoretical models. Because it is both empirical and highly controlled, laboratory experiments stand in the middle of this continuum between theory and reality. According to the seminal classification of Roth (1988), the three purposes that laboratory experiments are able to serve actually puts a bridge between theory and reality in both possible directions. First, experiments can be used for *testing theory*, i.e. assessing the empirical relevance of theoretical models. Second, they can be used to *search for facts*, in which case they use reality to inform theory – experiments then being used as 'exhibits' rather than 'tests' (Sugden, 2005). Last, building on both kinds of contribution, experiments can be used for *whispering in the ears of princes*, i.e. informing the decisions of policy-makers.

Testing theory

Theoretical models rely on behavioural assumptions to provide an understanding of the decisions of agents, and the resulting outcomes, induced by a given environment. They do so by restricting the economically relevant situation to a few key features. The Vickrey auction experiment reviewed in Chapter 2 is an example of such an exercise. Vickrey auction models reduce the auction environment to marginal values for the good, prices and monetary benefits. Based on the assumptions of utility maximisation and the axiomatic underlying the game-theoretic analysis of strategic interactions, it yields clear-cut predictions of both bidding behaviour and the properties of the resulting allocation.

As illustrated in Chapter 2, experiments exhibit two major advantages in that regard: the ability to both build an empirical situation that mimics the theoretical model, and measure or observe usually non-observable, or hardly measurable, dimensions (such as individual preferences towards the good, or individual prices posted). Experiments also get theory closer to reality by providing measures of individual preferences. As will be illustrated in later applications (see e.g. Sections 5.6, 6.6 and 7.4), such procedures rely on decision environments in which observed behaviour provides a direct measure of individual intrinsic attitudes. It not only allows us to assess whether the theoretical account of preferences actually makes empirical sense (e.g. to what extent is behaviour in risky environments actually described by the assumptions of expected utility), but also to assess whether predicted behaviour based on such preferences coincides with what theory predicts. In all these instances, experiments help in assessing the empirical relevance of theoretical results in terms of accuracy, precision and extent.

Searching for facts

On the other side of the continuum, there are many economic situations that are worth understanding, but which are too complicated and/or too specific to be covered by theory. Auctions again provide a useful illustration of such experiments: as the allocation mechanism, or the amount of information available to bidders, becomes more specific, auction models quickly become intractable. This does not mean, of course, that such specific auction markets are of no economic interest (even when there is no obvious reason why a market works as it does, the mere fact that it is used in practice is sometimes enough to make it worth investigating). In such cases, experiments can be used as a substitute for theoretical analysis. They are used to 'search for facts' in the sense that they allow us to mimic well-defined situations and measure behaviour as well as the outcomes they generate. In the absence of prior expectations based on theory, such observations provide empirical knowledge about how the environment works, and what are its most sensitive features. To serve this purpose, such evidence must be robust and conclusive enough to actually serve as a stylised fact. In that regard, the replicability of experimental data, and the possibility to assess the robustness of the results through variations of the environment, are important advantages of experiments.

Whispering in the ears of princes

This third purpose of experiments amounts to improving the decision-making process by informing regulators or decision-makers (Roth's 'princes') of the likely outcomes of new or existing public policies (see, e.g. Holt et al., 2006; Normann and Ricciuti, 2009, for surveys). The general principle is to use experiments to test-bed decision environments such as market mechanisms, policy changes or new organisational structures. Observed outcomes in the experiment provide insights into the likely changes in behaviour and economic outcomes raised by innovative decision environments. As such, this aim builds on the ability of experiments to both test theory and search for facts – depending on whether theoretical insights are available on the policy-relevant question under investigation. The specific contribution of experiments to policy design comes from the ability to answer the specific needs of decision-makers. Because all the parameters of the decision environment can be freely set in the laboratory, an experiment makes it possible to fully replicate the specific features of a given policy. Illustration 4.1 describes an early example of such a contribution. This ability to fine-tune the experimental environment according to the requirement of the policy-relevant questions stands in sharp contrast with observational data. As compared to field experiments, laboratory experiments are cheap and easily implementable. An additional contribution of the use of experiments to policy design is their use in an instructive function. Laboratory experiments make economic reasoning more intuitive and appealing for non-academics. Even without producing any new knowledge, they can be used to make a convincing case of what the consequences will be of an intended change in the environment.

4.2   Experiments, Theory and Reality: How Experiments Achieve Their Goals

The above-mentioned aims of laboratory experiments (testing theory, searching for facts and whispering in the ears of princes) all refer to some form of interaction between experiments on the one hand, and on the other hand either theory (first aim) or reality (second aim) or both (third aim). As a result, assessing the ability of experiments to achieve either of these goals requires an in-depth understanding of how '*reality*' and '*theory*' are defined from the point of view of economics.[1] We will discuss each of these separate elements in turn, before moving to a definition of laboratory experiments. This will allow us to clarify the interactions of experiments with theory and reality and characterise the main challenges they raise.

[1] This section relies on the framework and discussion presented in Samuelson (2005).

Illustration 4.1
Whispering in the ears of antitrust authorities

The 1979 *Ethyl Corporation* v. *Federal Trade Commission* case is one of the earliest examples of the use of experiments for policy design purpose (both the case and the experimental evidence are reported in Grether and Plott, 1984). This case opposed the FTC to producers of gasoline complements that were in widespread use at the time. The main concern of the FTC was about the possible anti-competitive effect of the contract practices used on this market. Three kinds of provision attracted attention:

- advanced notice and price announcement – any increase in price was announced at least 30 days in advance by producers;
- most-favoured-nation – producers commit to offer all buyers any discount subsequently offered to another;
- delivered pricing – producers post a list of price for a given compound, regardless of the location of the producer.

The FTC feared that such practices on a market with only a few producers might be used by firms as a means to maintain prices above their competitive level. But such an opinion was not grounded on either a rigorous theoretical analysis or any empirical knowledge. The FTC thus asked Grether and Plott to experimentally investigate this question. Based on experimental treatments replicating each of the above practices as well as various combinations of them, the authors show that they actually push prices upwards – as compared to the same competitive market without such provisions. This evidence subsequently stimulated a more formal analysis of the anti-competitive effects of such practices, showing that the theoretical evidence matches with the empirical strategies observed in the experiment (Holt and Scheffman, 1987). For the sake of completeness, it is worth noting that this experimental evidence was eventually not used as a piece of evidence during the judicial proceedings. However, it played a crucial role to reinforce the FTC in its will to open a case.

These definitions merit a few notations. We will denote $\mathcal{X}$ the inputs and $\mathcal{Y}$ the outcomes or consequences of a given situation (or environment). Both are defined as sets according to their K-dimensional combination:

$$\mathcal{X}^K = \prod_{k=1}^{K} \mathcal{X}_i \text{ and } \mathcal{Y}^K = \prod_{k=1}^{K} \mathcal{Y}_i$$

The set $\mathcal{X}^K$ thus denotes the combination of all the K inputs considered, and similarly $\mathcal{Y}^K$ is the set of all the K dimensions that are consequences of the situation.

4.2.1   What Is Reality?

Let's start with the most controversial definition: what is the real world? From the point of view of a scientist, who tries to understand why what happens happens, the answer is simpler than one would expect. In short, reality is no more than a set of causal relationships. This means that reality can be reduced to three elements: the causes $\mathcal{X}$, the consequences $\mathcal{Y}$ and a 'function', that transforms causes into consequences. What makes reality a complex object, even in this overly simplified representation, is that inputs and outputs are infinity-dimensional. Therefore, reality is the function:[2]

$$F: \mathcal{X}^\infty \to \mathcal{Y}^\infty$$

In words, the function F transforms inputs into outputs. Each particular combination of the content of $\mathcal{X}^\infty$, that defines a situation of interest, causes a particular output from the set of $\mathcal{Y}^\infty$. Social science can to a large extent be reduced to an attempt to understand this function F: how causes and consequences are related together in real life. As straightforward as it may seem, this definition makes an important methodological point: it is impossible to understand reality as it is. The input and output dimensions are infinite, because reality features an endless set of potentially relevant properties and characteristics. As an example, the relationship between employers and their employees involves paying a wage and exerting an effort, but also a relationship between two persons, the consequences for their family life, relations with co-workers, etc. As a result, neither theoretical nor experimental research could ever describe all aspects of reality. In a sense, the complexity of the real world is the very reason why science is needed: if the world were easy to understand as it is, no one would need the help of a science to elicit what happens and why it happened.

4.2.2   What Is a Model?

Because reality is such a complex object, science in general and economics in particular proceed by breaking down the real world into only a handful of its components. Therefore a model is, and must be, a simplified account of a real situation. As such, a built-in property of a model is to be false, i.e. to be unable to fully account for all subtle drivers and consequences of a situation. This determines the main ingredient of a model.

Like the function F that maps causes to consequences in the real world, a model seeks to capture a particular causal relationship between a number of inputs $\mathcal{X}$ (causes) and outputs $\mathcal{Y}$ (consequences). Reducing the real-world situation of interest, so as to make it intelligible, also amounts to restricting the dimensions of the sets. Rather than all causes and all possible consequences pertaining to the situation, a model will only focus on a few causes and a few of their consequences. This choice is part of the model: focusing, for instance, on performance and compensation schemes, as economics does, is obviously a restrictive view of work situations. But as stressed above, the challenge is not to understand reality as it is, but rather to enlighten some aspects of it and reduce the main mechanisms to a few channels – so that it becomes possible to think about the situation from inside the model. Illustration 4.2, for instance, shows how the behaviour of complex human organisation like firms, acting in many different ways on markets, are

---

[2] The aim of this discussion is definitely not to provide a full account of the epistemology of (social) sciences. We ignore, in particular, the important and interesting question whether one can actually separate reality and the tools and prism used to analyse it.

Illustration 4.2
Models as a reduction of reality: firms' behaviour in collusion theory

Collusion theory in industrial organisation differs from standard competition in that firms' decisions are assumed to be strategic – typically because only a few of them compete on the same market. We denote N the number of firms. The market is reduced to only a few dimensions, essentially prices and quantities, and the firms' behaviour is described by a profit function. The main focus here is to understand the difference in behaviour induced by the horizon of the decision-making. When competing in a one-shot set-up, each firm has an incentive to beat its competitor's decisions – resulting in the competitive, zero-profit, equilibrium if firms compete in price and the Cournot–Nash equilibrium if they compete on quantities. Let y be the quantities produced (and sold) and q the market price, $\pi(q, y)$ denotes the profit firms receive at the one-shot equilibrium, and $\pi_M(q, y)$ the one-shot monopoly profit. The important distinguishing feature of collusion is that firms are playing an indefinitely repeated game. Denoting δ the firms' exponential discount factor, collusion yields the following profit for each firm:

$$\sum_{t=0}^{\infty} \frac{\pi_M(q, y)}{N} \delta^t = \frac{1}{1-\delta} \frac{\pi_M(q, y)}{N}$$

Firms make this share of the monopoly profits as long as all firms collude and cooperate. As soon as one firm deviates from collusion, and cheats, all the other firms can use a (so-called) trigger punishment strategy, i.e. revert to the Cournot–Nash equilibrium from then on. The profit of a deviating firm is the sum of the one-shot monopoly profit $\pi_M(q, y)$ the firm gets when it deviates, and of the discounted sum of the future Nash–Cournot profit $\pi(q, y)$:

$$\pi_M(q, y) + \frac{\delta}{1-\delta} \frac{\pi(q, y)}{N}$$

Therefore, collusion is individually rational and can be sustained at equilibrium if no firm has an incentive to deviate:

$$\frac{1}{1-\delta} \frac{\pi_M(q, y)}{N} \geq \pi_M(q, y) + \frac{\delta}{1-\delta} \frac{\pi(q, y)}{N}$$

In the case of a Bertrand game in which firms compete in prices, the individual one-shot profit $\pi(q, y)$ is equal to 0. Therefore the collusion is sustainable if:

$$\delta \geq 1 - \frac{1}{N}$$

In the context of this model, collusion is a stable equilibrium (hence arising on actual markets) when the threat of punishment (through trigger strategies in this case) is large and credible enough. This is more likely to happen when the number of firms N is low and when δ is high, i.e. when firms only slightly discount the future. For future reference, it is worth noting that the model would write exactly the same if δ stood for the probability that the market survives for one more period at the end of each market period.

---

reduced to a few of its components in the analysis of collusive behaviour in industrial organisation.

This first step in theoretical analysis leads us to identify a few influential and/or interesting dimensions of the situation. On top of this finite number of inputs, denoted n_χ, and a finite number n_y of outputs, a model is again a causal relationship between the two:[3]

$$f : \mathcal{X}^{n_{\mathcal{X}}} \rightarrow \mathcal{Y}^{n_y}$$

The function f maps the set of inputs to the respective outcomes. Its aim is to be a 'sub-function' of F, hence to reflect part of the causal mechanisms at stake. The challenge in developing a model and assessing its quality is to solve the trade-off raised by the need to simplify reality. In the choice of $n_{\mathcal{X}}$ and n_y, the model must get rid of all unnecessary details, which would otherwise cloud the focus on the relationship between the causes and consequences of interest. But the theory cannot be too simplistic either, as it would then lose its explicative power, and its ability to be generalised. To sum up, without giving any definitive answer, a model must be as abstract as possible, and as detailed as necessary, in order to provide an accurate and closely focused account of reality.

4.2.3   What Is an Experiment?

An experiment is a controlled situation in which many features of the environment are implemented by design, so as to observe the resulting individual decisions and interactions. The aim of such observation is to infer the causal relationships between the environment and individual(s) behaviour. This can be easily embodied in the current notations: an experiment is nothing but a choice of a set of n inputs, defining the environment, associated with m measures of their consequences with the goal of inferring their causal relationship, F.

But, at the same time, an experiment deals with the decisions of human beings in a particular real-world environment – the laboratory. Thus, the measured outcomes in the laboratory are not only the results of the chosen controls, but also the consequence of an endless range of influences: from personal characteristics to anything the person may have experienced prior to coming to the laboratory, or any specificities of what happens inside and outside the laboratory during the experiment. An experiment is thus an almost-real situation, with many dimensions beyond the n inputs that are controlled and chosen actually influencing what happens. The situation built in the laboratory is thus defined by $x^\infty \in \mathcal{X}^\infty$, such that $x^\infty = x^n \cup x^{\infty - n}$, i.e. an element $\mathcal{X}^\infty$ that matches x^n (only) on the first n dimensions but leaves the others uncontrolled. Typical examples of such uncontrolled inputs are the level of noise inside and outside the laboratory, the mood of participants when arriving at the experiment, etc. These are all factors that possibly influence the behavioural response to the experimental situation, without belonging to the components that were chosen when designing it. In this setting, the outcome from an experiment is a set of measures m such that:

$$F^m(x^\infty)$$

This outcome must be thought of as a subset of the infinite-dimensional function F describing all the consequences of an experiment. Again, while individual decisions and payoffs will typically belong to the set of m measures that will be observed, there

---

[3] In order to better fit models that allow for heterogeneity, the definition can be easily generalised, as in Samuelson (2005), to a distribution over consequences rather than a deterministic relationship.

will always remain many consequences of the inputs of the situation that will not be observed: how the mood of participants changed during the experiment, what is the induced change in the room temperature, etc.

Two important lessons can be drawn from this definition. First, a critical aspect of the design of an experiment lies in the choice of the finite number of inputs, n, and the finite number of measures, m, on which the design is based – above and beyond the actual implementation of the input controls and the accurate observation of the outcomes of interest. The choice depends entirely on the relationship and phenomenon that the experiment seeks to measure – i.e. the research question. The case study presented in Section 4.3 illustrates this idea.

Second, this definition makes it clear that experiments share common features with both theoretical models and real economic life, as defined above. Like a model, an experiment focuses on a subset of relevant dimensions in order to study the phenomenon of interest. The aim is not to provide observations on all consequences induced by all relevant factors at stake in the empirical situation of reference, but rather to pin down a few driving forces and a few consequences, on which empirical evidence is needed. But at the same time, like in reality, what happens in the laboratory is made of an infinity of causes and consequences which no one is able to control or observe. Even with cleverly designed experiments, there will always be an infinity of inputs that will remain uncontrolled.

Because experiments have many of the same features as both theoretical models and reality, they can be seen as a way to establish a bilateral link between theory and the social reality this theory aims to understand (Croson and Gächter, 2010). This is the main reason why experiments are a particularly effective way of enriching and deepening, but also complementing or challenging, our understanding of the real world through economic theory and economic analysis. This is, in particular, the reason why they are well suited to achieve either of the goals described earlier. How they achieve it is derived from their attractive empirical properties in terms of identification, as described in length in Chapter 3. On this basis, experiments allow us to observe the consequences of the inputs involved – i.e. $F^m(x^\infty)$ – or the variation induced by different sets of inputs – through the comparison of $F^m(x^\infty)$ and $F^m(x'^\infty)$, i.e. the differences in outcomes under two sets of inputs x and x', which define treatment effects. Depending on the aim of the experiment, the inputs and measures will be defined according to either an underlying theory to be tested or a real-world phenomenon one seeks to understand better. The condition under which the outcome will be informative, however, strongly depends on the specific goal of the experiment. The remainder of the chapter considers each of them in turn.

4.3   *Case Study*: Deepening Understanding through Additional Controls and Measures: The Dictator Game

This section aims to illustrate how the choice of inputs and measures is part of the design of an experiment, and how it allows us to incrementally enrich the conclusions drawn from experimental observations. To that end, we focus on one of the most replicated game in the experimental economics literature: the dictator game (DG).

In this simple game, first introduced by Forsythe et al. (1994),[4] two players interact in a strictly anonymous setting. Both players do not know who their partner is, nor do they find out at any point. Within a pair of two subjects, one person is assigned to be the 'dictator', and the other one the 'receiver'. The dictator receives an endowment, e_i, and makes an offer $e_i \geq \ell_i \geq 0$ to the receiver. As a result, the dictator gets $e_i - \ell_i$ and the receiver gets the offer ℓ_i. There is no constraint on the split decided by the dictator. The open question in this environment is: how much money is the dictator willing to give to the receiver? Economic theory is of little help to answer the question – a point the experiment has been designed to make, as a matter of fact. Since there is neither any monetary benefit, nor any constraint on the amount given to the receiver, the dictator should 'theoretically' keep as much money as possible for him-/herself. This is obviously not what happens when people are asked to make such decisions in an experiment implementing the game.

Figure 4.1 provides an overview of the patterns of behaviour generally observed in this kind of experiment, based on a meta-analysis including more than 300 published studies all replicating the dictator game (Engel, 2011). While it comes as no surprise that some people do donate something to their receiver, the extent to which they do so is puzzling. On average, the dictators give 28.35% to a complete stranger whom they will never meet. It is not only the magnitude of the donation that sparked a great deal of interest in the literature, but also the strong heterogeneity in donation behaviour. One-third of people behave in accordance with a purely self-interested model of decision-making, one-sixth offer an equal split and one out of 20 even offers everything. These patterns are generally seen as robust stylised facts, thanks to the many replications of the same game with slight variations in the design (in different countries, with varying amounts of money to be split, etc.). In order to better understand the reason why such behaviour occurs, what are the motivations behind it and what fosters or undermines it, additional inputs and outputs have been considered in the literature.

4.3.1   Additional Inputs 1 – Social Distance

A first hypothesis is that donation behaviour is related to social relationships. In order to investigate this point, Hoffman et al. (1996) conducted six different versions of the dictator game, varying the dictator's degree of distance, isolation and anonymity – while maintaining the same decision-making structure.

The first treatment (denoted FHSS-R) is an exact replication of the Forsythe et al. (1994) experiment, the amount of the dictator's initial endowment being $e_i = \$10$. FHSS-V is a replication of the same game but uses neutral wording for what the game is about. The researchers did not use the 'sharing' language of the first version and instead asked the subject to 'divide' the preliminary allocation. Two further treatments strengthen the social distance involved in the dictator's decision-making by

---

[4] The Forsythe et al. (1994) game is itself a simplified version of a binary decision game introduced by Kahneman et al. (1986).

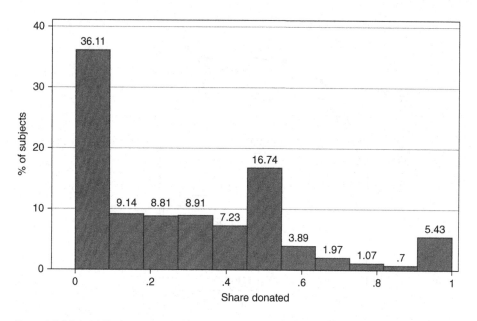

Figure 4.1 Meta-analysis results: the dictator game

Note. Empirical distribution of the population of dictators observed in more than 300 published studies, according to the share of the initial endowment given by the dictator to the receiver. *Source*: Engel (2011, p. 589, Figure 2).

implementing a double-blind donation. The procedures are drastically altered to achieve such isolation. First, the experiment is run by a subject, randomly selected to act as a monitor and paid to do so. But the most important changes are related to the elicitation of the donation decision. In an experiment involving 14 subjects playing as dictators, each subject draws an envelope from an urn. It is common knowledge that 12 of the envelopes in this urn contain 10 one dollar bills and 10 blank slips of paper, while the remaining two are filled with 20 blank slips of paper. Dictators then go to a separate room, keep as many bills as they wish and replace the bills with blank slips of paper. They seal the envelope, bring it back in a box, and leave the room. Once all dictators have made their decisions, the 14 subjects playing as receivers come one by one to draw an envelope from the box, show the content to the monitor and leave the room with it.

Thanks to the two blank envelopes, the procedures in this DB1 treatment imply that neither the experimenter nor the receiver is able to identify the individual decision of the dictators. Since it is common knowledge, it is expected to increase the social isolation of the dictators' donation decision. A second variation, DB2, weakens the anonymity achieved in this treatment by removing the paid monitor and the two blank envelopes – it is still the case that individual decisions are unobserved by both the receiver and the experimenter, but the distribution of decisions is now perfectly observed. Two additional treatments are meant to disentangle the components of social isolation induced by these treatments, by implementing a single-blind donation decision. In SB1, the experimenter opens up the envelope when the dictator brings it back, hence breaking

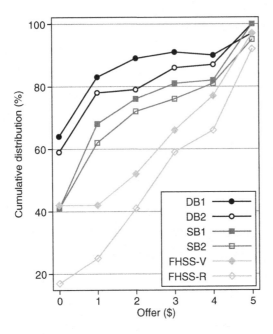

Figure 4.2 The effect of social distance on dictators' decisions
Note. Cumulative distribution of the amount donated by dictators in each treatment.
Source: Hoffman et al. (1996, p. 654, Figure 1).

the anonymity with the experimenter. Last, in SB2, the envelope into which the dictator puts the amount is replaced by a transaction form, which the dictator has to fill out and bring to the experimenter in an envelope so as to be paid the corresponding amount of money. The experimenter opens the envelope and notes the subject's name and decision and gives the dictator the sum $e_i - \ell_i$ they decided to keep. This procedure decreases the relative social distance, as the subject enters into a real transaction with the experimenter.

Figure 4.2 shows the cumulative distribution of donated amounts observed in the experiment (in this experiment, donations are never higher than five dollars, the equal split): the steeper the line, the less dictators keep for themselves. As compared to the baseline, the change in wording implemented in FHSS-V slightly decreases donations. But the most impressive change in behaviour comes with increased social isolation: there is a perfect first-order stochastic dominance relation in the distributions of dictators' behaviour according to the blindness of the donation decisions. In DB1, where the level of anonymity is the highest by design, only 40% of the dictators leave positive amounts to the receivers.

This experiment thus provides strong evidence that donation behaviour in dictator games is sensitive to social image. This is done by adding to the list an input, social distance, that wasn't part of the design of the baseline game. It is worth noting that such contrasting evidence between the two series of experiments does not dismiss any of the two results: surprisingly high donations in the baseline are an empirical fact, just as is the reduced donation when social distance is high. The actual, and more interesting, question is rather which one of the two kinds of behaviour is more relevant, and what each one of them tells us about the underlying reason behind the other.[5]

4.3.2   Additional Inputs 2: Earned money

Cherry et al. (2002) focus on another dimension of the original game: the property rights over the amount of money to be split by the dictator. In the baseline experiment, the endowment is 'windfall' as it comes to the participants from out of nowhere. Cherry et al. (2002) analyse the effect of changing windfall money into earned money.

This is achieved through a preliminary task, in which subjects earn their endowment according to a performance-based payoff. The issue with such an experimental treatment is that the size of the amount of money to be split can change donation behaviour by itself, beyond any effect of the property rights over this amount. To address this issue, the earned-money treatment relies on a tournament based on the performance at the preliminary task: those subjects whose performance is above the median are given $40, while other subjects are given $10. This treatment thus elicits observation on donation behaviour with earned money over two possible values of the endowment: high (EH treatment), or low (EL treatment). In order to measure the effect of windfall money on donation behaviour, two versions of the baseline treatment with windfall money are considered: BH (the windfall endowment is set equal to $40) and BL (the windfall endowment is set equal to $10). A third treatment couples the earned-money preliminary task and the double-blind treatment introduced by Hoffman et al. (1996), generating again observations of donations under two possible values of the endowment: DBH and DBL.

Observed donation behaviours in each treatment are organised in Figure 4.3 according to the amount of the endowment. In the baseline, cumulative distributions of donation behaviours again display strong heterogeneity, with 20% of the sample giving nothing to the receiver and the remaining offering up to half the endowment. Earned money drastically affects donation behaviour in both dimensions. The number of subjects who decide to give nothing in this case is three times higher, and positive amounts not only appear more often but also are of lower magnitude. When coupled with double blind procedures, earned money almost perfectly 'hardnoses' the dictator – only a few subjects still send small, but positive, amounts to receivers. These results unambiguously confirm that the legitimacy of the endowment plays a crucial role in shaping other-regarding behaviour. Again, the aim here is not to disqualify any of the two kinds of observation, but rather to characterise the dimensions of the environment that most crucially determine behaviour. Thanks to additional inputs in the experimental design, this experiment underlines the influence of the nature of the endowment.

---

[5] In the words of Hoffman et al. (1996, p. 654), 'this experimental exercise is fundamental to understanding the received evidence for other-regarding behaviour that is frequently manifest in bargaining game experiments, but in which strategic reciprocity and utilitarian elements are confounded in interpreting observed outcomes'.

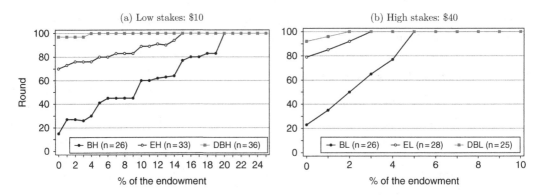

Figure 4.3 Offers in the dictator game with earned money
Note. Cumulative distributions of donation behaviours out of $10 in (a) or $40 in (b), endowment in the baseline (BH, BL), earned-money (EH, EL) and double-blind (DBH, DBL) treatments.
Source: Cherry et al. (2002, p. 1220, Figures 1 and 2).

4.3.3   Additional Inputs 3: Property rights on Player Positions

Beyond the nature of the endowment, another source of concern in the game is the strong asymmetry of positions between the dictator and the receiver: one subject is given full power over the outcome, while another is given no choice but to passively experience the decisions made by another person. Hoffman et al. (1994) study this dimension of the decision-making problem by introducing an additional treatment with earned entitlement to behave as a dictator. In a preliminary stage, all subjects are asked to answer a quiz on current events. After the quiz, subjects are ranked and then split into two groups: the top half of the subjects become dictators and the bottom half become receivers. Lastly, a matching procedure pairs the top-ranked dictator with the best receiver, the second-best dictator with the second-best receiver, and so forth.

Figure 4.4. shows the results of the experiment, along with those from the baseline treatment corresponding to the double-blind dictator game with windfall money as described in Hoffman et al. (1996; see Section 4.3.1 above). It clearly appears that the amounts shared are considerably lower when there is an earning stage which precedes this decision – one out of 10 subjects offers an equal split in the baseline treatment, while only 5% of subjects offer $4 out of $10 in the earned entitlement treatment. Property rights over the position in the game, which are ruled out in standard implementations of the dictator games by randomly allocating subjects to roles, thus foster selfishness.

4.3.4   Additional Measures: Response Times

Incrementally widening the set of inputs that are actually controlled in the experiment allows us to build more and more precise answers to research questions, by testing alternative hypotheses about the driving forces of behaviour. It is somehow too often neglected, but the exact same logic also applies to experimental outcomes. Among the many things that arise in the laboratory, and might be affected by the inputs involved, only a small subset is actually recorded so as to be part of the measures available. The

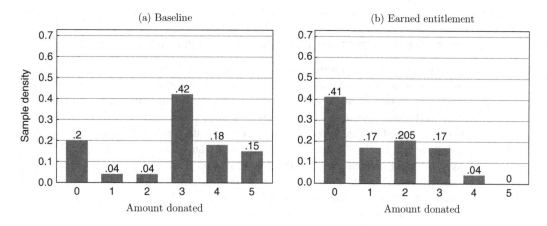

Figure 4.4 Donations from dictators who earned their position

Note. Empirical distribution of the amount donated by the dictator (in abscissa, out of an initial endowment of $10) in the control and earned-entitlement conditions.
Source: Hoffman et al. (1994, p. 365, Figure 4).

empirical answers generated by experiments can be very different depending on the pre-defined choice of measures. A typical example is the use of physiological measurement devices, such as skin conductance or eye tracking (see e.g. Sanfey, 2007, for a survey of applications to the dictator game), or the use of neurological measures (such as an fMRI), to investigate the brain activity while decisions occur. They all provide additional measures of the outcome from the experiment, that would always exist, but would have remained ignored, absent their implementation. Another example is response times.

The decision-making literature tends to relate different motives behind behaviour to the time spent on decision-making – as discussed in Focus 4.1. This can be easily investigated in the laboratory context, by keeping track of time elapsed from the beginning to the end of the decision task. Because it is simple and non-strategic, the dictator game is one of the first to which such measures have been applied. The results remain rather mixed. For example, the preliminary results obtained by Rubinstein (2006b, not reported in the 2007 published version of the paper) suggest that egotistic decisions are taken more slowly. On the other hand, the results obtained by Piovesan and Wengstrom (2009), and shown in Figure 4.5, tend to suggest the exact opposite: that egotistic decisions are taken faster than others. In both examples, however, the response time seems to have something to say about the type of decision the subjects take: decision times vary in a systematic manner across sub-samples of donation amounts. Focus 4.1 describes how such additional measures allow us to refine the interpretation of observed behaviour.

It goes without saying that additional inputs and additional measures are complementary in such a process. For instance, this same question of what kind of 'mode of thinking' drives donation behaviour has been addressed using additional inputs by Schulz et al. (2014). Instead of using time responses to classify observed decisions, they force different modes of thinking in order to observe their causal effect on donation behaviour. To that end, a preliminary task aims at affecting the cognitive load of subjects

---

Focus 4.1
On the use of response times to interpret observed behaviour in experiments

There is a growing interest in the correlation between economic behaviour and response times in both economics (e.g. Rand et al., 2012; Schotter and Trevino, 2012) and experimental psychology (Shalvi et al., 2012; Gino and Mogilner, 2014, among others). One of the psychological foundations of this focus on response times is based on the System 1/System 2 hypothesis raised by Kahneman (2003) – also known as the 'thinking-fast-and-slow' hypothesis (Kahneman, 2011). The model highlights a dichotomy between two modes of thought, System 1 being instinctive and emotional and System 2 more deliberative and logical. The main behavioural insight is that 'choices made instinctively, that is, on the basis of an emotional response, require less response time than choices that require the use of cognitive reasoning' (cited in Rubinstein, 2007, p. 1243). This pattern produces a strong correlation between mistakes and short decision times in decision problems where the solution is unambiguous. This leads Rubinstein (2007) to classify behaviour based on response times according to three types of action:

1. *cognitive*, for actions which involve a reasoning process;
2. *instinctive*, for actions which involves instinct;
3. *reasonless*, for actions which are likely to be the outcome of a random process with little or no reasoning about the decision problem.

Rubinstein (2013) collected the data on response times in a large-scale set of didactic online experiments. The evidence shows that the relationship between response time and error rates varies across tasks. For tasks where subjects can use a simple heuristic to avoid errors, response times are negatively correlated with error. This happens, for example, when participants have to choose repeatedly among alternatives. On the other hand, for tasks where the answers require a cognitive effort (coding letters, avoiding first-order stochastic dominance, assessing likelihood), response times are positive when correlated with errors. In the former case, simple heuristics benefit consistency. In the latter case, simple heuristics lead to mistakes. Lastly, and perhaps more importantly, the usual deviations from the expected utility observed in decision experiments (the Allais paradox, the three-colour Ellsberg paradox, Kahneman and Tversky's Asian disease problem) are not correlated with a given pattern of response times. The certainty effect, ambiguity aversion or framing effects are all compatible with fast and slow observed response times. For instance, Evans et al. (2015) suggest that response times might be related to decision conflicts rather than to dual thinking. Using a meta-analysis of existing experimental evidence, Rand (2016) confirms that favouring deliberation over intuition tends to push behaviour towards less pure cooperation, but leaves strategic cooperation unchanged.

---

when they enter the donation part of a binary dictator game – dictators are restricted to choosing between two possible allocations. During this task, subjects hear the sound of letters in headphones, and must press the corresponding letter on their keyboard but only for some of these letters – so that they need to stay focused and cannot just routinely press the key for all letters they hear. This treatment causes ego-depletion and lowers the ability to use deliberative decision as compared to the baseline, with no preliminary task. This cognitive load is applied to several conditions, in which the level

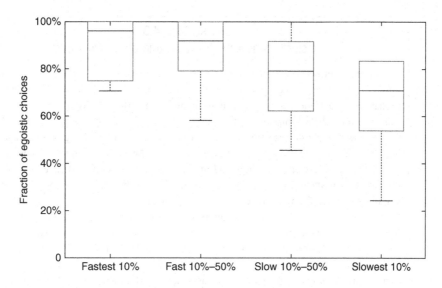

Figure 4.5 Generous decisions by dictators are taken slowly

Note. The figure reports the share of subjects who decide to behave selfishly in the dictator game in each subgroup defined by their quantile of response time (in abscissa). For each group, the straight line shows the median behaviour, the boxes cover the quartiles of the egoistic decisions distribution, and the vertical lines show the adjacent values.

Source: (Piovesan and Wengstrom, 2009, p. 195, Figure 2)

of inequality implemented by the two donation choices available to dictators is varied. The results show that lower deliberation leads to higher amounts of donations, and that deliberation leads to much more adjustment in the level of donation to the inequality of the allocation.

4.4   How Experiments Interact with Theory: Testing Models

Experiments share common features with both theory and reality, making it natural to use them to test-bed the empirical performance of theoretical models. The first challenge is to define an empirical environment that replicates the model assumptions. The interpretation of the results is heavily conditioned by the quality of the inference performed based on experimental data, i.e. the internal validity of the experiment.

4.4.1   Testing Theory

Theoretical models are most often way too general to be directly implemented: the actual decision-making environment must be simple enough to be described to people with no background in economics. The fair-wage-effort model described in Illustration 4.3 provides an example: the aim of the model is to underline the driving forces of a causal mechanism. For this purpose, the more general assumptions are, the more convincing and relevant is the model. But at the same time, such generality makes a theory compatible with many different specifications and concrete situations. The reason why

---

Illustration 4.3
Reciprocity at work: the fair-wage-effort hypothesis

The incentive effect of compensation schemes, illustrated all through Chapter 3, only goes through the change in consumption it offers to employees. Akerlof (1982) offers a 'gift exchange' model, the aim of which is to highlight the effect of norms and social relationships at work. The assumptions of the model are fairly simple. The worker's utility depends, as usual, negatively on the effort exerted on the job, ℓ_i, and positively on the wage w. But it also depends on a norm, ℓ_{norm}, which stands for the level of effort the worker sees as 'normal' given the work condition, and in particular the wage offered. The workers' utility function thus writes $u(\ell_{norm}, \ell_i, w)$. As is standard, a worker chooses the level of effort that maximises utility. The worker's choice of the utility-maximising level of effort is constrained by the minimum level of effort ℓ_{min} the firm requires – and implements through e.g. a control policy. The output of the firm depends on the work effort of all of its workers. The firm chooses the work rule ℓ_{min}, the wage function $w(\ell)$ and the number of workers it wishes to hire in order to maximise profit. The firm's behaviour is constrained by the worker participation constraint and takes the norm ℓ_{norm} as given. Akerlof (1982) considers several possible versions of labour market models based on this set of assumptions. They all illustrate the same main result: gift exchange at work as an incentive mechanism arising in equilibrium. One can assume, for instance, that all workers are homogeneous and exert an effort equal to the norm; and that this effort norm is a function of the firm wage relative to a reference wage w_0: $\ell_{norm} = -a + b(w/w_0)^\gamma$, with $\gamma < 1, a > 0, b > 0$. Akerlof (1982) defines the reference wage, w_0, as the geometric mean of the outside wage and the unemployment benefits. A direct consequence of this set of assumptions is that firms that pay a wage above the reference wage move the effort norm up and obtain extra effort. Firms thus optimally offer wages that are higher than w_0 – and fixed wages become incentive-compatible by inducing higher effort even if they do not directly link consumption and effort at work. This fair-wage mechanism is based on a 'gift-exchange' principle – a higher wage is considered a 'gift' by the employee, which reciprocates with higher levels of effort, to the benefit of the employer. Contrary to alternative models of efficiency wages (e.g. Shapiro and Stiglitz, 1984 in particular), the level of wage itself induces higher effort: not only will any wage cut reduce the effort of all the workers, but any positive wage shift will increase the effort of all the workers.

---

experiments nonetheless are an appropriate tool for testing theories is because general theories must also apply to simple cases they embed. In the words of Plott (1991, p. 902): 'General theories must apply to simple special cases. The laboratory technology can be used to create simple (but real) economies. These economies can then be used to test and evaluate the predictive capability of the general theories when they are applied to special cases'.[6] Experiments offer a simple way to create such simple situations. By doing so, they provide an empirical counterpart to theoretical models: they allow us to compare the empirical distribution of the behaviour obtained with the distribution predicted by theory; or to contrast the variation in empirical outcomes induced by an experimental treatment to the comparative statics generated by the model.

The gift exchange game described in Illustration 4.4 offers an example of such a process. It aims to provide an experimental implementation of the Akerlof fair-wage

---

[6] Also see Plott (1982; 1989) for earlier insightful discussions of the use of experiments to test theories.

Illustration 4.4
Experimental evidence on the fair-wage-effort hypothesis

Fehr et al. (1993) consider a very simple case of the Akerlof (1982) model in order to test its main lesson: that gift-exchange motives induce positive wage–performance relationships, so that high wages arise in equilibrium. Subjects are split into two groups: employees and employers, who play together a two-stage game. The first stage is a contracting game played in real time. Employers make increasing wage offers and employees either accept or reject the offers. Once an offer has been accepted, the employee is matched to the employer so that only unmatched subjects remain on the market. In the second stage, workers privately choose an effort level and receive the wage agreed upon in the first stage, whatever their effort decision. This wage is a cost for the employer, and a benefit for the employee. The payoffs are moreover designed in such a way that higher effort reduces the workers' payoffs and increases the employer's earnings. More precisely, the effort cost function $c(\ell_i)$ is a convex function defined from $\ell_i \in [0.1; 1]$ to $c(\ell_i) \in [0, 18]$. The payoff of worker i choosing effort ℓ_i and receiving wage w_j from employer j is $u_i = w_j - c(\ell_i) - a$, where a (set to 26) is a fixed cost of accepting a wage contract. On the firm side, the payoff of employer j is set to $\pi_j = (q - w_j)\ell_i$, where q is the unitary return to work (set to 126), and the wage cost is made proportional to effort of worker i so as to avoid losses (which reinforces the conflict of interest between employers and employees). If all subjects are pure payoff maximisers, the incentive structure of the experiment gives rise to clear-cut predictions: there is no incentive for workers to choose any level of effort higher than the minimum level, set equal to 0.1. This is further reinforced by the structure of the markets. In all experimental sessions, there is by design an excess supply of labour: the market always gathers more workers than employers. The ratio of excess labour supply is 9 workers for 6 employers in 3 out of the 4 sessions, and set to 8/5 in the fourth session. This, by itself, should push wages down by giving the whole bargaining power to employers. The first stage formally mimics a one-sided oral auction, which is known to converge theoretically and empirically to the competitive market price. Since the opportunity cost of accepting an offer is equal to 26, the competitive wage in the experiment is equal to 30 (since wages are chosen by step of five by design). Anticipating that no payoff-maximising worker would choose a level of effort higher than the minimum, this is the maximum level of wage employers should offer. The main results observed in the experiment are presented in the table below (from Fehr et al., 1993, p. 446, Table 2).

Wage	Average observed effort level	Median observed effort level
30–44	0.17	0.10
45–59	0.18	0.20
60–74	0.34	0.40
75–89	0.45	0.40
90–110	0.52	0.50

The results confirm the two main insights from the Akerlof (1982) model. First, the behavioural assumption that workers positively react to high wages through increased effort is confirmed – by looking at both the average and the median effort. Second, firms actually expect such an effect: despite the strong market forces pushing wages downwards, high levels of wages (up to almost four times the competitive level) are actually observed.

model. The experiment is designed in a such a way that the environment complies with the model's main assumptions – a work relationship with conflicting interests of the employer and the employee, competitive pressure on the choice of wage, non-contractible effort level, non-credible promises to exert high effort in exchange for a high level of wage due to the sequentiality of decisions. This environment is built in a way that is intuitive and simple enough to be easy to understand, and credible for subjects participating in the experiment. Observed behaviour can then be used to assess the validity of the model's main mechanisms and its predictions.

A testing process of this type is often seen as a simple accept-or-reject decision rule: theory is either confirmed, or challenged, depending on whether observed behaviour complies with the model predictions. As will be described in detail in Chapter 9, this question in itself is far from trivial. In a nutshell, this comes from three main reasons. First, no theory aims to perfectly predict behaviour, even in the simple world that directly stems from its assumptions. Deciding what is acceptable noise, and what observation definitely contradicts theoretical expectations, is often a difficult task. Second, the same kinds of theory often receive very different empirical assessments. As a simple example, double-auction theory (as studied by Smith, 1962, and described in Section 1.2.1) is generally seen as 'working': the induced behaviour of subjects in a double-auction, experiment in which both the buyers and sellers submit their bids, yields the same results as expected by economic theory. In contrast, the Nash equilibrium prediction in the prisoners' dilemma only holds to some extent in experiments (see Section 1.3.1). In both cases, the Nash equilibrium combining rationality assumptions and pure self-regarding preferences is the theoretical tool used to generate models' predictions. Testing models in such contexts often helps better characterise the situations to which theory applies and those in which it fails, rather than simply confirming or disparaging it.

But, perhaps more importantly, testing theory also means more than just seeking to accept or reject decisions. First, experiments can be used to disentangle competing models. Such an exercise is often hard to implement based on observational data, as competing models might rely on subtle assumption differences about the environment or economic agent's preferences. Experiments, by contrast, can be designed as simple cases in which observed outcomes can be contrasted with testable restrictions from each of the competing models. Second, an important role of testing theory is also to assess the empirical content and extent of theoretical assumptions (what Schram, 2005, labels 'stress tests of the theory'). Unrealistic assumptions abound in theoretical approaches. They are part of the process of simplifying and reducing real-world situations to get rid (deliberately) of part of this reality. To give just one example, atomicity on markets (leading to the important consequence that economic agents behave as price takers) is made of meaningless assumptions from an empirical point of view. The important and interesting question, however, is not that much whether each and every one of these assumptions has an actual empirical counterpart, but rather to document the kind of situations in which the actual behaviour is close enough to the behavioural insights from theory (price-taking behaviour in our example) for the model to actually make sense. Section 4.4.2 below provides an example of how experiments can be used to pin down the behavioural content of theoretical assumptions. Last, related to this point, experiments can also be used to assess the robustness of theoretical models in environment variations that are possibly not covered by the model – e.g., socio-personal characteristics of agents, norms or moral values associated with the situation, etc. This serves not only to document the scope of a model, i.e. the extent to which it accurately describes real-world situations, but also to identify parameters or dimensions that are influential on outcomes. When such unexpected influences have been identified in the laboratory, it can stimulate extensions of the theory.

4.4.2   *Case Study*: The Empirical Content of Collusion Theory

Among the most unrealistic, yet often made, assumptions in economics is the idea of infinitely lived agents and the resulting infinitely repeated games. This assumption may change dramatically the predictions of a repeated game. For instance, Illustration 4.2 shows in a simple collusion model that collusion may become a stable equilibrium outcome under this assumption. The stability of such a collusive outcome depends on whether firms are patient enough to refrain from deviating and whether market size is small enough to preserve high enough profits from collusion.

The result is both important and interesting, but relies on assumptions that make no empirical sense, because no economic agent can be reasonably thought of as infinitely lived. Still, the assumption is very useful, because it makes the model of repeated interactions easy to write down and solve. From an empirical point of view, what actually matters is not that much whether or not the assumption is 'realistic' but rather if it helps to describe empirically relevant situations. To that end, the behavioural mechanisms embedded in the assumptions matter more than their real-world counterpart. This question has sparked some debate in the example of infinitely repeated games. According to Martin J. Osborne, for instance, infinitely repeated games 'capture a very realistic feature of life, namely the fact that the existence of a pre-specified finite period may crucially affect people's behaviour (consider the last few months of a presidency or the fact that religions attempt to persuade their believers that there is life after death)' (Osborne and Rubinstein, 1994, p. 136; this is interestingly one of the issues on which the two authors of the book disagree). In terms of behaviour, the main difference between infinitely repeated games and finite horizon ones is thus whether or not current decisions account for what will happen at the last stage of the game. Translated into an empirical question, 'infinitely repeated' means that people do not take the last stage into account, or at least do not take it entirely into account when they decide what their current behaviour should be.

Unlike the formal assumption used in the theoretical model, this behavioural consequence makes a lot of empirical sense. Based on theoretical analysis, it will lead to drastically different outcomes – in a repeated prisoners' dilemma like the one presented in Section 1.3.1, Figure 1.6, for instance, it leads to non-cooperative decisions if people take the last stage into account in their current decision-making, to cooperative decisions otherwise. The open question thus is, what kind of environment fosters, or undermines, such a driving force of decision-making?

Normann and Wallace (2012) use this idea to provide an empirical test of the range of experimental situations that replicate the assumption of infinitely repeated games. The experiment looks at subjects' cooperative behaviour in a repeated 2*2 prisoners' dilemma game – the same players play together during all repetitions. Four treatments are defined according to different termination rules. In the first treatment (the KNOWN treatment) the fact that the game will last for 22 periods is common knowledge from the very start. In the second treatment (UNKNOWN), there are 28 periods and this is unknown to subjects. In the third treatment (RANDOM-LOW) there is a 1/6 probability that the game will end after 22 periods. In the fourth treatment (RANDOM-HIGH) there is a 5/6 probability that the game will end after 22 periods.[7]

Figure 4.6 shows the number of players who decide to cooperate over the first 22 periods of each treatment. For all termination rules, the initial responses as well as the time trend during the first 12 rounds are very similar. In the KNOWN treatment, cooperation subsequently decreases as a result of an end-game effect – current individual behaviour becomes more and more strongly influenced by the expected outcome at the last stage of the experiment. At the last period of the game, when it is common knowledge that there will be no further repetition of the game, the rate of cooperation is 50% lower than in other treatments.

Beyond this difference at the last stage of the KNOWN treatment, all four treatments generate the same pattern of cooperative behaviour. This has two important implications.

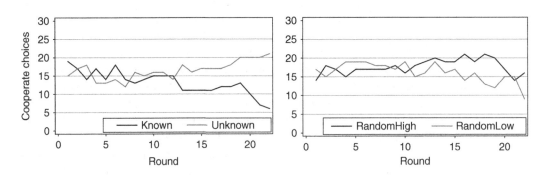

Figure 4.6 Cooperation in repeated games with different termination rules
Note. For each treatment, with varying termination rules, the figure reports the number of subjects who decide to cooperate at each round of a repeated prisoners' dilemma game.
Source: Normann and Wallace (2012, p. 713, Figure 1).

---

[7] As explained in Illustration 4.2, the random-termination rule used in these last two treatments replicates as closely as possible the model with infinitely lived agents.

First, the choice of a termination rule in experiments on repeated games does not significantly affect individual behaviour. A deterministic, but unknown, number of repetitions, or a random termination rule – or even the first periods of play with a long enough deterministic and common-knowledge termination – all induce subjects to disregard the last stage of the game to the same extent. Second, as shown by the end-game effect observed in the KNOWN treatment, these termination rules all induce the pattern of behaviour expected by infinitely repeated games: higher cooperation supported by the expected rents of cooperating in the future.

4.4.3 The Key Challenge: Internal Validity

Laboratory experiments are well suited to empirically test theoretical predictions because they allow us to build an empirical situation that reduces the environment to only those dimensions that are actually embedded in the model. Experiments thus provide an empirical counterfactual to theoretical models. Testing theory in this context amounts to either comparing behavioural outcomes to theoretical predictions, or performing such a comparison to assess the empirical content of simplifying theoretical assumptions.

In both cases, the process strongly relies on the ability to relate observed behaviour to those features of the environment that aim to replicate the model. If decision-making is rather induced by other dimensions, then observed behaviour has nothing to say about the model itself. In terms of the definitions stated above, this amounts to checking whether or not the experimental outcome $F^m(x^\infty)$ results from the n inputs chosen to replicate the theoretical causal mechanism $f : \mathcal{X}^{n_x} \to \mathcal{Y}^{n_y}$, rather than the $x^{\infty - n}$ inputs at stake in the experiment despite the control. This question is known as the experiment's **internal validity**.

Think, for instance, of an experiment with two treatments, with each session of the first treatment being scheduled early in the morning and all sessions of the other being scheduled in the afternoon. The slots may have an effect on both the kind of subject who shows up to the experiment and the degree of attention and focus during the session. Differences in behaviour between treatments will in this case not only reflect the treatment effects, but also this unwarranted variation between the two environments. In this example, the experiment has serious flaws in terms of internal validity. The main consequence is that the causal inference between the environment and the observed behaviour is challenged. Internal validity refers to how appropriately the causal relationship from inputs to outputs is measured, thanks to the design of the experiment. Since experiments testing theory aim to identify the theoretical causal mechanism, internal validity is the primary challenge.

This definition makes clear that the internal validity is a matter of identification in exactly the same sense as it has been defined and discussed in Chapter 3. When designing an experiment, the aim is to have the subjects' choices induced by the environment chosen, rather than by any other uncontrolled dimensions (such as the subjects' own understanding or interpretation of the game). Internal validity is challenged if the experimenter measures the consequences of a confounding factor rather than a proper causal effect, rendering the inference based on observed behaviour either invalid or meaning-less. The reference to identification helps us understand why the issue of internal validity is hard to tackle. Recall that the quality of identification relies on the exogeneity of the identifying variations, and such exogeneity can never be either proven or empirically tested. In just the same way, it is easy to define what a perfectly internally valid experiment would look like: in such an experiment, all inputs beyond the ones of interest would not interact with subject's responses to the controlled inputs – hence being exogenous. But it is far less easy, and in fact impossible, to definitely prove that an experiment is internally valid. We will devote a dedicated chapter to this issue (Chapter 5), and discuss how experiments can be designed and implemented in a way that enhances their internal validity.

4.5   How Experiments Interact with Reality: Searching for Facts

Experiments searching for facts seek to produce empirical knowledge on situations for which theory has little or nothing to say: either because no theory exists or because the existing theory makes predictions that are obviously inconsistent with behaviour. In these cases, experiments can be used to 'establish and document stylised facts, in the form of either observed phenomena or observed causal effects' (Schram, 2005, p. 232). The ability of experiments to test-bed such facts stands on the other side of the contin-uum between theory and reality. Experiments allow us to build pseudo-real situations, of which the set of inputs can be chosen in accordance with the main features of the situa-tion under study. The experiment then provides an empirical understanding of the kind of behaviour, decision and outcome induced by a given environment. Auction mechanisms, and the kind of bidding behaviour they induce, can, for instance, quickly become highly technical from a theoretical point of view. Once the boundaries have been reached of the ability of theory to actually predict how bidders will behave when faced, e.g., with a given set of rules, and under a specific information set, experiments searching for facts can produce useful knowledge. To that end, it is enough to experimentally build the auction situation and observe both the bidding behaviour and the market conditions it gives rise to. Illustration 4.5 describes a typical example of a well-known experiment searching for facts.

An important feature of experiments serving this purpose is the ability to replicate the results. The more often a given behaviour arises in subsequent implementations of a given experiment (possibly with slight variations), the more these observations become actual regularities, giving rise to stylised fact. This is one reason for using meta-analysis (see e.g. the results of the dictator game presented in Section 4.3 for an example, and Chapter 8, Section 8.4, for a detailed discussion).

4.5.1   The Key Challenge: External Validity

Accumulated evidence from such experiments aims to produce empirically based knowledge about the behaviour and outcomes generated by a given environment. Internal validity is obviously a necessary condition for this empirical knowledge to be

Illustration 4.5
Trust: evidence from the lab

The trust game has been purposefully introduced by Berg et al. (1995) to provide empirical facts on the existence and extent of trust and trustworthiness in economic relationships. In this experiment, each subject first receives a $10 windfall endowment. Subjects are then randomly split into two groups, defining their role as either senders or receivers. Senders have to decide to give any share (including 0) of their $10 endowment to an anonymous, and randomly matched, receiver. The experimenter then triples any amount sent by the sender to the receiver – i.e. the actual amount a receiver receives is three times the amount sent by the sender. Last, receivers are asked which part of the tripled amount they want to send back to the sender. Standard economic theory, based on self-regarding preferences, allows for neither trustworthiness nor trustfulness. Applied to this situation, it thus predicts that no cooperation should occur: the sender should keep everything, because the receiver is expected to return nothing. But this game is built in such a way that the rent from trust is huge: the question is thus how much of this economic value, created by trust, can be achieved by human beings despite the incentives to behave selfishly. The answer from simple economic theory is way too extreme to be informative. The results from the experiment, presented in the figure below (from Berg et al., 1995, p. 130, Figure 2), confirm that a large share of this benefit is actually realised.

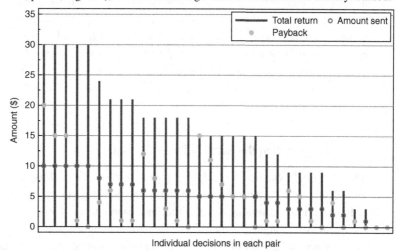

Individual decisions in each pair

The figure shows the decisions made in each of the 32 pairs of subjects, in decreasing order of the amount sent (white circles) and the resulting amount received (height of the bars). The amounts sent back are shown with black circles. On average, senders 'invest' about 50% of their endowment in a transfer to the receiver. There is a large heterogeneity in terms of what receivers sent back. About 20% of receivers send back no money at all, while a large majority send back something. Trustworthiness thus seems less widespread than trustfulness. The main outcome from these two behaviours is that the return to trust is on average 0: around 95% of what is invested (from senders to receivers) is repaid. At the same time, the average total return is $15 – from an endowment equal to 10. Trust is thus beneficial for the economy as a whole, leading to a 50% increase in the monetary value to be split between players.

sound – as the experiment would otherwise document the effect of inputs different from the ones under study. But, in the case of experiments searching for facts, it is far from being the end of the story. If the experimental outcome is actually conclusive, then it provides observations on the behaviour of those individuals who participated in the experiment, facing the artificial institutions built in the laboratory. Each element of the sentence can be a matter of concern. Do the experimental subjects behave in the same way as the actual economic agents would? Isn't the game too abstract to induce the same kind of behaviour that would occur in the real world?

Answering this kind of question is of utmost importance in the case of experiments searching for facts – just because these facts are meaningless if they have nothing to do with real-world situations. This issue is known as **external validity**, in reference to what happens outside the experimental environment. The two kinds of validity refer to what can be made of the laboratory observations, but while internal validity refers to the quality of the empirical measure generated by the experiment, external validity is rather related to its relevance. The strength and range of external validity of the results of an experiment thus mainly condition its interpretation. The question is no easier to deal with than that of internal validity. But the reason why it is the case is quite different. The answer to the external-validity question is in a sense as simple as whether or not it is the case that the causal relationship measured in the experiment is specific to the laboratory context or would occur as well in the real world. What makes the question hard is the many ways in which the words *'specific'*, *'as well'* and *'real world'* can be understood when assessing external validity. This discussion, and what is currently known about the external validity of laboratory experiments, will be the topic of Chapter 8, of which the case study below provides an example.

4.5.2   *Case Study*: Testing the Reciprocity Model in the Field

The empirical evidence from the trust game (presented in Illustration 4.5) echoes the Fehr et al. (1993) experiment in support of the fair-wage-effort hypothesis. Both potentially have huge consequences for the understanding of labour contracts. From these results, it is no longer true that flat wages are unable to foster performance at work. It strongly widens the set of incentive-compatible compensation devices. This is indeed one of the reasons why this behaviour has been so widely studied in the economics literature. But this all is true only if it is actually the case that this kind of behaviour occurs in actual work relationships – if these results have external validity.

Gneezy and List (2006) offer an empirical investigation of this question – 'is the behaviour of laboratory subjects, who are asked to choose an effort or wage level (by circling or jotting down a number) in response to pecuniary incentive structures, a good indicator of actual behaviour in labour markets?' (p. 1366). To that end, one needs to define what a labour market is in the real world, i.e. what makes it specific as regards the behaviour studied in the laboratory. Gneezy and List focus on the duration of the work relationships.

The empirical investigation relies on an experiment implemented in the field. Students are recruited through advertisements to computerise the holdings of the university's library. The advert announcing the experiment offers a $12 wage per hour of work, so that this wage rate is known by all the students who come to participate. In the control group (NO GIFT treatment), students who come on the morning of the experiment are invited to sit in front of a computer and are paid $12 per hour. They work for a total of six hours, and the number of books correctly entered into the system is recorded by the computer. This number is an observable measure of work performance and is used as the main outcome variable of the experiment. In the treatment group (GIFT), the experiment works exactly the same except for one feature. Upon arrival, students are told that the wage rate has been revised upward to $20 per hour. In terms of Akerlof's gift-exchange model, the initially announced wage sets the reference wage of subjects coming to participate. The good surprise implemented in the treatment thus replicates the fair-wage condition of the model.

The main results observed in the experiment are shown in Figure 4.7. The lines are drawn separately for each group according to the duration of the experiment and show the evolution of the performance measured every 90 minutes. In the first 90 minutes, the treated subjects in the treatment group produce around 25% more output per hour than those in the control group, which is consistent with the standard results on the fair-wage-effort hypothesis. In the next portion of 90 minutes, the difference falls to 10%, and becomes (almost exactly) 0 afterwards, in such a way that the performance of 'workers' is now the same whatever the level of the fixed wage they are offered. The experiment thus shows that the effect of a higher fixed wage eventually fades away as the duration of the contract increases. This is obviously a strong limitation to the ability of the fair-wage-effort hypothesis to describe work relationships, and is actually taken by Gneezy and List as strong evidence against the external validity of experiments supporting the existence of such behaviour.

In response to Gneezy and List, Falk (2007) notes that, strictly speaking, the external validity of experimental results is satisfied if the consequences are the same when the inputs controlled for in the experiment are also at stake in the field. To make the point, Falk offers an alternative test of the external validity of these results, based on a one-shot interaction. The experiment is designed jointly with a charitable organisation, whose aim is to help children in need. The experiment consists of sending solicitation letters to a random sample of households in Zurich (Switzerland). The letters ask for donations for funding schools for street children in Dhaka, Bangladesh. The households are randomly assigned to three treatment groups. The first group receives only the solicitation letters asking for donations. The second group receives the letter and a 'small gift' – a nice postcard. The third group gets the letter and a pen, which represents a 'large gift'. The letter makes it clear that the presents are free and for the recipients to keep, regardless of whether they decide to donate or not. The experiment thus replicates a one-shot real-world fair-wage-effort relationship: the solicitation letter stands for a work contract; the amount of the donation is a non-contractable effort; and the gift, when there is one, is an unexpected compensation for this effort.

Table 4.1 Gift exchange in the field: donation patterns

	No gift	Small gift	Large gift
Number of solicitation letters	3.262	3.237	3.347
Number of donations	397	465	691
Relative frequency of donations	0.12	0.14	0.21

Note. For each treatment group in a column, the table reports the sample size and the the number of households who donate in return to the letter.
Source: Falk (2007, p. 1505, Table 1).

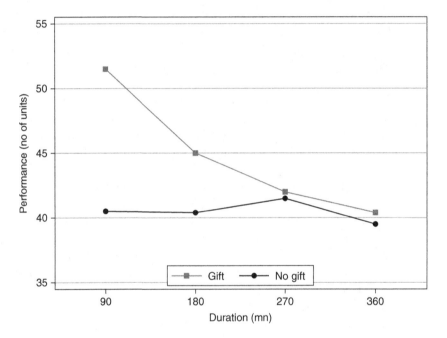

Figure 4.7 Reciprocity in the field
Note. The figure shows the average performance (number of books entered in the system) measured every 90 minutes, respectively in the control (NO GIFT) and in the treatment group (GIFT) according to the duration of the experiment.
Source: Gneezy and List (2006, p. 1371, Figure 1).

Table 4.1 reports the donation patterns observed in each of the three treatment groups. Clearly, donation frequencies increase with the inclusion of a gift as well as with the value of the gift. While the donation frequency only slightly increases when a postcard is associated with the letter, it almost doubles when the letter includes a bigger gift. This increase in the extensive margin of the donation does not crowd out the amount of the donations: no treatment effect shows up when comparing the distribution of the amount donated in each treatment (see Falk, 2007, Figure 2, p. 1506).

Because they happen in the field, and involve real-word decisions in a real context, these results substantiate that laboratory behaviour has some external validity. The same kind of behaviour observed in the laboratory is generated by the same set of outputs.

This is actually consistent with the Gneezy and List (2006) results, if one focuses on the first 90 minutes of the experiment – the maximum duration of the target task of the vast majority of laboratory experiments. Both these results thus confirm that the gift-exchange mechanism is one driving force of real-word economic behaviour, although it is not the case that the mechanism works under all possible circumstances – it is strongly sensitive, in particular, to the duration of the relationship.

Beyond the case of the gift-exchange mechanism itself, these results illustrate how controversial the question of external validity can be. The good news, however, is that in the end it always boils down to an empirical question. It thus stimulates an informed debate involving laboratory studies to assess the robustness of observed behaviour to alternative inputs in a highly controlled environment as well as field experiments to confront such effects in real-world behaviour. The gift-exchange model is a typical example of how the experimental literature evolves over the years according to this process. The experimental research on reciprocity has originated from theoretical models (Akerlof, 1982; Akerlof and Yellen, 1990; Shapiro and Stiglitz, 1984), which were then put to the test in laboratory experiments. These results were then challenged and tested for robustness through field experiments. This process is still ongoing.

Summary

The core of economic science is to understand social reality based on theoretical models. Experiments are central to this process, contributing to each of its directions. Following Roth's (1988) seminal classification, experiments can serve three different purposes: testing theory, i.e. assessing the empirical relevance of theoretical models; searching for facts, by documenting situations that are ill-covered by economic theory; or supporting the design of public policies, which is a combination of the first two. The ability of experiments to achieve these goals raises the question of the interaction between theory, experiments and reality and how they inform one another. This chapter introduced an integrated framework on what an experiment, a theoretical model and reality are, showing that both theory and experiments are restricted environments designed to simplify reality – a must-have to be able to understand it despite its complexity.

This is the building block of a discussion of how theory and experiments, together or separately, inform our understanding of the real world. First, testing theory in the laboratory amounts to building an empirical counterfactual to the theoretical causal mechanism. This is achieved based on causal inference between observed behaviour and the institutions purposefully implemented in the laboratory in order to replicate the model's assumptions. As a result, the big challenge faced by these kinds of experiment is their internal validity, i.e. whether or not observed behaviour is induced by the chosen institutions rather than by uncontrolled dimensions. This issue is at the heart of how experiments are designed and put in practice. This is the topic of Part III. Chapter 5, in particular, describes both the main impediments to internal validity and how to solve them. The practicalities of experiments, described in Chapters 6 and 7, put these principles in practice.

Internal validity is obviously important as well for experiments searching for facts. They aim to provide stylised facts about situations that are poorly covered by economic theory. This amounts to creating a pseudo-real situation, focusing on a few dimensions of interest of the environment, in order to document the outcomes and behaviour they generate. They can be seen as an empirical model, with observed behaviour standing for the predictions. But such experiments are informative about real-world mechanisms only if what happens in the laboratory also happens outside – i.e. if the experiment is externally valid. This raises the question of what experiments tell us, the focus of Part IV. It opens with a focus on the real world in Chapter 8, addressing the question of the external validity of the results raised by laboratory experiments. The will to challenge and refine external validity stimulates an empirical process going back and forth from the laboratory to the field in order to stabilise and refine empirical knowledge. The final stage of this process is eventually to close the loop and get back to theory, to adjust for the empirical phenomenon it pinpointed. How such induction can and may occur is discussed in the first part of Chapter 9. Then, ultimately, the experimental empirical phenomenon becomes part of the toolbox of the economic analysis of the outcomes generated by different kinds of institution. This serves as a basis for policy design. The second part of Chapter 9 focuses on this third aim of laboratory experiments, discussing how well-designed and externally valid experiments, either testing theory or searching for facts, improve our understanding of public policies.

Part III

How? Laboratory Experiments in Practice

5 Designing an Experiment: Internal-Validity Issues

Discussing the need for experiments in the previous part delivered two take-home messages. First, from an empirical point of view, an experiment allows us to choose the data-generating process – the properties of which are the core of the inference properties of any empirical strategy. Second, at the same time, an experiment is also a pseudo-real situation which shares features with both theoretical models – some of the driving forces of behaviour are chosen – and the real world – there will always be some feature that remains beyond control but nowadays influences behaviour. The aim of this chapter is to operationalise these two observations by describing how the DGP can be chosen in such a way that identification is achieved despite the inevitable uncontrolled driving forces of behaviour.

This concern is often referred to as the internal validity of the experiment: does the experimental environment produce convincing outcome measures? Answering this question comes down to asking how experimenters can create a world in the laboratory that best fits their observational needs. As a result, this chapter will also be about how to make the laboratory best suited to its measurement objectives: how do we concretely **design** an experiment? What are the main concerns and pitfalls? What are the choices and trade-offs to be made? To facilitate the discussion, it will be helpful to more precisely describe the components of the experimental DGP, which is the aim of Section 5.1. This will help understand more precisely how the internal-validity issue arises, and how it can be dealt with. This will lead to two complementary answers: internal validity requires controlled dimensions to drive outcome behaviour, and uncontrolled ones not to be confounding. The main feature of experimental designs used to fulfil the first dimension is the use of monetary incentives, which we describe in Section 5.2, and the implementation of exogenous changes through experimental treatments (Section 5.3). We then move to the features that are likely to induce uncontrolled and confounding variations: the perceived experiment induced by how the experiment is described to human beings asked to behave in the experiment, and beliefs about others' behaviour. Through this review, this chapter will thus describe the most crucial best practices in the implementation of experiments, and discuss their rationale.

5.1   What Is an Experiment? How Is It Linked to Internal Validity?

In one of the classics of the methodological literature in experimental economics, Smith (1982) defines an experiment as a 'microeconomic system' made up of three components (the environment, the institutions and the resulting behaviour). While the terminology is different, this definition is very close to the one we introduced in Chapter 4 (Section 4.2.3). The first two components – the environment and the institutions – are nothing but a partition of what we introduced as *inputs*, deciding on the pseudo-real situation that subjects are faced with. The dividing line between these two components is the following: the environment encompasses all the initial circumstances of the experimental system, while the institutions frame its dynamic evolution.

The last component is the same as the transformation function, through which these inputs result in specific occurrences of the experimental measures. Each definition serves its own purpose. In Chapter 4, the definition helped contrast experiments with the two main objects of economic science – real economic life and theoretical models. The main contribution of Smith's definition, in terms of components, is to describe more precisely the ingredients involved in the choice of inputs, and how influential they are on laboratory outcomes. It emphasises that an experiment is a closed system. This will prove very helpful to discussing internal validity – the accuracy of the link between the chosen structure of an experiment and the decisions it elicits from subjects, and how to best choose this structure in that regard.

5.1.1   Experiments as 'Microeconomic Systems': The Components of an Experiment

The *environment* is the collection of all characteristics describing what the system is made of. Important pieces in this collection are: the number of agents (players in a game, buyers and sellers on a market, etc.), the specification of the commodities (tokens and their face value in a trust game, abstract good in an induced-value auction, etc.), and agent-specific endowments in terms of resources, preferences (over allocations, i.e. utility functions) and technology (e.g. skills and knowledge). This defines the givens of the system, some of which are individual-specific. As such, they might be private information.

The second constituent of a microeconomic system is made of the *institutions*, which define the functioning of the system. This first amounts to specifying the ways agents act together: how they communicate and decide (what is the set of available messages, what is the order in which they are decided) and how they interact (who knows what, and when) within the environment. The consequences of these actions for the state of the system are driven by the allocation rules set by the institution. This determines how the initial endowments are affected by agents, messages and decisions, and how property rights over this allocation are distributed among agents. This is coupled with cost-imputation rules, specifying how agent resources are impacted by the change in the allocation. Last, the dynamic of the system is decided by the set of adjustment-process rules, including the initial rules (how the system is initiated), the transition rule (how messages drive the system from one state to another) and the stopping rule (deciding when the exchange of messages is terminated).

These elements are general and precise enough to characterise any microeconomic system. Applied to a laboratory experiment, they highlight the complete set of characteristics that are to be decided on when 'designing' or 'building' an experiment.

Focus 5.1
Cold versus hot: available measures of outcome behaviour

One important dimension on which controlled experiments enhance the observation possibilities is the set of decisions elicited from subjects. In sequential games, the most natural way of eliciting decisions in a game is to ask subjects to make a choice when they have to. In a seminal paper, Selten (1967) introduced an alternative elicitation scheme called the *strategy method*. It amounts to asking subjects to post the full set of contingent actions they would make at any possible node in the game. The outcomes are then determined by having each subject's full set of actions play against one another. Consider, for instance, the four-moves centipede game presented in Chapter 1, Section 1.3.2. Applying the strategy method would amount to asking Player 1 whether Take or Pass would be chosen at nodes 1 and 3, were it reached in the course of the game; and similarly Player 2 about nodes 2 and 4 – both without knowing anything about the choice of the other. The actual outcome for these players then results from the intersection of their contingent plan of actions. The strategy method thus widens the scope of observed outcomes to choices that never have to be actually made. The two methods do not exactly coincide in terms of the driving forces of behaviour they elicit: direct answers are 'hot' – decided spontaneously as the decision problem arises – while decisions elicited through the strategy method can be seen as 'cold' – they force subjects to consider all possibilities at once (Brandts and Charness, 2000). The two methods can easily be compared within an experiment: it amounts to having different subjects play the exact same game, but under each of the two elicitation methods. Brandts and Charness (2011) provide a literature review of existing comparisons and show that little quantitative difference, and no qualitative variation, are generally observed. When a difference is to be expected, a choice needs to be made about the accuracy of either of the two methods to best answer the empirical research question.

The ability to choose the specification of each and every of these components is what makes experiments a highly controlled empirical setting: deciding on the environment and the institutions amounts to deciding on the specification of the microeconomic system. But this same control over the system is also what makes the empirical evidence highly sensitive to the accuracy of this choice. As in any microeconomic system, an experiment is closed by *agents' behaviour*. Under the rules set by the institutions, and the endowments set by the environment, the state of the system evolves according to agents' individual decisions. This includes two different kinds of outcome: the final state of the system, reached thanks to all previous decisions and interactions; and agents' response behaviour, governing individual reactions in the course of the experiment. Both are the behaviours elicited by the system, which can thus be seen as the empirical reaction functions of the experiment's subjects to the environment and the institutions they faced in the laboratory. As explained in Focus 5.1, several methods are available to design the measures of outcome behaviour.

This view of an experiment as a microeconomic system helps characterise the empirical approach. The experimenter has control over the environment and the institutions, which together result in agents' behaviour. The aim is to infer the empirical properties of the chosen environment and the institutions from observed behaviour. Such inference is accurate only if behaviour is actually induced by the chosen microeconomic system. Here stands the core of the internal validity of an experiment. There are two necessary conditions for the experiment to achieve this goal. First, internal validity requires that decisions from subjects occur within the system, i.e. that behaviour responds to the chosen microeconomic system. The remainder of this chapter describes the building blocks of how experiments are designed to that purpose. Second, this is not enough to achieve proper inference if uncontrolled dimensions occur in a way that is confounding. The design choices of experiments aim to fulfil both conditions.

5.1.2   Internal Validity and the Design of Experiments

Because it is a matter of inference, internal validity shares a lot with the idea of endogeneity in econometrics, as introduced in Chapter 3. Identification is challenged as soon as unobserved variations contributing to the outcome occur at the same time as experimental controls. In the framework of the estimation of causal treatment effects, for instance, the data do not deliver identification of the causal parameter if unobservables systematically change in line with the implementation of the treatment. One take-home lesson from this discussion is that identification is achieved if the true data-generating process – what makes outcomes what they are – complies with some assumptions on the determinants of the outcome variable – what we called the assumed DGP. In an experiment, the true DGP is chosen on purpose, by choosing the microeconomic system described above. In the experimental economics literature, such a choice of the specifications of the system (how decisions are elicited and taken in the laboratory) is referred to as the *design of the experiment*. Proper identification in this context implies choosing the specification of the microeconomic system, the experimental design, in order to comply with identifying assumptions. This is the crucial criterion governing the experimental design: choosing the experimental data-generating process in order to achieve, for the best, proper identification of the relevant parameter(s).

Although it may be disturbing at first glance, 'for the best' in the previous sentence will come as no surprise to the reader aware of the discussion in Chapter 3. Identifying assumptions hold on the mechanisms that actually generate outcome behaviour. There would be no need for empirical research if such mechanisms were either perfectly known or observable. Any effort to achieve identification thus relies on a pre-existing knowledge or understanding of what these actual mechanisms are. In the same way as identification properties of estimators are conditional on non-testable identifying assumptions, internal validity relies on assumed properties of agents' responses to the microeconomic system they face. This remark has two important consequences. First, internal validity always reduces to a matter of faith. One will never be able to prove that the unobservable true DGP actually matches the assumed one (again, in the same way as exogeneity cannot be tested or proven). The reverse is not true, however, as it is enough to show that a confounding effect does have an influence on behaviour to establish that internal validity is challenged. Illustration 5.2 provides an example of such empirical test of internal validity, applied to the WTA/WTP discrepancy discussed in Illustration 5.1 and Focus 5.2. But there is an endless list of such unobservables, so that testing them

---

Illustration 5.1
Endowment effects in market behaviour

The Coase 'theorem' (Coase, 1960) states that in the absence of any transaction cost, the allocation of property rights does not matter to the efficiency of the final allocation. This is one of the building blocks of public economics. The seminal experiment by Kahneman et al. (1990) provides strong evidence against this principle. In this market experiment, the subject pool is divided at random into two sub-populations: subjects are sellers in the first one, buyers in the second. We herein focus on the last four periods of the experiment, in which sellers receive a coffee mug. The market value of this object is $6 in the university book store at the time of the experiment. Sellers are asked to state the minimum price they need to receive to agree to sell the good – their *willingness to accept* (WTA) – while buyers are asked to state the maximum price they would like to pay to acquire the good – their *willingness to pay* (WTP). Based on elicited answers, the market is cleared and transactions are accordingly implemented. The main results from this experiment are summarised in the table below (Kahneman et al. 1990, p. 1332, Table 2) displaying the average price chosen by buyers and sellers.

Trial	Trades	Price	Median buyer reservation price	Median seller reservation price
			Mugs (expected trades = 9.5)	
4	3	3.75	1.75	4.75
5	3	3.25	2.25	4.75
6	2	3.25	2.25	4.75
7	2	3.25	2.25	4.25

Since the good is the same and subjects are allocated randomly to groups, prices should – by design – be the same in both groups in a Coasian world. This is by far not the case: the WTA is more than twice the WTP. The behavioural interpretation of this discrepancy is known as the endowment effect: the property of the object generates value on its own. This contradicts the Coase theorem, as the initial allocation of property rights matters for the final allocation through market transactions.

---

all one after the other is a hopeless avenue. Second, for this same reason, an experiment will never be 'perfectly internally valid'. The best one can do is to choose the design as carefully as possible so as to (i) make it likely that the chosen environment does matter for behaviour and (ii) discard influences that are likely to be confounding.

5.1.3   Indirect Controls: Block Everything You Can, Randomise Otherwise

Despite the wide scope of controls offered by the experimental environment, there always remain many features of the context of the decisions that are uncontrollable. This is highlighted in Chapter 4's definition of what an experiment is: no matter how large the set of the controlled inputs, the actual input of an experimental situation is

---

Focus 5.2
Loss aversion: a behavioural foundation for the endowment effect

The endowment effect giving rise to the WTP/WTA discrepancy shown in Illustration 5.1 can be rationalised by a model of loss aversion (Kahneman and Tversky, 1979; Tversky and Kahneman, 1992), according to which subjects dislike losing what they already have even if traded against something else of the exact same value. For example, Knetsch (1989) elicits the willingness to exchange goods (the experiment is based on exchanges between candy and a mug) and shows it strongly depends on initial endowments. Indeed, 89% of those initially given a mug opted to keep it while only 10% of those initially given candy opted to exchange it. As a consequence, exchange appears as a loss of the endowment and is rejected by most of the subjects, whatever their initial endowment. For example, in Kahneman et al. (1990) the value of a good is much higher for sellers than for buyers, because the former ask to be largely compensated for their loss. When an individual is loss-averse, 'losses loom larger than gains': losses are weighted much more heavily than objectively identical gains in the evaluation of prospects. This occurs whether such prospects are risky or not. Loss aversion results in a utility function that is steeper for losses than for gains. A common graphical representation of loss aversion is shown in the figure below. When facing a loss x_L, a much larger gain $x_G \gg x_L$ is needed to compensate the individual from the negative value associated with the loss.

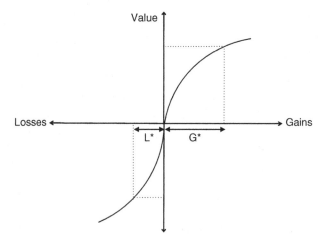

This utility function is reference-dependent in the sense that gains and losses are defined relative to a reference point. In the figure, the reference point is set to 0 and the utility function (which is sometimes called the 'value function' in reference-dependence models) is assumed to be concave for gains and convex for losses. This shape corresponds to a diminishing sensitivity towards gains and losses. The kink at the reference point represents loss aversion: as the individual valuations depend on a reference situation, the asymmetric shape induces loss aversion and therefore an endowment effect. Subjects prefer to keep what they have than to lose it in favour of something of the same value.

Illustration 5.2
Identified failures of internal validity: misconceptions about the endowment effect

In a series of articles, Plott and Zeiler (2005, 2007) question the internal validity of the endowment effect observed in market experiments. Based on a literature review of existing experiments, four main dimensions of the experimental design are found to influence the WTA–WTP gap:

- the elicitation device (in particular, whether or not it is incentive-compatible),
- the extent of subject's training with the mechanism,
- whether practice rounds are paid, and
- whether anonymity is ensured.

These features are hypothesised to affect subjects' understanding about the environment. To investigate whether misconceptions might occur when some of these features are missing, the experimental design consider them all at the same time in a replication of the Kahneman et al. (1990) mug experiment described in Illustration 5.1. The table below displays the main result from the study (from Plott and Zeiler, 2005, p. 539, Experiment 1, Table 4).

	N	Individual decisions (in USD)	Mean	Median	Std. dev.
WTP	15	0, 1, 1.62, 3.5, 4, 4, 4.17, 5, 6, 6, 6.5, 8, 8.75, 9.5, 10	5.20	5.00	3.04
WTA	16	0, 0.01, 3, 3.75, 3.75, 3.75, 5, 5, 5, 6, 6, 6, 7, 11, 12, 13.75	5.69	5.00	3.83

This implementation of the experiment gets rid of any evidence of a WTA–WTP gap: in terms of mean price, median price and dispersion, all outcomes are very similar when elicited from either buyers or sellers – all comparisons are non-significantly different. This result is highly controversial given the influence of the endowment effect on both the theoretical and empirical literature. The nature of the good, in particular, has been shown to be crucial as the gap seems more robust to the procedures when lotteries, rather than consumption goods, are exchanged on the market (e.g. Isoni et al., 2011; Plott and Zeiler, 2011).

$x^\infty = x^n \cup x^{\infty-n}$, because it belongs to the real world (see Section 4.2.3). Leading examples of such inputs are subject-specific heterogeneity, like their beliefs (about the behaviour of others but also, for instance, about how trustable is the information coming from the experimenter), or their mood or emotions when arriving; but this also includes experimenter-specific heterogeneity (e.g. how clear is the reading of the instructions, how 'serious' or trustable the experimenter seems to be), lab-specific characteristics (location, comfort, etc.). All these examples are sources of noise in the experimental observations: decisions will likely not be the same, within the same experimental design, when either of these features changes. They are also both unobservable and generally impossible to control – one cannot choose to implement a given level of trust towards the experimenter: subjects are endowed with their own, which can hardly be measured. But such noise is not confounding per se. As such, it only affects statistical inference (the precision of the estimated effects). Reducing the intensity of the noise improves the quality of experimental outcomes, by delivering more precise estimates.

But what matters for identification is whether such noise is correlated with the variables of interest. To make things concrete, take an experiment that aims to measure gender effects by comparing behaviour between only-males and only-females versions of the experiment. If the male version always take place before lunch, and the female version just after, this very fact might induce noise in observed behaviour. But the chosen implementation moreover generates a correlation between noise and gender. The observed differences in outcomes between the two versions will not be an accurate measure of gender effects. It is so because changes in the outcome (through the noise) occur at the same time as variations of the target variables, hence misleadingly suggesting a relationship between the two while both variations are in fact caused by the noise. Such a correlation between the noise and the outcome is said to be confounding and challenges identification. The concern for internal validity leads to preventing correlations between the noise arising in the experiment and the variables of interest. While there are as many internal-validity issues as the number of known or expected confounding mechanisms, two kinds of strategy introduced in Section 3.4 circumvent them. The best practices in the design of experiments operationalise these strategies.

'*Blocking*' strategies aim to hold constant nuisance dimensions of the experiment: nuisance is still there, and is not observed in any way, but since it no longer varies, it is no longer confounding – hence implementing the identification strategy described in Section 3.4.3. Blocking amounts, for instance, to avoiding using several different physical laboratories to run several sessions of the same experiment, or changing the identity of the experimenter. The more such features remain the same, the more likely it is that changes in outcome behaviour are immune to their effect, because they hold constant across all instances in which the outcome variable is observed. For this same reason, this also achieves better precision in the measure of the relationship of interest.

The alternative design strategy, '*randomisation*', is used when variation in nuisances cannot be avoided. As shown in Section 3.4.1, if such variations happen but are uncorrelated with the target determinants of behaviour, they induce noise in the data and less precision in the econometric analysis, but they are no longer confounding. This concretely implies choosing the value taken by these nuisance variables according to a random draw. Many dimensions of an experiment can be chosen in this way (and the general principle is to follow a random-allocation rule in all instances in which blocking is not available). This is the reason why, in particular, computers in the laboratory are allocated to subjects by asking them to draw an assignment card before entering the lab – in such a way that they do not choose where they sit, and who the neighbours are. Similarly, in those experiments featuring different kinds of position in the game (like sender/receiver, for instance) these roles are not attributed based e.g. on the location of the computer in the room, or to subjects based on their arrival order, but rather by random assignment across all subjects to the session – in such a way that any systematic relationships between location-specific or subject-specific heterogeneity and role in the game are broken.

On a final note, it is worth stressing that any choice of an experimental design can only be assessed as regards the specific research question the experiment aims to address. The research question is what defines the outcome, the noise, and relevant variables of the experiment – hence what might, or might not, be confounding. As an example, when experiments seek to measure the causal effect of changes in the environment or institution, the outcome variable is the difference in behaviour between two settings. The relevant noise is those unobservables that make the *difference* in outcome change at the same time as the relevant *change* in the context. Basically, any noise influencing the outcome levels in the same way in the two settings cannot be confounding. In contrast, the case study below provides an example of a *measurement experiment*, in which observed behaviour per se is the outcome of interest. In a measurement experiment the identifying assumptions are more demanding, because any unobservable influencing behaviour belongs to the relevant noise term, and might thus be confounding. As suggested by these examples, a sensible choice of design for one experimental investigation can thus be just obviously wrong for another one. Consequently, the insights developed in this chapter should be seen as neither absolute principles any experiment must comply with – as a matter of fact, the chapter will describe plenty of counterexamples to the general discussion – or an exhaustive review of confounding effects found in experiments – as each new design is likely to raise its own. They describe the set of tools available to undermine the effect of usual suspects challenging internal validity, and illustrate the practical consequences of the principles discussed here on how experiments are designed.

5.1.4 *Case Study*: A Measurement Experiment: The Voluntary-Contribution Mechanism

Public goods in microeconomic theory share two specific features: they are non-rival and non-excludable. Non-rivalry means that any unit of the good that is consumed by an economic agent still remains available for consumption for another one; non-excludability happens when there is no way to prevent an agent consuming available units of the good. National security is a prototypical example of a public good. First, it is non-rival because one person enjoying domestic safety does not hinder another person from 'consuming' this same safety. The important consequence in terms of microeconomic analysis is that the cost of providing national security to an additional inhabitant is 0. This stands in sharp contrast with private goods, for which serving more consumers requires producing more of the good. Second, national security is also non-excludable, as anyone living in the area will benefit from it. Again, this is a huge departure from standard analysis of private goods, for which consumption can be made conditional on paying a price for each unit of the good that is consumed.

The main consequence of these two features (together, as none of them alone is enough to define a public good) is that the allocation of public goods is a typical example of a market failure: the number of units produced and consumed in the economy if economic agents behave in an unconstrained and decentralised way is not the best they can achieve together with the available resources. The intuitive reason for that is easy to understand: because of non-rivalry, the number of units that should be produced is determined by the sum of all consumers' willingness to pay for each of these units – because all consumers will then be able to consume each and every unit of the good. To achieve such a level of production, each consumer should thus be asked to pay an individualised price exactly equal to one's own preferences towards the good. But because of non-excludability, consumers can enjoy any unit of the good once available in the economy at no cost – just because there is no way to constrain people to pay for a non-excludable good. On a free market, everybody will thus hope to rely on others to pay for the production cost of the good, while enjoying those units that eventually become available. This obviously results in no production at all. In behavioural terms, the key mechanism in this reasoning is free-riding behaviour: if asked to freely choose whether or not they want to contribute to funding the production of a public good, rational consumers will give the least possible. The empirical content of the microeconomics of public goods, and the design of institutions aimed to enhance the allocation, crucially depend on the relevance and extent of such behaviour.

The Voluntary-Contribution Mechanism (VCM) is an experimental game purposefully designed to provide an empirical measure of free-riding behaviour (Isaac et al., 1984). This game gathers N players who each receive an endowment denoted e_i. Each player is asked to decide on the allocation of this endowment between two possible investments: a private or a public one. The per-unit individual return of the private good is q (> 1): each dollar put by individual i in the private investment increases i's earning by $\$q$. The public good, by contrast, benefits anyone: the return on each dollar invested in the public good is Q but this amount is equally split between all members of the group, increasing the individual earnings of each one of them by $\$Q/n$. We denote ℓ_i, with $0 \leq \ell_i \leq e_i$, the level of 'contribution' to the public good (the amount allocated to the public investment). Once all allocation decisions have been made in the group, the individual payoff resulting from them is thus:

$$\underbrace{q(e_i - \ell_i)}_{\text{Return from private good}} + \underbrace{\frac{Q\left(\ell_i + \sum_{j \neq i} \ell_j\right)}{N}}_{\text{Return from public good}}$$

As simple as it is, this game replicates the main features of the social dilemma raised by public-good provision in an economy. It is usual to refer to $Q/(qN)$ as the MPCR, marginal per capita return. As soon as the returns and group size are such that $1/N < MPCR < 1$ (see Focus 5.3 for details), it is individually rational to put the whole endowment in the private investment, although everyone in the group would be better off by favouring the public investment. The driving force of this result is free-riding: rational individuals only take into account the private return of their investment when considering the public investment. No matter what others do, it is payoff-improving to benefit from others' investment (if any) and invest everything in the private good and enjoy the private return from the private investment.

Isaac et al. (1984) is among the earliest attempts to experimentally investigate the empirical relevance of such behaviour (see, e.g. Ledyard, 1995, for a review of the literature). They consider repeated VCM games in which the same four players interact 10 times together. Two versions of the game are considered: one with low MPCR (equal to 0.3), another with a higher one, equal to 0.75. According to theory, the closer the MPCR

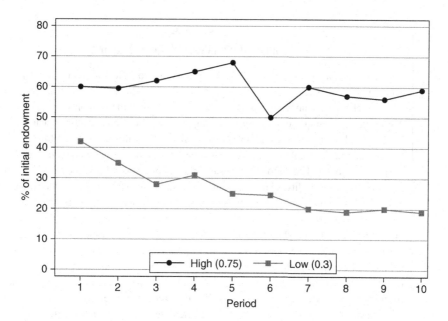

Figure 5.1 Empirical free riding in VCM games

Note. For each period in abscissa, the figure shows the average group contributions as a percentage of the optimal one (investing the whole endowment). Each line refers to a different treatment, with varying levels of the MPCR.

Source: Isaac et al. (1984, p. 135, Figure 4).

is to 0.25 (= $1/N$ in the experiment), the stronger are the incentives to free-ride – conversely, cooperation becomes more and more likely as the MPCR becomes closer to 1, where individually rational behaviour spontaneously switches to the public investment. Several interesting lessons arise from the results, presented in Figure 5.1.

First focusing on the low-MPCR treatment, empirical behaviour clearly contrasts with the theoretical prediction: the contribution rates are strictly positive and amount to 40% to 20% of the initial endowment. It is worth noting that, although far from the Nash equilibrium, this behaviour is just as far from the fully cooperative outcome one would obtain if people cared about others just as much as they care about themselves. The pattern over time is also worth noting: the cooperation rate is decreasing over time, reaching its lowest level at the final stage of the experiment. This is a typical outcome in this kind of experiment, called an *end-game effect*. Overall, these results show that the free-riding issue in public-good-provision problems might well be weaker than expected. It does not rule out any explanatory power of theory, though. Turning to a comparison between the two treatments, it clearly appears also that insights about how behaviour changes according to the value of the MPCR are accurate. Contributions are much higher when the MPCR in higher (equivalently, contributions are much lower when incentives to free-ride are higher), and the decrease over time is also more attenuated. The general lesson from this seminal work is twofold: theory accurately describes how behaviour is adjusted to the monetary incentives at stake, but definitely misses something in driving forces of behaviour itself.

Focus 5.3
Equilibrium analysis of the VCM game

The theoretical analysis of the VCM aims to answer two different questions: what can small economy of N people best achieve given the available endowment? And what they will actually do if choices are not constrained – i.e. what allocation will result on a competitive market? Answering the first question amounts to comparing what can be collectively achieved according to the whole set of possible investments. Since the return rates all are linear, the answer is quite simple. One dollar from the endowment results in a wealth equal to q if invested in the private good, and equal to Q if invested in the public good. These are the public returns of the investment possibility, as they measure the overall change in wealth in the whole community associated with each possibility. The resources are thus best used by investing anything in the public good when $Q > q \Leftrightarrow Q/(qN) > 1/N$, and by opting for the private investment otherwise. This is the efficient-allocation rule (which corresponds to what is known as the Bowen–Lindahl–Samuelson condition in public economics). Let's now investigate how people will be individually willing to behave in this environment. Again, the linearity of the returns makes the problem straightforward. While deciding on the investment of each dollar from one's own endowment, each member of the group compares the private returns from the investment – by how much one's own wealth increases. As stated in the text, this return is still q for the private good, but is equal to Q/N for the public investment. The individually rational strategy is thus driven by the rate of substitution between the public good and the private good, usually called the *marginal per capita return* in the literature: $MPCR = Q/(qN)$. The private investment dominates the public one at the individual level if the MPCR is lower than 1 ($Q/N < q$). Each individual will then decide to opt for the private investment, resulting in equilibrium contributions $\ell_i^* = 0$, $\forall i$ (and $\ell_i^* = e_i$, $\forall i$ as soon as $MPCR > 1$). The discussion is summarised in the figure below.

Efficient (collectively rational) allocation

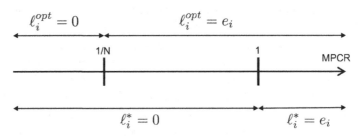

Equilibrium (individually rational) allocation

Not all ranges of the parameters give rise to a market failure. If $MPCR < 1/N$ or $MPCR > 1$, individually rational decisions coincide with the efficient allocation and there is nothing to worry about. But if $1/N < MPCR < 1$, a social dilemma arises: individual decisions no longer match the efficient allocation, because individuals fail to take into account the consequences of their investment for the rest of the community. Each individual is better off opting out of the provision of the public good.

In terms of internal validity, the two kinds of result make use of different identifying assumptions. Comparisons between treatments only require that no confounding effect is correlated with the treatment – if the room temperature influences behaviour in a particular way, and both treatments have been implemented in the same experimental lab, then it is neutral on inferences based on behavioural variations. Inference about free-riding behaviour per se, by contrast, is a measurement problem. It requires that observed choices are induced by the chosen environment. If people rather react to features beyond the experimenter's control, then observed choices do not inform about target behaviour.

Andreoni (1995) designed an experiment aimed at addressing this second issue. The main research question is whether observed contributions from participants to VCM experiments are actually motivated by non-purely selfish preferences, like kindness or altruism. If not, in Andreoni's (1995 p. 893) own words, 'a second hypothesis is that experimenters have somehow failed to convey the incentives adequately to the subjects ... subjects have somehow not grasped the true monetary incentives'. Andreoni labels this failure of internal validity 'confusion'. To that end, the experiment considers three treatments. The standard public-good game (treatment REGULAR) is similar to the ones considered above – groups are made of five subjects playing 10 VCM games with an MPCR of 0.5. The main difference is that subjects play with different others in each game. The main treatment of interest, labelled RANK, aims to eliminate any other-regarding motive while maintaining the same incentive structure of the game. In this treatment, subject's final earnings do not depend on their absolute earnings from the game, but rather on how their earnings compare to other subjects in their group. A list of fixed prizes is announced before the game takes place. In each period of play, the subject ranked first gets the highest pay-off, the subject ranked second gets the second-highest payoff and so forth. The incentive structure of the game remains the same: the dominant strategy, just like in the REGULAR treatment, is to contribute nothing to the public good. But the incentive to contribute due to other-regarding motives is now arguably eliminated from the game: since the public investment earns just as much for anybody in the group, contributing does not benefit others and just harms the investor's ranking. Positive contributions in this treatment thus cannot be interpreted as a departure from free riding due to kindness towards others.

Thanks to this feature of the RANK treatment, the comparison between these two treatments aims to identify the extent of contribution that is actually due to kindness – and what share of the usually observed level of cooperation can actually be attributed to confusion or error. There is, however, a potential confounder in this comparison. There are two actual changes in the decision environment between the two treatments. One is the change in the compensation scheme, which is implemented on purpose. But this requires a second change: the ranking information becomes available to subjects. If such information has an influence on behaviour (e.g. by fostering relative comparisons), there is no way to disentangle the two effects based on a simple comparison between RANK and REGULAR. A third treatment is designed to address this issue: the REGRANK treatment implements the same compensation rule as the REGULAR treatment, but provides subjects with the ranking information at the end of each round of play.

Table 5.1 Voluntary contributions without altruism

| Condition | Percentage of endowment contributed to the public good, by round | | | | | | | | | | |
	1	2	3	4	5	6	7	8	9	10	All
REGULAR	56.0	59.8	55.2	49.6	48.1	41.0	36.0	35.1	33.4	26.5	44.07
REGRANK	45.8	45.4	32.6	25.0	23.1	17.8	11.3	9.5	8.3	9.0	22.79
RANK	32.7	20.3	17.7	9.9	9.2	6.9	8.1	8.3	7.1	5.4	12.55
$\neq$	13.2	25.1	15.0	15.1	13.9	11.0	3.2	1.3	1.2	3.6	10.24
% Regular	23.5	42.0	27.1	30.4	28.9	26.7	8.9	3.6	3.6	13.5	20.82

| Condition | Percentage of subjects contributing zero to the public good | | | | | | | | | | |
	1	2	3	4	5	6	7	8	9	10	All
REGULAR	20	12.5	17.5	25	25	30	30	37.5	35	45	27.75
REGRANK	10	22.5	27.5	40	35	45	50	67.5	70	65	43.25
RANK	35	52.5	65	72.5	80	85	85	85	92.5	92.5	74.50

Note. For each round of play (in column) and in each treatment (in row) the upper part provides the average observed contribution as a percentage of total endowment. The lower part displays the share of subjects who behave as perfect free-riders – i.e. contribute exactly 0.
Source: Andreoni (1995, p. 896, Tables 1 and 2).

The results are shown in Table 5.1, providing both the average level of contribution in each round, and the share of subjects who behave as perfect free-riders. According to both outcomes, the three treatments are perfectly ordered: contributions are always higher in REGULAR as compared to REGRANK, and higher in REGRANK than in RANK. The change in behaviour from REGULAR to REGRANK confirms that informing subjects about their relative performance changes contributions – but it cannot be attributed with certainty to either kindness or confusion. By contrast, only confusion can explain positive contributions in the RANK condition. The average behaviour in this treatment, in terms of both contribution level and perfect free-rider distribution, amounts to half the one observed in REGRANK. This implies that half the contributions observed in this treatment (and almost one-third of those observed in REGULAR) have nothing to do with subjects' willingness to improve the group's outcome. This is only the empty part of the glass, of course; the full part is that half of observed contributions can be taken as accurate measures of people's tendency to spontaneously overcome the free-rider problem. This is large enough to deserve attention – and did elicit a large body of literature in the last three decades.

5.2   The Incentive Structure of Experiments

Smith's view of an experiment as a microeconomic system identifies the main building blocks of empirical identification based on experiments. Inference is based on outcome behaviour, supposedly generated by the environment and institutions implemented in the laboratory. The link between the two, which makes the whole work as a system, is individual behaviour: outcome behaviour results from decisions by people, in response

Table 5.2 Smith (1982) precepts: three incentive-compatibility criteria

Criterion	Description
Non-satiation	More is always better than less
Saliency	Payoff differences are such that choices are worth it
Dominance	The whole experiment is attractive enough to compensate for the opportunity cost of participation

to the experiment rules. There is one driving force in this system that remains beyond control: individual preferences over outcomes. Such a system is closed only if preferences driving decisions are well defined over outcomes. This is the main rationale for the use of monetary incentives in experimental economics – how much people lose or win according to what happens in the course of an experiment. These principles are described in the next subsection. As all methodological rules described in this chapter, this one has pros and cons and experiences famous exceptions. The most noticeable is even the field as a whole, as the use of incentives is to a large extent specific to economics among all experimental social sciences. Beyond this variety across fields, the choice of incentive structure raises practical issues within economics, which we describe in the last two sections.

5.2.1   The Logic of Incentives

The choice of the incentive structure of an experiment has been introduced as the core internal-validity issue in Smith's (1982) seminal article.[1] This choice is very much like a mechanism design problem: the incentive structure is what makes individual decisions driven by the environment and the institutions. Smith characterises the properties of the incentive structure according to three precepts – i.e. criteria, rather than rules – to assess the accuracy of the incentive structure. They are summarised in Table 5.2.

The first criterion is '*non-satiation*', which prescribes that more must always be better for everyone, and at any point, in the experiment. In case of a costless choice between two possible options, where the second is offering a higher reward, non-satiation thus requires this second alternative to be strictly preferred to the first one. The risk otherwise is to see people in the experiment not caring about the consequences of their own choices – possibly without any possibility to identify them. The application of this precept might seem very intuitive and almost overly obvious. One common limitation to non-satiation comes from threshold effects. For example, when exam grades are used as a rewarding currency, the reward increases to the extent the grade does. However, above a certain threshold, students might no longer care about additional gains. Giving a bonus

---

[1] In the words of Smith (1982, p. 935), non-satiation and saliency precepts are 'sufficient conditions for the existence of an experimental micro-economy, that is, motivated individuals acting within the framework of an institution'. With the addition of dominance (and privacy, to be discussed in Section 5.2.4), the experiment is a 'controlled microeconomic experiment [overcoming the possibility that] individuals may experience important subjective costs or values in transacting, and may bring invidious ... taste to the laboratory from everyday social life'. In Smith's paper, a fifth precept is introduced, 'parallelism', which refers to external validity and will hence be discussed in Chapter 8 – Section 8.1 in particular.

of 20 points to all subjects gives rise to satiation for a student who already got 90/100, resulting in a flat compensation system once 10 additional units have been accumulated in the course of the experiment.

A second criterion is '*saliency*', meaning that the decisions in the experiment must be unambiguously linked with rewards. This implies that the differences in payoffs, or the marginal utility of the compensation scheme, must noticeably vary according to choices. For example, if one decision implies earning $2, and the next-best decision implies earning $2.25, it is not clear that for all agents this will be a sensible increase, as not even a cup of coffee can be bought with a quarter. Although the principle is that difference in level should be convincing, and make a difference for the decision-maker, there is no clearly and universally defined criterion to assess saliency. Illustration 5.3 provides an example of how sensitive outcome behaviour can be to the saliency of the experimental stakes.

A last criterion in the design of incentives is '*dominance*', which implies that the reward structure dominates any cost associated with participation in the experiment, both inside and outside the experiment. This criterion is akin to a participation constraint in microeconomic theory. Dominance implies a set of conditions on the compensation scheme used in the experiment. First, the compensation scheme must compensate the agent for the cognitive effort underlying decision-making in the experiment. Second, the compensation scheme must compensate the opportunity cost of participating in the experiment. The risk incurred in case of failure of the dominance principle is essentially a matter of selection bias and heterogeneity, as only those people for whom it is worth it will actually care about their decisions, or even come to the laboratory. As for all the precepts described here, there is no clear-cut reference that can be used to establish how much people should be compensated. It depends in particular on the market wage, the value of time and individual characteristics (such as human capital) of the subject pool, as they might all potentially affect the opportunity cost of individuals.

The three precepts together provide guidelines over the choice of the incentive structure of the experiment: how to design, in level and variation, the relationships between the states of the system and individual payoffs. In the terminology of the mechanism-design literature, compliance with the precepts makes the experiment incentive-compatible. Thanks to this property, the experiment offers control of preferences through the control of incentives.

5.2.2   Why Incentives after All?

Based on the above logic, the use of monetary incentives is almost systematic in experimental economics (at least to the extent that not using incentives must be strongly justified). Ortmann (2010), for instance, reports that all experimental studies published in the *American Economic Review* between 1970 and 2008 paid subjects according to their performance. It is, however, a matter of intense debate, both within economics and between economics and other experimental social sciences – psychology in particular. Within economics, one of the most convincing advocates against the use of monetary incentives is Ariel Rubinstein (2013, p. 541), who for instance notes,

---

Illustration 5.3
Saliency and coordination: experimental evidence based on the stag hunt game

The stag hunt game is a famous coordination game drawing back to the French philosopher Jean-Jacques Rousseau, who introduced it as a metaphor of collective action and social cooperation. Two players have the choice between hunting a stag or a hare. Hunting a stag (action A) is hard and requires the joint effort of both players, but then the reward is relatively high – large meal. Hunting a hare (action B) is easy and each player can succeed on their own, but then the reward is relatively low – small meal. The actions in this game strongly depend on beliefs about what the other player will do. The game has two symmetric equilibria: the outcome maximises payoff if both players hunt a stag (the outcome is said payoff-dominant), but if there is any doubt about what others will do, then hunting a hare is a riskless action (this outcome is hence the risk-dominant equilibrium of the game). Which of the two will be selected is an empirical question. Battalio et al. (2001) consider three variations of this game, presented below.

	Game 2R			Game R			Game 0.6R	
	A	B		A	B		A	B
A	45, 45	0, 35	A	45, 45	0, 40	A	45, 45	0, 42
B	35, 0	40, 40	B	40, 0	20, 20	B	42, 0	12, 12

While the strategic structures of all three instances are the same, the size of the incentives strongly differs. The *optimisation premium* – i.e. the difference between the payoff of the best response to an opponent's strategy and the inferior response – is twice as large in game 2R as it is in game R, and six-tenths as large in game 0.6R as it is in game R. The experimental implementation of these games aims to assess to what extent a change in incentives induces a change in coordination, based on three main theoretical hypotheses: (i) the larger the optimisation premium, the more responsive the subjects' behaviour will be to beliefs; (ii) the larger the optimisation premium (i.e. higher sensitivity to the history of one's opponent's play), the faster behaviour converges on an equilibrium; (iii) the smaller the optimisation premium, the more likely the behaviour converges on the payoff-dominant equilibrium (A, A). Eight cohorts of eight subjects are randomly paired and play one of the three games seventy-five times. Observed behaviour is summarised in the table below (from Battalio et al. 2001, p. 754, Tables 1 and 2).

	Period 1		Period 75	
	A	B	A	B
0.6R	41 (0.64)	23 (0.36)	28 (0.44)	36 (0.56)
R	45 (0.70)	19 (0.30)	16 (0.25)	48 (0.75)
2R	34 (0.53)	30 (0.47)	3 (0.05)	61 (0.95)
Total	120 (0.63)	72 (0.73)	47 (0.24)	145 (0.76)

Two important results emerge: while initial behaviour is the same across treatments, it converges on very different outcomes after some repetitions. After a while, participants play the

> payoff-dominant action more often the larger the optimisation premium is. The study of the dynamics of behaviour between these two time periods provides support to the three above hypotheses. The general lesson from this experimental evidence is that the size of the stakes strongly influences strategic behaviour in the laboratory. The open question is then which of the observed behaviours is more informative about game-theoretical predictions.

I have never understood how the myth arose that paying a few dollars (with some probability) will more successfully induce real life behavior in a subject. I would say that the opposite is the case. Human beings generally have an excellent imagination and starting a question with 'Imagine that . . .' achieves a degree of focus at least equal to that created by a small monetary incentive.

As a matter of fact, there are noticeable exceptions to this rule, which even elicited a large literature in behavioural economics. Illustration 5.4 provides an example of such a very influential laboratory experiment which does not make use of economic incentives – and only relies on fictitious scenarios.

This kind of counterargument echoes the view of incentives that dominate the experimental literature in psychology. This has been popularised, for instance, by Tversky and Kahneman (1986, p. 274), who conclude a survey on the topic by noting, 'Experimental findings provide little support to [the] view . . . that the observed failures of rational models are attributable to the cost of thinking and will thus be eliminated by proper incentives'. This methodological debate is still ongoing, and is likely to remain open for a long time. It amounts to an empirical question: is behaviour less or more conclusive as an empirical outcome of the experiment system when performance is incentivised? Several attempts to answer the question have been made in recent years, of which Illustration 5.5 provides an example. Two different cases have to be distinguished in order to make a choice in this regard. The first question is whether or not the use of incentives harms inference based on experimental behaviour. Although a few examples go in this direction, there is very little evidence supporting this (other) view (as well). On the other extreme, it is rather clear that not incentivising performance leads to more noise in the data (Smith and Walker, 1993). Since decisions of the agents no longer have monetary consequences for them, the motivations behind individual behaviour are more likely to be idiosyncratic and diverse. In the extreme case of surveys based on purely declarative answers, the resulting measures will likely not be very informative about the underlying true attitude. If one asks subjects whether they feel happy in the experiment, the observed level of happiness will be regarded as a poor measure of the true mental state of the subjects by most empirical economists. Any systematic change in behaviour, however, like the difference in self-reported happiness between two treatments, is hardly induced by such noise and provides convincing cues about the actual happiness effect of the treatments. This again illustrates that the choice of incentivising behaviour has to be mainly driven by the research question. More generally, it also points to the answer, giving rise to the current consensus in the experimental economics community. If (when) incentives do not harm, they at worst are innocuous on behaviour and at best enhance

---

Illustration 5.4
Evidence from non-incentivised behaviour: the status quo effect

The *status quo bias* is another striking behavioural consequence of prospect theory presented in Focus 5.2. One of the earliest empirical studies documenting this phenomenon is due to Samuelson and Zeckhauser (1988), based on two simple surveys. The first survey tells the respondent: *You are a serious reader of the financial pages but until recently have had few funds to invest. That is when you inherited a large sum of money from your great-uncle. You are considering different portfolios. Your choices are*:

___ a Invest in moderate-risk Co. A over a year's time; the stock has 0.5 chance of increasing 30% in value, a 0.5 chance of being unchanged, and a 0.3 chance of declining 20% in value.

___ b Invest in high-risk Co. B over a year's time; the stock has a 0.4 chance of doubling in value, a 0.3 chance of being unchanged, and a 0.3 chance of declining 40% in value.

___ c Invest in treasury bills. Over a year's time, these will yield a nearly certain return of 9%.

___ d Invest in municipal bonds. Over a year's time, they will yield a tax-free return of 6%.

In the second questionnaire, the text includes a slight modification with respect to the initial conditions: '*You are a serious reader of the financial pages but until recently have had few funds to invest. That is when you inherited a portfolio of cash and securities from your great-uncle. A significant portion of this portfolio is invested in a moderate-risk Company A (option (a)). You are deliberating whether to leave the portfolio intact or to change it by investing in other securities (the tax and broker commission consequences of any change are insignificant).* The proposed choices are identical to the one shown along with the first questionnaire. In one case (the second survey) the money has already been invested, whereas in the other case (the first survey), the money has not been invested yet. Obviously, this leaves unchanged the comparison between all options and the instructions aim to make clear that changes to the portfolio induce no monetary cost. While economic theory imposes no condition about the choice between the four options (this entirely depends on the shape of individual preferences), it should, however, be the case that the arbitrage decisions of the subjects in the two situations are the same. Observed behaviour strongly contradicts this prediction, with an average 20% more choices of the default option in the second survey. This is consistent with loss aversion deduced from prospect theory – the default investment working as a reference point from which departures are evaluated in the loss domain. Alternative explanations have been raised in the literature, such as costs of thinking, small transaction costs or psychological commitments to prior choices.

---

the quality of inferences based on behaviour. So just use it, for the same outcome if not for a better one.

5.2.3   Implementation Issues: Multiple Play Incentives

In many experiments, the decision task is repeated in an effort to allow for some learning and to avoid focusing only on initial responses (see Section 5.5 for a discussion about

---

Illustration 5.5
The effect of incentives on experimental outcomes

Camerer and Hogarth (1999) review 74 studies published in the *American Economic Review*, *Econometrica*, the *Journal of Political Economy* and the *Quarterly Journal of Economics* between 1990 and 1998. Studies were included if they compared behaviour of subjects according to their performance with different levels of incentives ranging from no incentives to high monetary incentives. Camerer and Hogarth (1999) classify the studies in three broad classes depending on the effect of incentives. In the first class of studies, incentives help improve performance in experimental tasks. This appears to be the case for judgement and decision tasks: incentives promote effort in memory and recall tasks of past events, as well as increasing attention. Incentives are important to increase effort in mundane clerical tasks (coding words or numbers, building things). In this class, the main effect on effort is obtained by raising incentives from hypothetical choice to incentivised choice. Increasing the level of incentives appears to have limited effect. In the second class of studies, incentives do not appear to matter much because the marginal return on effort is low. According to Camerer and Hogarth (1999), this is the most common result. This class regroups studies in experimental games, auctions and preference elicitation. The marginal return on effort is low when it is hard to improve performance (computing all the equilibrium strategies of a game) or when performance is easy to attain (when the strategy is obvious to most participants). If incentive does not improve or hurt average performance they decrease the variation in performance, a point raised early by Fiorina and Plott (1978). In the third class, incentives do hurt performance. This class is the smallest one and regroups mostly judgement and decision tasks. Incentives hurt here because of a number of reasons: they push subjects to stick to a given heuristic, they make subjects overreact to feedback, and they make participants self-conscious about tasks which should be automatic. The general lesson thus is that incentives generally seem a good idea to get data of better quality, but different research questions and researcher belief about the true (behavioural) data-generating process might well lead to different choices.

---

the implementation of repetition itself). The same players are then involved in the same task (either decisional or strategic) several times. The general principles behind the use of incentives applies to each one of these multiple decisions. In this case, subjects would earn some money based on their performance at each stage of the repetition, and their overall compensation for participating in the experiment would be computed as the sum of their earnings over all instances of the decision task. Such a compensation scheme, however, raises important internal-validity issues.

When subjects face real play in several successive tasks, the outcome obtained in the earlier tasks can contaminate behaviour in the subsequent tasks and lead to biased measurement. Several well-documented phenomena can give rise to such carry-over or contamination effects: wealth effects, house-money effects and portfolio effects. *Wealth effects* are the most obvious consequence of paying subjects for the sum of their earnings in all decision tasks. As the experiment evolves towards subsequent decision stages, the level of wealth of the subjects increases thanks to accumulated earnings (either known or expected) at each stage. If wealth has an effect on decision-making (income effects in the utility function are an obvious reason for this to occur), then decisions at later stages are not similar to decisions made earlier in the experiment: there is serial correlation in decisions due to the design of performance-based incentives. Such a wealth effect is also likely to occur in decision experiments involving uncertainty as soon as risk aversion changes with wealth. When subjects have decreasing risk aversion, experiencing prior gains increases wealth and potentially leads to higher risk taking in subsequent tasks. On the other hand, it could also be the case that subjects show a propensity to break even after a prior loss and take more risks as the experiment progresses. Thaler and Johnson (1990) show evidence of such an effect of prior gains on risk behaviour, and label *house-money effects* biases arising from the fact that subjects consider prior outcomes as windfall money and take more risk with it.[2] *Portfolio effects* come from the fact that changing behaviour provides a natural hedge in experiments where uncertainty plays a role. For example, in an experiment involving an unknown urn filled with two balls of different colours, taking two complementary positions on and against a colour in two choices provides a hedge against uncertainty.

Because of these likely failures of the internal validity of multiple decisions, the implementation of incentives is often adapted accordingly. One of the most widely used compensation schemes to circumvent these caveats is the so-called *random incentive system* (RIS), which amounts to paying for real only one of these tasks, chosen at random, at the end of the experiment. The main advantage of such a system is to isolate, through randomisation, one choice from another. The intuition is rather straightforward: if the experiment involves two decision tasks, each one compensated with a one-half probability, then an expected utility maximiser will put exactly the same weight on the two outcomes. Focus 5.4 summarises the main methodological drawbacks of this procedure.

Another drawback of random incentives lies in their saliency. Randomisation decreases the expected value of the incentives, as each task is paid with a probability lower than 1. The size of the stakes thus has to be adjusted accordingly. Conversely, for this same reason, RIS also allows us to study decision tasks with big monetary consequences at a reasonable cost. This need to adjust compensation for decreased saliency is shared by all random incentive compensation schemes. It is even more stringent for between-subjects RIS, in which one decision for only one player out of all participants is compensated. In an experiment involving J decisions and N participants, pure between-subject randomisation induces a $1/(NJ)$ probability that each decision actually counts in terms of payoff. On top of this saliency issue, a violation of dominance can also potentially arise when using this mechanism if subjects who happen not to be paid *ex post*

---

[2] A possibility to mitigate this income effect is to postpone the disclosure of the draws in the chosen lotteries to the end of the experiment. Another possibility, introduced by Holt and Laury (2002), is to require the subjects to give up previous gains in order to answer to subsequent tasks. However, in practice, any perceived change in the expected value of the experiment can influence risk attitudes, as stressed by e.g. Grether and Plott (1979).

Focus 5.4

Incentive-compatible compensation of repeated choices: the random incentive system

Baltussen et al. (2012) list at least five different names for the random incentive system described in the text, among them 'random lottery incentive system', 'random lottery selection method', 'random problem selection procedure' and 'random round payoff mechanism'. This incentive scheme blocks the changes in wealth over the course of the experiment. According to Holt (1986), however, subjects might consider the experiment a meta-lottery where each task can be selected with equal probability. More generally, subjects can consider the experiment a meta-lottery with any probability distribution over the different tasks depending, for example on the precise form of the random incentive system or on their beliefs. As a consequence, subjects might no longer perceive each task in isolation and integrate all the choices in the meta-lottery, leading to carry-over effects similar to the ones identified when all tasks are paid. Because each task corresponds to a given outcome in a (meta-)lottery, these complementarities exist when the independence axiom for choice under risk is violated. Several studies have investigated the internal validity of the random incentive system. Bardsley et al. (2010, p. 269), show that the preceding speculations are incorrect. In their words, 'It is easy to see, however, that the RLI [RIS] could be unbiased in the presence of any form of non-EU preferences given different assumptions about how agents mentally process tasks.' Starmer and Sugden (1991) show that these potential problems are of little concern and that isolation can be assumed. A large body of literature has confirmed this finding (Cubitt et al., 1998; Hey and Lee, 2005; Lee, 2008; Baltussen et al., 2012). The overall picture is that for simple binary choices under risk with a high number of repeated measurements, the random incentive system is compatible with the isolation hypothesis. In more complex tasks or dynamic tasks, or in case of between-subject randomisation, however, the existing evidence shows that isolation might not be as strong and carry-over effects can appear (see Beattie and Loomes, 1997; Baltussen et al., 2012, for further details). Cox et al. (2015) provide an empirical investigation of the incentive properties of a wide variety of compensation mechanisms.

---

see their participation as a pure waste of time. The anticipation of such a feeling in the course of the experiment might undermine the ability of incentives to compensate the opportunity cost of taking part in the experiment.

5.2.4 Other-Regarding Preferences and the Incentive Compatibility of Experiments

The logic behind the use of monetary incentives is to provide control of subjects' preferences over outcomes in such a way that the experimental situation implements an actual microeconomic system. The experiment then provides evidence on the outcomes raised by a given combination of the environment and the institutions. This aims to mimic the way theory works, in which preferences are given. Accumulated evidence over the last decades, however, tends to challenge the idea that individual monetary payoffs are enough to describe preferences (see e.g., the discussion associated with the prisoners' dilemma game in Section 1.3.1 or the VCM game in Section 5.1.4). Rather, in many circumstances, people seem to behave differently according to the consequences

of their decisions for others. Such motives are often labelled other-regarding preferences to point out the departure from the standard self-interested representation of
individual preferences. Illustration 5.6 describes the ultimatum-bargaining game, which
contributed to stimulating interest in this topic.

As an illustrative example, consider an outcome-based model of social preferences
(Focus 5.5 describes an example from the alternative class of intention-based models).
Individual utility, U_i, is defined over two attributes: one's own payoff, x_i, and other
players' payoff, x_{-i}. Various representations of the dependency of agent i utility on x_{-i}
exists in the literature. If the utility is independent of x_{-i}, the model coincides with
the standard self-interest assumption. Alternatively, the utility can be defined over the
total surplus ($\sum_j x_j$), so that social preferences mimic a utilitarian social planner. In
Bolton and Ockenfels (2000), utility is a function of the share of agent i in the allocation
($x_i/\sum_j x_j$). In Charness and Rabin (2002) utility is a function of a disinterested social-
welfare criterion, i.e. a weighted sum of the total surplus and of the payoff of the least
well-off agent ($min\{x_i, x_{-i}\}$).

One of the most widely used outcome-based models is the aversion-to-inequality
model introduced by Fehr and Schmidt (1999), in which utility is a function of payoff differences between the agents. In this model, the utility function is defined over the
vector of individual monetary payoffs according to:

$$U_i(x_i, x_{-i}) = x_i - \theta_i^- \underbrace{\frac{1}{N-1} \sum_{j \neq i} \max\{x_j - x_i, 0\}}_{\text{loss from disadvantageous inequality}} - \theta_i^+ \underbrace{\frac{1}{N-1} \sum_{j \neq i} \max\{x_i - x_j, 0\}}_{\text{loss from advantageous inequality}}$$

Each agent thus has three sources of utility: one's own individual payoff and two functions of payoff differences leading to utility losses in case of both disadvantageous
inequality ($x_j > x_i$) and advantageous inequality ($x_j < x_i$). The original model adds
three assumptions to the parameters value: (i) agents suffer more from disadvantageous
inequality than from advantageous inequality: $\theta_i^+ \leq \theta_i^-$, (ii) agents do not like advantageous inequality: $\theta_i^+ \geq 0$, and (iii) no agent is willing to burn money in order to reduce
inequality: $\theta_i^+ < 1$.[3] Under this set of assumptions, agents endowed with such preferences exhibit aversion to inequality: there is a trade-off between one's own payoff and
the fairness of the resulting allocation.

The main point as regards performance-based incentives in experiments is that if
subjects exhibit this kind of preference, then part of the control implemented through
the use of monetary incentives is lost. As an example, consider a prisoners' dilemma
game. Table 5.3.a shows the typical payoff matrix of the game, in which each player
can choose between two actions: cooperate (Coop) or defect (Def). As discussed in
Section 1.3.1, empirical behaviour often does not coincide with the Nash equilibrium
of this game: while defecting is the individually rational action, many people decide
to cooperate. This is a departure from the Nash equilibrium when payoff accurately
describes individual preferences. But for inequity-averse subjects, the game played is
actually the one described in Table 5.3.b. For such a payoff structure, cooperating is a

---

[3] The model embeds other kinds of psychological motive with alternative parameterisation: individual
preferences exhibit guilt if $\theta_i^+ < 0$ and is envious if $\theta_i^- < 0$.

Illustration 5.6
Social preferences and strategic uncertainty: the ultimatum-bargaining game

The ultimatum-bargaining game (UBG) introduced by Guth et al. (1982) is an early experiment that stimulated research into social preferences. It focuses on a simple two-player game. One player is the sender, the other is the receiver. The sender receives an initial endowment and is asked how much is sent to the receiver. The receiver then decides whether to accept or reject the offer of the sender. The offer is implemented if the receiver accepts it, and each player gets the corresponding payoff. But if the receiver rejects the offer, both players get 0. The sub-game perfect equilibrium is rather simple: the receiver should accept any positive offer, leading the sender to offer the smallest possible share of the endowment. The game thus replicates a situation in which the sender has full bargaining power. The figure below (from Guth et al., 1982, p. 375, Table 5) shows the number of experimental subjects who decide to offer or reject the share of the endowment shown in the *x*-axis.

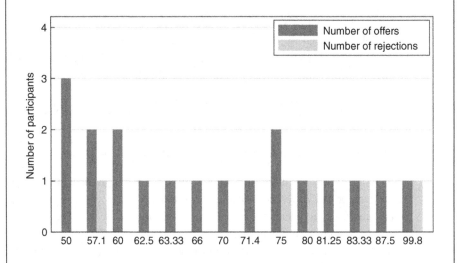

First, it is common for receivers to reject offers below 20% of the endowment. Moreover, most offers from senders lie in the [40%, 50%] interval, with no offers above 50% and very few below 20%. There are thus two deviations from the behaviour predicted by sub-game perfectness. While pure selfishness can hardly explain receivers' behaviour, one can wonder whether senders' behaviour is induced by other-regarding concerns or a best reply to rejection behaviour. This early evidence has been replicated many times since the appearance of the paper, with always the same patterns. In particular, this result appears robust to the level of incentives: in an experiment that raises the stakes to three times the monthly expenditure of the average participant, Camerer and Hogarth (1999) replicate the evidence on proposal rates.

Focus 5.5
Intention-based social-preference models

The altruism-based model has been later generalised to highlight intention-based social preferences. In such a model, what matters to an agent is not only the payoffs but also the intention behind others' actions. In Rabin's (1993) model of intention-based reciprocity, it is for instance assumed that people want to be nice to those who are nice to them, and punish those who are mean to them. In order to account for such behavioural motives, the standard game-theoretic approach must be generalised. To that end, Geanakoplos et al. (1989) introduce psychological games, in which payoffs depend not only on actions, as in traditional game theory, but also on beliefs about actions. Rabin (1993) applies these ideas in the simple context of a two-player game (later on generalised as a sequential game by Dufwenberg and Kirchsteiger, 2004). Let a_i denote the strategy chosen by Player i in their action set, b_{ij} denote Player i's belief about the strategy Player j is choosing and c_{ij} denote Player i's belief about what Player j believes Player i's strategy is; i.e. a_i are standard strategies, b_{ij} are first-order beliefs and c_{ij} are second-order beliefs. The kindness of Player i towards Player j is the difference between the material payoff to Player j, x_j, minus the equitable, or fair, payoff to Player j. The fair payoff to j is the average payoff of the lowest and the highest payoff Player i could have secured to Player j. The fair payoff corresponds to an average point on the Pareto frontier for Player j's payoffs and serves as a reference point to measure how generous Player i is to Player j. Formally, the kindness of Player i towards Player j is a function of both Player i's strategy, a_i, and the belief b_{ij} about Player j's strategy:

$$k_{ij}(a_i, b_{ij}) = \underbrace{x_j(a_i, b_{ij})}_{\text{payoff to Player } j} - \underbrace{\frac{1}{2}[\max_{a_i \in A_i} x_j(a_i, b_{ij}) + \min_{a_i \in A_i} x_j(a_i, b_{ij})]}_{\text{fair payoff}}$$

This function is equal to 0 if Player i's strategy gives Player j their fair payoff, negative if Player i's strategy gives Player j less than their fair payoff, and positive if Player i's strategy gives Player j more than their fair payoff (if possible). Player i also has beliefs about how kind Player j is to him. This belief function depends on first-order beliefs b_{ij} and on second-order beliefs c_{ij}. Formally, Player i's belief about Player j's kindness towards him is

$$h_{ji}(b_{ij}, c_{ij}) = \underbrace{x_i(b_{ij}, c_{ij})}_{\text{payoff to Player } i} - \underbrace{\frac{1}{2}[\max_{b_j \in A_j} x_i(b_j, c_{ij}) + \min_{b_j \in A_j} x_i(b_j, c_{ij})]}_{\text{fair payoff}}$$

The sign of the belief function reflects Player i's opinion about Player j's behaviour. For example, it is negative if Player i believes Player j is treating him badly. Utility functions driving behaviour in this context are augmented with kindness functions:

$$U_i(a_i, b_{ij}, c_{ij}) = \underbrace{x_i(a_i, b_{ij})}_{\text{material well-being}} + \underbrace{\theta_i k_{ij}(a_i, b_{ij}) h_{ji}(a_i, b_{ij})}_{\text{fairness}}$$

where θ measures how sensitive agent i is to reciprocity towards agent j. For each player, the strategies depend not only on material payoffs but also on beliefs about the other subject's intentions. For instance, if Player i believes that Player j is treating him kindly, then $h_{ij}(a_i, b_{ij}) > 0$ so that Player i will choose a strategy a_i such that $k_{ij}(a_i, b_{ij}) > 0$. Conversely, if Player i believes that Player j is treating him badly, then $h_{ij}(a_i, b_{ij}) < 0$ and Player i will choose a strategy a_i such that $k_{ij}(a_i, b_{ij}) < 0$. Rabin (1993) shows that there exists a 'fairness equilibrium' such that each player maximises utility and intentions are self-fulfilling and compatible ($a_i = b_{ij} = c_{ij}$). It can also be shown that fairness equilibria in games include Nash equilibria as specific cases where players mutually maximise or minimise each other's material payoffs.

Table 5.3 Outcome-based social preferences in the prisoners' dilemma game

	(a) Standard game		(b) Game played by inequity-averse subjects	
	Coop	Def	Coop	Def
Coop	5,5	−10, 10	5, 5	$-10 - 20\theta_1^-, 10 - 20\theta_2^+$
Def	10, −10	−5, −5	$10 - 20\theta_1^+, -10 - 20\theta_2^-$	−5, −5

Nash equilibrium if $\theta_i^+ > 1/4$.[4] As a result, there is a discrepancy between the game subjects are actually playing and the one analysed by the theoretical model – as illustrated by Illustration 5.7, the same kind of issue arises if one assumes alternative sources of other-regarding concern, like altruism. This has important consequences for the conclusions that can be drawn from such data: one cannot test at the same time theoretical assumptions about preferences and theoretical predictions about strategic interaction. If preferences are the main focus of the experiment, their occurrence does not challenge internal validity, provided their source is accurately controlled. Illustration 5.8 provides an example of such an experiment, which tries to disentangle intention- and outcome-based social preferences. But non-monetary motives will be confounding if behaviour is to be interpreted as conditional on the control over preferences offered by monetary incentives.

Beyond the case of social preferences in games, this feature has many consequences in the way experiments are designed and implemented. The general aim is to design and implement the incentive scheme of the experiment in order to minimise the confounding effects of any uncontrolled non-monetary motive of behaviour. First, this is the main reason why compensation rules and payoffs are described aloud publicly in experiments. This makes the incentive scheme common knowledge among participants in the experiment and prevents subjects forming beliefs about how well or badly they are treated as compared to others. Second, it is also sometimes useful to rescale the payoffs associated with decisions in the experiment using an abstract currency. Subjects then play with tokens rather than actual money, with possibly absolute values that are much higher

---

[4] Similarly, in the ultimatum-bargaining game presented in Illustration 5.6, observed behaviour is compatible with preferences such that $\theta^+ < 0.5$ for the sender and $\theta^- > 1/3$ for the receiver. If $\theta^+ > 0.5$, the sender always offers 50%, which is always accepted.

Illustration 5.7
Altruism in the prisoners' dilemma game

Altruism-based approaches have been developed as an alternative to outcome-based models. They assume that people care about the well-being of others. In its simplest, two-agent, version, utility has the following additive representation: $U_i = u(x_i) + \theta v(x_j)$. Here the total utility of the agent involves two components: the selfish part of utility, $u(x_i)$, is derived from one's own payoff, but, due to altruism, agent i also cares about the payoff of agent j. This is reflected by the second term, $\theta v(x_j)$. For the sake of simplicity, assume that utility is linear for both the selfish term and the altruistic term. In the prisoners' dilemma game described in Table 5.3.a, the actual game played by altruistic agents when faced with the monetary rewards of their actions is therefore:

	Left	Right
Top	$5 + 5\theta_1, 5 + 5\theta_2$	$-10 + 10\theta_1, 10 - 10\theta_2$
Bottom	$10 - 10\theta_1, -10 + 10\theta_2$	$-5 - 5\theta_1, -5 - 5\theta_2$

As for the inequity-averse example in Table 5.3.b, the incentive structure no longer provides perfect control of individual preferences – social preferences induce a discrepancy between the game actually played and the one described by monetary incentives. In this example, cooperation is an equilibrium if both players have a high enough level of altruism and discount the other rewards as at least one-third of their own rewards (*i.e*, if $\theta > 1/3$).

---

than their monetary equivalent. The monetary value of such '*experimental currency unit*' used to measure the payoffs in the experiment is generally announced before the start of the experiment, and gains are converted when subjects are informed about their overall performance. This is sometimes used to inflate the payoff, in order to improve saliency thanks to an illusion that amounts at stake are big even if they are associated with rather small monetary amounts. This is also useful if one needs to vary the monetary incentives across subjects or across implementations of the experiment (in the course of cross-cultural comparison, for instance; see Chapter 8, Section 8.3.3) while maintaining the currency used to label earnings in the experiment constant. Third, individual earnings from the experiment are confidential and private information of the owner. This avoids interpersonal comparisons, the anticipation of which might induce unwarranted competition between subjects during the experiment. Fourth, payment generally occurs in a separate room, where subjects enter individually to receive their payment. Fifth, this is also the reason why roles assigned to subjects are generally held constant when the experiment features roles that are not symmetric – i.e. a receiver and a sender. The main rationale is to avoid empathy, i.e. that a subject better cares about the partner's situation if playing in this position occurred earlier, or will occur later, in the course of the experiment. In a UBG game, for instance, it is likely people will behave differently depending whether they always decide as a sender, or are forced to put themselves in the shoes of the receiver by knowing they will be one at some point, or have been one before.

Illustration 5.8
Outcome versus intention: an experiment on the nature of social preferences

In order to disentangle outcome-and intention-based social preferences, Falk et al. (2003) design an experiment in which a given choice–outcome combination is associated with varying intentions. Subjects play a UBG with 10 tokens to split. Instead of implementing the usual choice of offers inside the range of all possible values, the experiment elicits a series of four binary choices. In all choices, one option is to divide the 10 tokens by keeping eight and leaving two to the receiver – allocation $(8, 2)$. Four possible alternatives are considered in turn: $(5, 5), (2, 8), (8, 2)$ or $(10, 0)$. Clearly, different behavioural models lead to different predictions of receivers' behaviour: a standard model involving self-interested agents predicts that the allocation $(8, 2)$ is never rejected by receivers; an outcome-based model (e.g. Fehr–Schmidt or Bolton–Ockenfels) predicts rejection of the unequal allocation $(8, 2)$ due to aversion to inequity whatever the alternative choice among the four is considered; last, an intention-based model predicts different rejection rates of the $(8, 2)$ allocation, depending on the alternative against which it has been chosen. The figure below (from Falk et al., 2003, p. 24, Figure 2) shows the observed rejection rates of the $(8, 2)$ offered in the four different choice configurations.

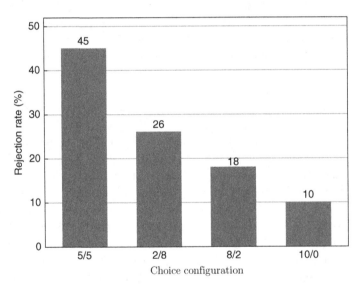

Overall, 55% of receivers reject the $(8, 2)$ allocation if the alternative share is $(5, 5)$, but only 10% do the same against a $(10, 0)$ alternative. Such a shift unambiguously supports the position that intentions matter in rejection behaviour. There is also evidence of pure aversion to inequitable shares, since 18% of the receivers reject the $(8, 2)$ allocation when $(8, 2)$ is the alternative – in this configuration the sender has no choice and cannot signal any intention.

These results provide evidence of outcome-based reasoning which contradicts a pure intention-based model. The general conclusion drawn by Falk et al. (2003) is that social preferences in this game are mainly driven by intentions, but influenced by outcomes. The experiment also provides evidence that senders rationally respond to empirical rejection behaviour. As shown in the table below (from Falk et al., 2003, p. 24, Figure 1), the likelihood of the $(8, 2)$ offer strictly increases in its expected return according to the empirical probability of acceptance.

Game	Expected payoff of the $(8, 2)$ offer	Expected payoff of the alternative offer	Percentage of $(8, 2)$ proposals
$(5, 5)$ game	4.44	5.00	31
$(2, 8)$ game	5.87	1.96	73
$(10, 0)$ game	7.29	1.11	100

It is a well-document fact that roles interact with decision-making (see Illustration 5.9 for one of the most famous examples in social psychology). Finally, the nature of decision outcomes can be modified to control for unobserved preferences. For instance, Roth and Malouf (1979) use binary lotteries in bargaining games to control for risk aversion. With binary lotteries, the outcomes associated with decisions are lottery tickets, and payoffs are chances to obtain a fixed prize. If subjects are expected-utility maximisers and therefore reduce compound lotteries, the utility associated with the fixed prize is equal to the probability of winning that prize. For example, in an experimental bargaining game, the utility associated with an agreement would be equal to the percentage of lottery tickets received from this agreement (Murnighan et al., 1988). Because elicited probabilities capture von Neuman and Morgenstern utilities, binary lotteries are often used as devices to induce risk neutrality. Krawczyk and Le Lec (2015) show this design can also be used to induce more selfish behaviour in experimental games.

5.3   Parameters and Experimental Treatments

The use of performance-based compensation is a way to ensure the incentive compatibility of the experiment, i.e. that the chosen combination of the environment and institutions does induce individual behaviour. We now turn to the specification of these environment and institutions, and how it relates to internal validity. An important distinction needs to be made among the features of the system that are directly controlled by the experimenter. Some of them, called '(control) parameters', are set at the same value in all instances of the experiment. Others, called 'treatment variables', are purposefully varied across several instances of the experiment. The aim of this variation is to measure its effect on outcome behaviour. In order to provide proper identification of this effect, implementation of the treatment relies on the identification strategies described in Section 5.1.3.

Illustration 5.9
The effect of roles on behaviour: the Stanford prison (aborted) experiment

In a famous experiment, Stanford University psychologist Philip Zimbardo showed how far the disconnection of social and moral values can go when people are involved in alienating contexts – social positions driving decisions more strongly than individual preferences. The experiment took place in 1971 in the basement of Stanford University, which was equipped as a prison facility (the full story of the experiment is reported in Zimbardo, 2007). The participants were 24 students who responded to advertisements in local newspapers. The selected candidates were all male, mostly-middle class white, and were chosen conditional on a strong mental and emotional stability. The volunteers, who were all paid $15 per day for the experiment (which was supposed to last two weeks), were split into two groups: 12 were asked to play the role of 'guards', the other half were 'prisoners'. The guards were dressed in military uniforms, wore mirrored sunglasses to hide their eyes and carried wooden bats to intimidate the prisoners. No physical punishment was allowed but this was basically the only rule: for the rest, the guards were free to rule the 'prison' according to their own judgement. Conversely, the prisoners lived in tough conditions. Only cheap coveralls, very basic facilities and plain food were provided. A chain around their ankle was there to underline their status. Only identity numbers were used, instead of names. Upon students' agreement and thanks to the support of the local police, prisoners started the experiment without any warning, with a simulated raid of the policemen in their homes and a routine for real suspects, including fingerprinting. Zimbardo himself acted as a prison warden, so that he was able to directly observe the course of the study. The experiment degenerated very quickly and was suspended by Zimbardo after only six days. On one hand, guards quickly got carried away with a cruel authority, using punishments (mattresses were confiscated, access to the toilet was arbitrarily denied, etc.) and different kinds of humiliation. Overall, one-third of the guards began to show clear signs of sadism. On the other hand, many of the prisoners started to show symptoms of emotional and mental distress. Two of them were removed before the end of the experiment. Although a riot arose on the second day, none of the prisoners decided to leave the experiment before its end. Guards developed antisocial attitudes and showed no sympathy for individual protests. The main conclusion drawn from Zimbardo is that people who are drawn into some particular situations tend to adapt their behaviour to a role, instead of using their own judgement and moral values. Social and ideological factors shape this role, and consequently submerge individual personalities.

5.3.1   Direct Controls

All dimensions of the experiment that can be chosen by design are parameters of the experiment (those are the 'controlled inputs' of the framework developed in Chapter 4). Examples include, among many (many) others, the nature of the subject pool who will be invited to come to the laboratory, the number of periods of play, the exchange rate of the experimental currency, the number of subjects sitting in each section. Choosing the value taken by each such parameter in the experiment amounts to choosing the experimental DGP, hence providing direct control over the environment. Any different choice in the value of one parameter is likely to change the outcome behaviour. For instance, designing an experiment implies making a choice as regards the size of incentives. Too low incentives may fail to implement salient enough decisions, while too high ones may mistakenly stimulate pay-off maximising behaviour (see Illustration 5.2 for an example). Whether the appropriate choice is closer to one extreme or the other has to be decided by sound judgement – according to a trade-off as regards internal validity which, in this case, also has to be weighted with the consequences in terms of the cost of the experiment.

The experimental setting widens the set of dimensions that can actually be chosen. Induced-value designs (Smith, 1976), in particular, allow preference parameters to be chosen thanks to the incentive scheme. As shown in the auction example of Chapter 2, for instance, the marginal utility of subjects for the experimental good can be 'induced' by setting the price at which a unit of the good can be sold to the experimenter. Similarly, experiments focusing on effort at work often induce the marginal cost of effort (see Illustration 4.4 for an example): in this context, the effort at work is implemented as a simple number with positive monetary consequences for the employer and negative ones for the employee. In a non-laboratory context, these preference parameters are not only private and unobservable information, but also heterogeneous between subjects. Laboratory experiments, by contrast, allow one to include these dimensions in the set of chosen parameters.

Beyond the direct choice of the components of the decision-making environment, the design of the experiment also involves the set of measurement tools used to measure the existing heterogeneity leading to the outcome variable. This includes simple questionnaires collecting data on subject's socio-demographic characteristics like age, gender, field of study, etc. To this basic information, more specialised questionnaires can be added to measure specific dimensions of subjects' personality traits, morality or values (typically, based on questionnaires developed in psychology, see e.g. Borghans et al., 2008) or their cognitive skills – using, e.g., the cognitive reflection test (Frederick, 2005) or Raven's progressive matrices test (Raven, 2008). Illustration 5.10 provides an example of a measure of intensity of social relationships taken from social psychology. A recent trend in experimental economics also includes measurements of the physiological process and consequences of decision-making. For example, skin-conductance responses allow us to keep track of subjects' emotions (see Bach, 2016, for a discussion of how it helps interpret data from economic experiments), and eye-tracking techniques for instance allow us to record how information is collected by participants in the course of the experiment (see Lahey and Oxley, 2016, for a review). Such measurement tools deliver 'control variables': empirical measures of the components of decision heterogeneity. In line with the identification strategy described in Section 3.4.2, these control variables narrow the scope of the unobserved variations leading to the outcome, thus enhancing the quality of inference. They can also be used to better interpret the results, by assessing the role played by such heterogeneity in the variations of interest in the outcome variable.

Illustration 5.10
Controlling for closeness: the inclusion-of-the-other-in-the-self scale

An important question in behavioural economics is the effect of pre-existing relationships between people – to what extent and why do members of the same family, friends, employees of the same organisation, people from the same country, etc., interact differently together. The usual way of studying this dimension is to ask people to report the nature of their relationship with others (or, similarly, to organise the experiment in such a way that people with a given pre-existing relationship come to participate). Such information provides a proxy variable of how people are linked together, but does not measures the actual strength of this link. To overcome this issue, Gächter et al. (2015b) develop a measure of intensity borrowed from social psychology, the 'inclusion-of-the-other-in-the-self' (IOS) task (Aron et al., 1992), based on the figure below.

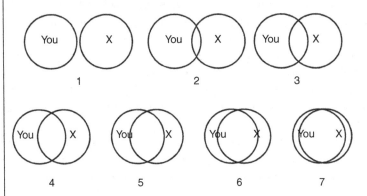

For each possible choice, one circle refers to the respondent and one circle refers to another person, *X*. For a clearly designated participant, respondents are asked to 'consider which of these pairs of circles best describes your relationship with [this individual] in all questions that follow. In the figure "X" serves as a placeholder for [this individual], that is, you should think of "X" being [this individual]. By selecting the appropriate number please indicate to what extent you and [this individual] are connected'. Gächter et al. (2015b) confirm empirically the psychometric properties of the original scale, and show it describes not only 'close relationships' (typically, romantic ones) but also non-close relationships, in particular friends and acquaintances.

5.3.2   Treatment Parameters and Experimental Treatments

Examples abound in the experiments described in previous parts of the book of parameters that are purposefully set at different values. To name a few: the marginal per capita return in Isaac et al.'s (1984) experiment described in Section 5.1.4 is a treatment variable set equal to either 0.3 or 0.75; the alternative split against which subjects must choose in the discrete version of the UBG of Falk et al.'s (2003) experiment described in Illustration 5.8 is another example of *one* treatment variable, which takes *four possible values*: $(5,5),(2,8),(8,2)$ or $(10,0)$. Due to the frequent use of experiments in medical sciences, these kinds of parameter, which take more than one value according to the design of the experiment, are called *treatment parameters* (sometimes also called treatment variables) – while parameters that remain constant in all instances of the experiment will be called *control parameters* (or control variables).

Treatment parameters need to be distinguished from *experimental treatments*: an experimental treatment usually refers to a unique combination of all the parameters' values. In the last example, one treatment variable defines four experimental treatments – the sender chooses between $(8, 2)$ and $(5, 5)$ in the first treatment, between $(8, 2)$ and $(2, 8)$ in the second, etc. In the first example, the two values for the MPCR define two experimental treatments.[5]

The main difference between control and treatment parameters is that treatment parameters aim to generate variations in the outcome, in order to provide identification of their causal effect. The causal effect of control parameters cannot be measured, precisely because they remain constant at a given value in all instances in which outcome behaviour is observed. But their effect can always be measured by implementing them as treatments rather than controls. As a matter of fact, the classification between controls and treatments belongs to the experimental design in just the same way as the value at which they are set: all examples of control parameters given above can be implemented as treatments, if measuring their effect on outcome behaviour is relevant or interesting. For this reason it is often very tempting to widen the set of treatment variables, and the number of values considered for each them. This temptation has to be resisted, due to the data requirements implied by such an inflation in treatment dimensions. The reason lies in the resulting rise in the number of experimental treatments necessary to provide identification – a question to which we now turn.

5.3.3   Between-Subject Designs: Identification of Treatment Effects through Randomisation

Consider an experiment with one treatment variable fixed at two possible values (as the MPCR example discussed above, for instance). This defines two versions of the experiment called experimental treatments (or sometimes experimental *conditions*):[6] one condition for each possible value of the treatment, with all other parameters fixed at a constant value. The open question we want to discuss in the reminder is: how should the two conditions be implemented to achieve identification of the effect of this treatment on outcome behaviour?

The discussions in Chapter 3, Section 3.4.1 in particular, provide a natural answer to this question. Identification is achieved if subjects are allocated to one condition or another according to a random rule. This produces two kinds of individual: those involved in the 'baseline', or 'control', condition and those involved in the 'treatment' condition. Denoting $T_i = 0, 1$ the group variable indicating the condition individual i is involved in, the effect of the treatment on the outcome variable y_i can be estimated by simple mean comparisons:

---

[5] Treatment parameters and experimental treatments trivially coincide in experiments that consider two possible values for a unique treatment variable; the two wordings are often used as synonyms in such circumstances.

[6] In general, economists say 'treatment' where psychologists say 'condition'.

$$\widehat{\Delta} = \frac{1}{N_{T_i=1}} \sum_{i \in T_i=1} y_i - \frac{1}{N_{T_i=0}} \sum_{i \in T_i=0} y_i$$

Since the allocation to one group or another is random, the individual heterogeneity that makes y vary for unobserved reasons is not correlated to the experimental condition. This simple comparison thus provides an unbiased estimate of the mean causal effect of the treatment on behaviour. This identification strategy is identical to the cross-section estimator $\widehat{\Delta}^{Cross}$ introduced in Chapter 3. Randomisation of treatment groups achieves the identifying assumption of this estimator, i.e. that there is no selection into the treatment groups.

In the experimental literature, this implementation is often referred to as a 'between-subjects' design, since individuals involved in each condition are different people. People generally refrain from having different treatments implemented in the same session, in order to preserve common knowledge of equal treatment between subjects. As a result, between-subject experiments generally implement one condition per session. Identification requires the experimental treatment implemented in a given session to be chosen at 'random', i.e. in a way that is uncorrelated with any unobserved factor that might have an effect on behaviour. To get back to a previous example, if some sessions are scheduled early in the morning and others just after lunch, the mapping of these slots with the treatments should be chosen in such a way that there is no systematic relationship between the two. If it is the case, then people in the two groups are statistically the same: the distribution of noise in the treatment sub-samples is identical. Because the counterfactual is statistical in nature, between-subject designs are demanding in terms of sample size.

5.3.4   Within-Subject Designs: Identification of Treatment Effects through Blocking Strategies

The alternative to a statistical counterfactual based on randomisation is to get rid of the confounding effect of individual unobserved heterogeneity by just having the very same people behaving in all decision environments. In this way, unobservable individual heterogeneity would no longer interact with the treatment by remaining constant in all decision environments. This can be achieved by implementing experimental treatments one after the other in the same experimental session, with the same subjects. In the example of two experimental treatments, decision periods denoted t are associated with the first of them ($T_{i,t} = 0$, $\forall i$), and decision periods denoted $\bar{t}$ are associated with the second ($T_{i,\bar{t}} = 1$, $\forall i$). The effect of the treatment can be measured by a simple comparison of outcomes between the two situations:

$$\widehat{\Delta} = \frac{1}{N} \sum_i y_{i,\bar{t}} - \frac{1}{N} \sum_i y_{i,t}$$

Since the same individuals are observed in two different periods of time, this formally amounts to relying on the before–after estimator introduced in Chapter 3, Focus 3.4. It uses the past behaviour of treated subjects as a counterfactual for their behaviour after the treatment. This discussion underlined that this estimator thus identifies a mix between the treatment effect of interest and the variation in unobserved heterogeneity in the group of treated individuals, from before ($\varepsilon(1)_{t=\underline{t}}$) to after ($\varepsilon(1)_{t=\bar{t}}$) the treatment. Since the same individuals are making decisions in the two situations, the difference $\varepsilon(1)_{t=\bar{t}} - \varepsilon(1)_{t=\underline{t}}$ eliminates any permanent heterogeneity. Individual-specific determinants of behaviour, in particular, disappear thanks to this comparison. Because the comparison occurs for the same individuals observed in different conditions, this design is often labelled a *within-subject* implementation of the treatment.

One advantage of this design is to achieve a higher statistical power than the between-subject design, thanks to both lower noise in the data and more individual observations delivered by a given sample of participants. First, within-subject designs generate observations associated with several different treatments based on the same individuals – i.e. it increases the number of subjects who participate in each treatment for a given size of the subject pool. Second, since individual-specific heterogeneity remains constant across decision stages, variations in the outcome variable are conditional on these unobservables, resulting in lower variance of the noise as compared to between-subject designs. Illustration 5.11 provides an example of how this conditioning on individual heterogeneity widens the sets of research questions that can be addressed.

The price for this increased power is that identification is weaker, as the identifying assumption is more likely to be violated. The identification assumption amounts to requiring that the treatment is the only influential change over time in the experiment. Any change in unobserved heterogeneity that happens at the same time as a new experimental treatment is introduced will thus be confounding. Typically, if repetition itself induces a change in decision-making, because subjects learn how to best decide, or get tired or bored with the experimental exercise, the estimator will confound this effect and the causal effect of behaving in environment $\underline{t}$ rather than $\bar{t}$. A major source of such a change over time is the sequence of the treatments themselves. If there is any permanent effect of being exposed to a treatment on subsequent behaviour, then the comparison no longer elicits the pure effect of behaving in one environment as compared to behaving in another, but rather a combination of the treatment effect of interest and this change in unobserved heterogeneity over the course of the experiment. Because such a confounding effect arises due to the order in which the treatments are implemented, it is known as *order effects* in the experimental literature (see Illustration 5.12 for an empirical example, in which order effects are induced on purpose).

As for any confounding mechanism, order effect can be indirectly controlled through either blocking or randomisation. Randomisation in this context implies choosing randomly the order in which treatments are implemented. There will be change over time in unobserved heterogeneity, but randomisation will ensure that this change is not systematically correlated with the occurrence of the treatments, hence achieving identification. As before, this identifying assumption is statistical in nature, hence requiring gathering enough data for the assumption to be empirically meaningful. Alternatively, a blocking design will systematically balance the order in which treatments are implemented.

Illustration 5.11
Individual consistency of social preferences: a within-subject design

The inequality-aversion model of Fehr and Schmidt, presented in Section 5.2.4, rationalises behaviour in social-preference games by extending the specification of individual preferences to additional parameters, θ^-, θ^+, that relate individual well-being to the distribution of outcomes. The model has been shown to perform well in describing the observed distribution of decisions in social-preference games. Blanco et al. (2011) aim to assess whether such predictive power holds at the individual level. To that end, they design an experiment eliciting behaviour in social-preference games for the same individuals. This within-subject design allows us to measure the consistency of individual preferences across games. In this experiment, the same subjects plays the following games one after the other:

Game	Label	Description
Ultimatum-bargaining game	UBG	£20 pie, proposer gets £$(20 - s)$ and responder s if the respondent accepts, both get 0 otherwise
Modified dictator game	MDG	dictator chooses between £20 and £0 and equitable outcomes ranging from £0–£0 to £20–£20
Sequential-move prisoners' dilemma	SPD	both defect: £10–£10; both cooperate: £14–£14; one defects, one cooperates: £17–£17
Public-good game	PG	two players, £10 endowment per player, marginal per capita return on contributions is 0.7

From these data, individual preferences (i.e. estimates of θ_i^-, θ_i^+ for each subject i) are estimated based on behaviour as receiver in the UBG and as proposer in the DG. This provides a distribution of preferences in the sample of subjects. The analysis then proceeds in two steps. First, the distribution of preferences is used to assess its ability to predict aggregate behaviour: this amounts to comparing the actual distribution of preferences to the distribution required in order to generate the observed distribution of behaviour in each game. The model performs well in that regard in the ultimatum-bargaining game, the public-good game and the first-mover strategy of the sequential prisoners' dilemma, confirming previous analysis. The second step makes use of the within-subject dimension of the data. Individual decisions in each game are compared to the prediction from the individual-specific estimated preferences. Based on this within-subject consistency criterion, the model performance is very low. As an illustration, we focus on the results from the public-good game. People who exhibit a high level of guilt about advantageous inequalities ($\theta_i^+ > 0.3$) should make a positive contribution to the public good. On the other hand, people with a low guilt parameter are expected to free-ride on the public good. In the sample, 20 subjects are characterised by preferences such that $\theta_i^+ < 0.3$, and 17 subjects contributed zero, confirming the good performance of the model in aggregate. However, only 13 of the 20 subjects with low θ^+ belong to the group of zero contributors. The hypothesis that a low θ^+ implies free riding at the individual level thus is rejected by the data.

Illustration 5.12
Evidence of order effects: rationality spillovers

Cherry et al. (2003) rely on a within-subject design to test a 'rationality spillover hypothesis', i.e. that non-market behaviour changes when rationality is fostered through a market setting. The hypothesis is tested in the context of a preference-reversal game. The baseline, T1, features no arbitrage and real choices – i.e. choices affect take-home pay. Subjects play 15 rounds. In each of them, subjects choose between two lotteries (A and B) with the same expected value, first in a market setting and secondly in a non-market setting. At the beginning of each round, they are endowed with an initial balance of $10. In both settings, subjects are asked to order their preferences between the first lottery (A) – which is a low-risk lottery – and the second lottery (B) – which is a high-risk lottery. Then, they are asked to report their fair value for both lotteries in both settings. Finally, an offer price is randomly drawn for each lottery in the market setting and the subject is sold the lottery if the stated value was higher or equal to the price – the price is subtracted from the round balance – and the buyer becomes the owner of the lottery: the lottery is played, and earnings are determined according to a draw in the lottery. Arbitrage is introduced in T2, in order to test the rationality spillover hypothesis. Starting at round 6 in the market setting, preference reversals are automatically arbitraged: the lottery with the lowest price is sold to the subject, and traded against the preferred lottery. This realises the monetary cost of preference reversals. Two further treatments provide robustness checks. In T3, everything is similar to T2 except that in the non-market setting subjects make hypothetical choices instead of real choices. In T4, everything is similar to T3 except that subjects make a choice over environmental lotteries instead of monetary lotteries as in all other treatments. For example, a subject is asked to choose between seeing a grizzly bear with a 30% chance and catching a cut-throat trout with a 70% chance.

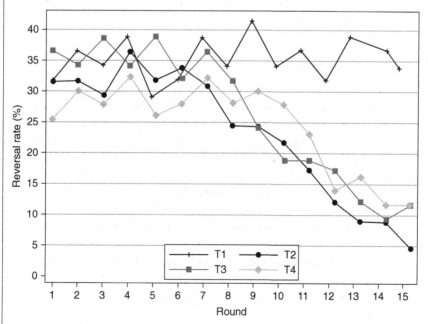

The main results from the experiment are provided in the figure above (from Cherry et al., 2003, p. 71, Figure 2). Thanks to the within-subject design, subjects serve as their own control in the non-market setting. Comparing the trends between T1 and T2, shows a strong discrepancy after 6 rounds (when arbitrage is introduced), in the number of observed preference reversals: the double difference confirms the rationality-spillovers hypothesis. This decrease in reversal rates is observed even when the choice is hypothetical (T3) and when the lotteries are environmental instead of monetary (T4).

In the example of two experimental conditions, this amounts to balancing the number of sessions between the two orders $\{T_{i,\underline{t}} = 1; T_{i,\bar{t}} = 0\}$ and $\{T_{i,\underline{t}} = 0; T_{i,\bar{t}} = 1\}$. The identifying assumption is more restrictive than the one associated with randomisation: it achieves identification only if the time-varying confounding mechanisms are the same in the two sequences – for instance: if it is not the case that one of the two conditions fosters quicker learning than the other. The design, however, extends the scope of the robustness check that can be performed in that regard. One can use only the data from the first half of each sequence to perform a between-subject analysis of the treatment effects. Cross-sequence comparisons can also be used to assess whether behaviour is different over time by comparing $T_{i,\bar{t}} = 1$ to $T_{i,\underline{t}} = 1$ and $T_{i,\bar{t}} = 0$ to $T_{i,\underline{t}} = 0$ (to distinguish order effects from pure learning effects, it might be necessary to consider another sequence, $\{T_{i,\bar{t}} = 0; T_{i,\underline{t}} = 0\}$ in order to produce the counterfactual behaviour in treatments $T_{i,\underline{t}} = 0$ without order effects). Either of the two choices implies complementing the within-subject design by additional treatments with different orders. In the end, the number of experimental treatments, and thus participants, required for a within-subject design is thus the same as for a between-subject design.

5.3.5   Multiple Treatments

The distinction between treatment variables and experimental treatments is mainly relevant when there are more than two values of the treatment parameters. This happens when one treatment variable is set to more than two possible values, but more often so when several variables are used as treatments. Illustration 5.13 provides an example that combines the two cases – with two treatment variables in a VCM game, the MPCR and the group size, one of them associated with two possible values while the other can take either of four levels. To make things concrete, consider two treatment variables denoted T_a and T_b, each associated with two values of the corresponding treatment variable, which we denote as usual as $T_a = \{0, 1\}$ and $T_b = \{0, 1\}$. The challenge is to define experimental treatments in such a way that the causal effect of each one can be identified from observed behaviour. Strict randomisation of the treatment variables would imply independently randomly choosing the parameter value of each treatment variable. The main drawback of this procedure is that it allows several treatment variables to change simultaneously.

The implementation rule circumventing this issue amounts to defining experimental treatments according to a *factorial design*: an experimental treatment is defined for

Illustration 5.13
VCM: a 4 × 2 factorial design

As shown in Focus 5.3, the intensity of the social dilemma raised by a VCM game crucially depends on how the MPCR compares to the individual shares in the group, $1/N$. Isaac et al. (1994) further investigate the empirical content of this prediction by considering variations in both dimensions. The core game is the one described in Section 5.1.4. Two dimensions are used as treatment variables: the MPCR is set at either 0.3 or 0.75, and the group size takes four possible values: 4, 10, 40 and 100. Together these two treatment variables define a 4 × 2 factorial design, resulting in eight experimental treatments. The figure below (from Isaac et al., 1994, p. 14, Figure 6) shows the share of contribution elicited over time in each treatment.

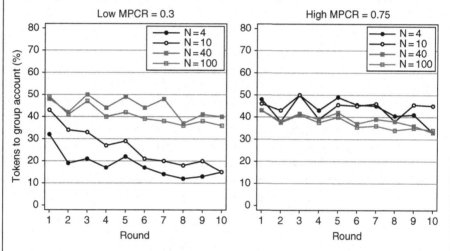

For a given private return to the public good, group size does not decrease subjects' contribution per se. In particular, for large groups, an increase in the group size has a positive influence on the contribution to the public good. Therefore, large groups can be more efficient at providing public goods than small groups. Two additional features appear from the figure. First, with a low marginal per capita return, large groups are more cooperative than small groups, but this effect disappears when the marginal per capita return increases to 0.75. Second, the positive link between the marginal per capita return and the contribution to the public good that existed in small groups vanishes in large groups.

each and every combination of all treatment variables. Table 5.4 illustrates the factorial design associated with the above example, with two treatment parameters each set to two possible values. This 2×2 factorial design results in four experimental treatments. The advantage of a factorial design is to build a control situation for each treatment condition: comparisons across cells in the table identify the marginal effect of switching the value of one treatment variable, conditional on some value for the other. It also delivers more: as shown by the comparisons in the outer row and column of Table 5.4, as many estimates of the treatment effects as the number of parameter values (two in our example) are observed thanks to this design. For instance, $\Delta_{\mathcal{T}_a|\mathcal{T}_b=0}$ and $\Delta_{\mathcal{T}_a|\mathcal{T}_b=1}$

Table 5.4 Multiple treatment variables: a 2 × 2 factorial design

		Treatment variable 2		
		$T_b = 0$	$T_b = 1$	$\neq$
Treatment	$T_a = 0$	Experimental treatment 1	Experimental treatment 2	$\Delta T_b \vert T_a = 0$
variable 1	$T_a = 1$	Experimental treatment 3	Experimental treatment 4	$\Delta T_b \vert T_a = 1$
	$\neq$	$\Delta T_a \vert T_b = 0$	$\Delta T_a \vert T_b = 1$	Δ^{DD}

both are measures of the effect of the treatment variable T_a, but each is generated by a different decision environment in terms of the value of T_b. The difference between the two provides a measure of the interaction between the treatments. It amounts to relying on the difference-in-difference estimator (DD), i.e.:

$$\widehat{\Delta}^{DD} = \left(\overline{Y}_{T_a=1,T_b=1} - \overline{Y}_{T_a=1,T_b=0}\right) - \left(\overline{Y}_{T_a=0,T_b=1} - \overline{Y}_{T_a=0,T_b=0}\right)$$
$$= \left(\overline{Y}_{T_a=1,T_b=1} - \overline{Y}_{T_a=0,T_b=1}\right) - \left(\overline{Y}_{T_a=1,T_b=0} - \overline{Y}_{T_a=0,T_b=0}\right)$$

When applied to a design in which the treatments all are target variables, this estimator measures the joint contribution of the two treatments, i.e. how the outcome varies when the two treatments are simultaneously influential, as compared to their own marginal effect. This same strategy is sometimes applied to designs in which one of the two treatment variables is used to generate the baseline: the target outcome, on which the treatment effect is to be identified, is the change in behaviour between two baseline conditions. It is the case, for instance, in experiments described in Section 2.4, trying to measure the hypothetical bias in preference elicitation. In this case, the variation in behaviour depending on whether incentives are real or hypothetical (say, treatment variable T_a) serves as a benchmark for the investigation. The main treatment variable of interest is another dimension of the environment (T_b, such as a priming task, or a certainty question) of which the design aims to measure the effect on hypothetical bias in elicited preferences. In circumstances like this, the difference-in-difference estimation strategy is applied in order to measure the effect of the treatment variable of interest (T_b) on the variation of behaviour. As shown in Chapter 3, Focus 3.4, the identifying assumption is then the so-called parallel-trend assumption: that the change in unobserved heterogeneity that occurs in line with the 'nuisance' treatment variable is not affected by the change in the target one.

The factorial design implementation of multiple-treatments experiments is the main reason why the choice of treatment variables, and their individual values, must be made with parsimony. In the general case, with K treatment variables with n_k ($k = 1, \ldots K$) individual values each, a factorial implementation requires as much as $\prod_{k=1}^{K} n_k$ experimental treatments, defining the set of all feasible combinations of the treatment variables. For a given number of observations, this implies an important loss of statistical power as additional treatment dimensions are added; conversely, for a given statistical power, the required sample size explodes as the number of dimensions increases. As an example, adding one value to one of the two treatment variables in a 2×2 design increases the number of treatments from 4 to 6 (2×3), and adding a third binary variable increases the number of conditions from 4 to 8 ($2 \times 2 \times 2$).

5.4   The Perceived Experiment

The quality of identification in an experiment is based on two building blocks. The first is a well-designed decision environment, as discussed up to now. But the actual decision environment is not quite the experiment that has been designed and implemented. What actually generates outcome behaviour is rather the experiment in which participants *think* they are involved. This perceived experiment is the second building block of internal validity. For instance, if subjects believe they will not get paid at the end of the experiment, then the performance-based reward will not incentivise behaviour; if they think the worst outcome is always to be drawn to manipulate their payoffs, then the experiment will not deliver their actual decisions under risk, etc. No matter how clever the actual design is, outcome behaviour will only result from what people have in mind – see Illustration 5.14 for an application to the incentive-compatibility of the compensation scheme. As a result, control over subjects' perceived experiment is a very important part of experimental designs, and their internal validity.

5.4.1   The Perceived Situation: Experimental Instructions

Within the set of controls over the perceived experiment, the leading one is the way the experiment is explained to the subjects. This is usually referred to as the '*experimental instructions*', and generally takes the form of a printed sheet of paper that is distributed to subjects before the experiment starts. Section 2.1 provided a concrete example applied to a second-price Vickrey auction; Section 6.2.1 provides practical advice about its structure and content. What matters in terms of internal validity is that this document is the main source of information for subjects about how the experiment proceeds. As such, it has to be written in such a way as to fulfil two basic aims: (i) that the experiment is well understood by each and every subject, and (ii) that all subjects are given the same information about the experiment. Each of the two conditions has its own consequences on the internal validity of the outcome behaviour. Condition (i) guarantees that the decision environment that subjects have in mind is the one that ought to be implemented. Otherwise, observed behaviour will either be generated by another experiment (the one subjects think they behave in) or, even worse, by random behaviour in an environment subjects simply did not get. Condition (ii) applies a blocking strategy. The aim is to avoid idiosyncratic noise in the perceived experiment that would be induced by a heterogeneous understanding of the rules – hence preventing correlation with any change in target outcomes. Each condition also has its own implications on how experimental instructions are written and communicated to subjects.

Illustration 5.14
Identified failures of internal validity: confusion in VCM games

Ferraro and Vossler (2010) further explore Andreoni's (1995) hypothesis presented in Section 5.1.4 by considering whether players' inability to distinguish the relationship between their choice and the game's incentives plays a role in cooperation behaviour in VCM games – a feature they label '*confusion*'. They design a series of experiments which compare VCM outcomes when the game is played with other humans or with virtual players. Virtual players are designed to perform predetermined contribution sequences. Subjects are informed whether they are matched with real people or with robots. In a virtual-player treatment, other-regarding preferences should play no role.

To test this hypothesis, participants are involved in 15 VCM games, with varying MPCR and group sizes – in order to check the robustness of the difference in changes in the incentives. The nature of other players (whether they are automatons or real human beings), by contrast, remains the same in all decision rounds. The main results are shown on the figure (from Ferraro and Vossler, 2010, p. 9, Figure 1).

Based on the comparison between the two treatments, confusion accounts for half the average contribution – equal to 25% in the human treatments, 12.5% in the virtual-player treatments. What is more, confusion does not seem to disappear with repetition.

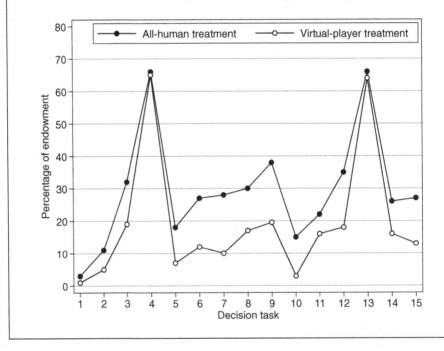

The second condition, requiring that the same information is given to all subjects, is the main reason why experimental instructions are actually written and distributed to subjects. Thanks to this document, explaining the experimental procedures to subjects amounts to reading the same text to all subjects: the same wording, the same order, the same sentences, the same examples will thus be used to communicate the decision